Mixed-Mode Modelling:
Mixing Methodologies For Organisational Intervention

Applied Optimization

Volume 58

The titles published in this series are listed at the end of this volume.

Mixed-Mode Modelling: Mixing Methodologies For Organisational Intervention

Edited by

Miles G. Nicholls

Steve Clarke

Brian Lehaney

KLUWER ACADEMIC PUBLISHERS

DORDRECHT / BOSTON / LONDON

A C.I.P. Catalogue record for this book is available from the Library of Congress.

ISBN-13:978-1-4613-7980-5 e-ISBN-13:978-1-4613-0289-6
DOI:10.1007/978-1-4613-0289-6

Published by Kluwer Academic Publishers,
P.O. Box 17, 3300 AA Dordrecht, The Netherlands.

Sold and distributed in North, Central and South America
by Kluwer Academic Publishers,
101 Philip Drive, Norwell, MA 02061, U.S.A.

In all other countries, sold and distributed
by Kluwer Academic Publishers,
P.O. Box 322, 3300 AH Dordrecht, The Netherlands.

Printed on acid-free paper

CONTENTS

CONTRIBUTORS

Steve Clarke
Luton Business School
The University of Luton
Department of Finance, Systems and Operations
Park Square, Luton,
United Kingdom
email: steve.clarke@luton.ac.uk

Gary Bell
School of Computing, Information Systems and Mathematics
South Bank University
London, UK
email: bellgaa@sbu.ac.uk

Jon Warwick
School of Computing, Information Systems and Mathematics
South Bank University
London, UK
email: warwick@sbu.ac.uk

Mike Kennedy
School of Computing, Information Systems and Mathematics
South Bank University
London, UK
email: kennedms@sbu.ac.uk

Maggie Cooper
Department of Computing
City University
London, UK
email: maggie@soi.city.ac.uk

John Davies
School of Business and Public Management
Victoria University of Wellington
PO Box 600, Wellington, New Zealand.
email: john.davies@vuw.ac.nz

Vicky Mabin
School of Business and Public Management
Victoria University of Wellington
PO Box 600, Wellington, New Zealand.
email:vicky.mabin@vuw.ac.nz

John E Boylan
Buckinghamshire Chilterns University College
Buckinghamshire, England
email: jboyla01@bcuc.ac.uk

Mark A Williams
MRC Business Information Group, Oxford, England
email: mark.williams@mrcinfo.com

Krishna S. Dhir
Berry College, Mount Berry, Georgia, USA
email: kdhir@berry.edu

Michael Enright
School of Business
Swinburne University of Technology, Melbourne, Australia
email: menright@swin.edu.au

Ian Yeoman
Napier University Business School
Edinburgh, UK
email: I.Yeoman@Central.Napier.AC.UK

Anthony Ingold
Napier University Business School
Edinburgh, UK
email:a.ingold@which.net

Brian Lehaney
Centre for Knowledge Management,
University of Luton,
Park Square, Luton
United Kingdom
email: brian.lehaney@luton.ac.uk

Gillian Jack
Centre for Knowledge Management,
University of Luton,
Park Square, Luton
United Kingdom
email: gillian.jack@luton.ac.uk

Miles G. Nicholls
School of Business
Swinburne University of Technology, Melbourne, Australia
email: mnicholls@swin.edu.au

Barbara J. Cargill
School of Business
Swinburne University of Technology, Melbourne, Australia
email: bcargill@swin.edu.au

M. Gordon Hunter
Management Information Systems
The University of Lethbridge
Lethbridge, Alberta, Canada
email: ghunter@uleth.ca

PREFACE

The 1980s and 1990s have seen a growing interest in research and practice in the use of methodologies within problem contexts characterised by a primary focus on technology, human issues, or power. During the last five to ten years, this has given rise to challenges regarding the ability of a single methodology to address all such contexts, and the consequent development of approaches which aim to mix methodologies within a single problem situation. This has been particularly so where the situation has called for a mix of technological (the so-called 'hard') and human-centred (so-called 'soft') methods. The approach developed has been termed *mixed-mode modelling*.

The area of mixed-mode modelling is relatively new, with the phrase being coined approximately four years ago by Brian Lehaney in a keynote paper published at the 1996 Annual Conference of the UK Operational Research Society. Mixed-mode modelling, as suggested above, is a new way of considering problem situations faced by organisations. Traditional technological approaches used in management science have suffered criticisms relating to their adequacy in the past few decades, and these hard approaches have been replaced by soft methods, which consider process more relevant than outcome. However, the sole use of human-centred approaches to organisational problems has also proved to be inadequate. Mixed-mode modelling accepts the importance of both process and outcome, and provides enabling mechanisms for hard and soft investigation to be undertaken.

This book addresses the conceptual, methodological, and empirical aspects of *mixing methodologies for organisational intervention* in a business and management environment. The emphasis on organisational intervention has been deliberately selected since this is an area increasingly recognised as critical to the success of businesses and public sector bodies. It is also an area very suited to the application of mixed-mode modelling and aptly illustrates its value. Additionally, organisational intervention has been the most difficult to deal with using 'traditional' approaches.

The book has been loosely segregated into three main sections. The first section is concerned with an overview of mixed mode-modelling and intervention frameworks (Chapters 1, 2 and 3). The second section addresses general applications of mixed-mode modelling (Chapters 3, 4, 5 and 6) while the third section deals with mixed-mode modelling and human resources (Chapters 8, 9 and 10), an area specifically related to a unique aspect of organisational intervention.

In the first grouping of chapters (overview and framework oriented), Steve Clarke provides an overview that traces the historical development of mixed-mode modelling from both theoretical and practical perspectives and argues a logical future direction for mixed-mode modelling (grounded on theories of communicative action) (*Chapter 1; Mixing Methods for Organisational Intervention: Background and Current Status*). Gary Bell, Jon Warwick, Mike Kennedy and Maggie Cooper introduce the concept of the Holon Framework that aims to improve and control human activity systems by combining aspects of Soft Systems Thinking and Hard Systems Thinking (*Chapter 2; Towards a General Holistic Framework for Improving and Controlling Human Activity Systems*). John Davies and Vicky Mabin investigate framing as a meta-framework for the use of mixed-mode modelling (*Chapter 3; Framing: A Meta-Framework for the Use of Mixed-Mode Modelling*).

In the second grouping of chapters (applications oriented), John Boylan and Mark Williams show how mixing methodologies from systems thinking and soft systems methodology helps focus on how forecasts should be used and who should be responsible for forecasting and monitoring (*Chapter 4; Introducing Forecasting and Monitoring Methods to an SME: the Role of Soft Systems Methodology*). Krishna Dhir applies a mixed-mode approach to the assessment of the value of knowledge developed and transferred within an organisation (*Chapter 5; Assessment of the Value of Knowledge Transferred: a Mixed-Mode Approach*). Michael Enright argues for the use of human-centred methodologies as the basis for marketing decision-making in small firms especially in the area of new product development (*Chapter 6; Hard Decisions, Soft Data: Localised Context-Rich Solutions to Problems of New Product Development*). Ian Yeoman and Anthony Ingold discuss the fundamentals of yield management and illustrate its holistic nature and the need for yield management systems incorporating soft and hard aspects (*Chapter 7; The Fundamentals of Yield Management*).

In the third grouping of chapters (mixed-mode modelling and human resources oriented applications) Gillian Jack and Brian Lehaney consider the increasing complexity of internal and external influences on organisational management and behaviour and show that different management approaches impact in different ways on the wellbeing of the workforce. By the use of a mixture of methodologies, an approach is developed that improves wellbeing, and through this, performance in the work place (*Chapter 8; Management and Wellbeing in the UK*). Miles Nicholls and Barbara Cargill develop an approach that allows the soft area of human resources management to be inter-related with the hard production planning function of a business. The resultant mixed-mode model and its solution heuristic is shown to provide a holistic approach to determining business best practice (*Chapter 9; The Use of Mixed-Mode Modelling in Determining Best Practice for a Business*). Finally, M. Gordon Hunter mixes a number of methodologies to form an approach (model) that develops a skill assessment process for information systems professionals (*Chapter 10; A Skill Assessment Process for Information Systems Professionals*).

This book aims to summarise and consolidate the work in the mixed-mode modelling field to date and provide a springboard for future development. It is also hoped that this collection of chapters written by experts in their fields will assist operational research practitioners, managers, as well as practitioners in all the fields covered in this book, to better understand what can be gained from the mixing of methodologies in the pursuit of a holistic 'best practice' solution. Additionally, it is hoped that the reader will see that the mere *application* of a mixed-mode modelling approach will engender an appreciation of a problem and its interrelatedness with other facets of the business. Mixed-mode modelling still has some exciting developments to undergo, but this text, at the very least, serves to illustrate its enormous potential.

We would like to take this opportunity to thank the authors, the anonymous referees, the School of Business at Swinburne University of Technology and most of all Ms Sharman Feinberg for her tireless effort in the preparation of this book.

Miles G. Nicholls
Steve Clarke
Brian Lehaney

April 2001.

1

MIXING METHODS FOR ORGANISATIONAL INTERVENTION: BACKGROUND AND CURRENT STATUS

Steve Clarke

Luton Business School
The University of Luton
United Kingdom

ABSTRACT

Tracing the historical development of mixed-mode modelling from a theoretical and practical perspective leads to an understanding of the domain as substantially underpinned by critical social theory. A 'natural' progression is discerned, from which it is argued that the logical future direction for mixed-mode modelling is one grounded on theories of communicative action.

The beginnings of a framework for such a project are outlined, together with the plans for the next stage of this project. This future is seen to lie, not in the development of a methodology, but rather in guidelines for communicative action which can be followed irrespective of methodological choice.

Keywords: mixed-mode modelling, complementarism, social theory, critical theory, methodology.

M.G. Nicholls et al. (eds.),
Mixed-Mode Modelling: Mixing Methodologies for Organisational Intervention, 1–18.

INTRODUCTION

The aim of this chapter is to present a brief outline of the thinking underpinning mixed-mode modelling, and to point to possible future directions for the domain.

The term 'mixed-mode modelling' was introduced in a paper presented at the annual conference of the U.K. Operational Research Society at Warwick, England in 1996. See Lehaney [1]. Subsequently, the concept of mixing methods within a single organisational intervention has gathered pace, being now represented by the two domains of mixed-mode modelling and multi-methodology, which for the purposes of this chapter will be assumed synonymous.

The impetus for these developments can be characterised by the view that, whilst the idea, and arguably the practice, of mixing methods has been around for as long as organisational intervention itself, the theoretical and pragmatic difficulties of such an approach have been substantially underplayed. In this chapter an attempt is made to summarise these difficulties, using the summaries to point to improved practice in the future.

To set mixed-mode modelling in context, first the perceived problem issues which have given rise to the domain are outlined, followed by a review of the background and history to its development. Finally, a discussion and critique of current thinking is undertaken, from which potential future directions are proposed.

MIXED-MODE MODELLING: THE PROBLEM

Whilst at a pragmatic, common-sense level, mixing methods in organisational intervention is mostly seen to be unproblematic, this chapter, by reviewing the development of mixed-mode modelling, seeks to demonstrate that there are difficulties to be overcome which require more than a pragmatic approach. This development is presented first below in the form of a historical sketch, which embraces both empirical and theoretical issues, and outlines the key approaches used.

History and Background

For the purposes of this section, the position taken is that, in organisational intervention:

- Up to the 1950s, interventions were dominated by hard, pseudo-scientific methods, mitigated only minimally by inputs from the human relations school.
- In the 1960s and 1970s, these approaches were challenged by the so-called 'soft' methods, which privileged human viewpoints and activities ahead of an instrumental concentration on (for example) the use of technology.
- The 1980s onward has seen increasing concentration on ways of combining these, and other, methods so as to be able to address all aspects of a given problem context with one 'overarching' approach.

Mixed-mode modelling is concerned with the last of these: the ways in which methodologies, methods or techniques are combined within an intervention. The history and background is pursued through key approaches to methodological mixing, the first of which is the system of systems methodologies.

THE SYSTEMS OF SYSTEMS METHODOLOGIES

A convenient starting point for mixed-mode modelling is to be found in the work of Jackson and Keys [2], and the 'system of systems methodologies' (SOSM).

The SOSM (Figure 1) is used as the basis for an argument that the application of methodologies can be understood through determination of the problem contexts to which they are applied. The SOSM is therefore, first and foremost, a problem context classification, through which it is argued that problem contexts can be categorised according to the extent to which they exhibit a 'people complexity', from unitary to coercive, and a 'systems complexity', from simple to complex.

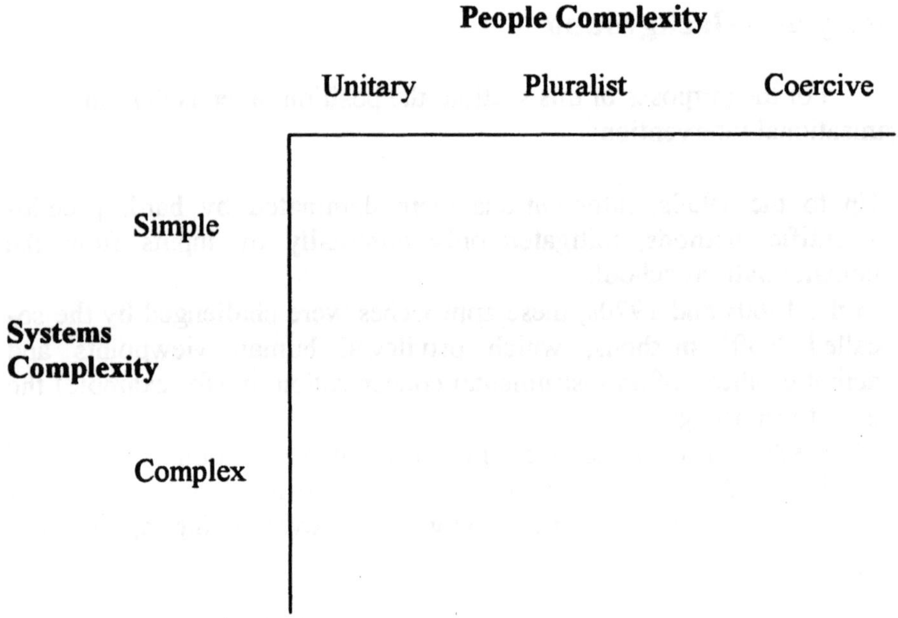

Figure 1. The System of Systems Methodologies
(Based on Jackson and Keys [2]; Jackson [3]; Jackson [4]).

So, for example, a 'problem' may be seen as 'simple-unitary': 'simple' in the sense that it has few elements and few interactions between elements; 'unitary' in terms of people complexity in that there is only one agreed viewpoint. Such 'problems', it is argued, do not require discussion, and can be 'solved' using hard, scientific, 'design-based' methods. By contrast, a 'complex-coercive' context not only exhibits system characteristics of high complexity (many elements, many interactions), but also cannot be progressed until the power issues (hence high 'people complexity') dominating the context are resolved (for a more detailed analysis applying the use of the SOSM. See Clarke and Lehaney [5].

Application

In use, this problem context classification forms a basis for determining the methodology to be used in the intervention. So, for example, a 'simple-unitary' problem context will demand the use of a methodology which focuses on design issues, and does not seek to address multiple viewpoints, since these are seen not to exist within the context identified. The system of systems methodologies is silent on *how* such methodologies should be applied, leaving this to the individual methodology.

A PRAGMATIC APPROACH

Ormerod, see Mingers and Gill [6] (pp29-58), through the presentation of a number of case studies, presents a compelling argument for an essentially pragmatic approach to methodological mixing across subjective and objective paradigms. In particular, the arguments that "with hard methods the choice is often a response to the issue faced", and "a hard approach had been successfully embedded in a soft approach (strategic choice)", Mingers and Gill [6] (pp47-48), support the view that in the Sainsbury's intervention the approach was predominantly pragmatic, whilst offering as a way forward the potential for treating hard methods as operating within a soft framework. There can be little question that Ormerod's command of, and use of the methods outlined is, in comparison to the average commercial consultant, quite remarkable. This command, he seems to see as almost a set of skills to be learnt:

> "Indeed, I would encourage OR consultants to adopt an eclectic approach. The key is to hone one's craft skills, learn a number of methods and note when and where they seem to work." Mingers and Gill [6] (pp56-57).

Application

In use, then, the pragmatic approach is straightforward. The consultant should gain mastery of a wide variety of methodologies, methods and techniques, and apply them in a contingent fashion to the problems encountered.

TOTAL SYSTEMS INTERVENTION AND THE COMPLEMENTARIST FRAMEWORK

In this early work, the paradigm position taken by the SOSM was core to the approaches recommended. That is to say, it was accepted that different problem contexts 'inhabited' different paradigms, and further that communication across paradigms was difficult if not impossible. So, for example, a problem context characterised by high levels of disagreement among participants, in which debate might be seen as a way forward, might prove difficult to combine with a requirement to produce a technical system, where focus is on design, and agreement as to means and ends is typically assumed.

Whilst 'paradigm incommensurability' was the normal view in these approaches, a way out of the problem was proposed through Habermas' theory of knowledge constitutive interests. In essence, this theory was that, at a fundamental level, human beings, in carrying out any task, seek to satisfy three interests: technical, practical and emancipatory. If this could be shown to be so, then the incommensurability of paradigms becomes a human construction, rather than something fundamental to human activity, and by acceding to approaches which take account of Habermas' interest constitution theory, such incommensurability could be overcome.

The most comprehensive attempt at applying this theory to organisations was undertaken through total systems intervention, TSI:Flood [7], where 'complementarism' was promoted as a way forward, enabling methodologies from different paradigms to be used together in a single intervention, applied to the same problem situation (for an example of TSI in use, see Clarke and Lehaney [8]).

Total systems intervention (TSI), offered a 'critical complementarist' approach which was seen to be capable of resolving both the theoretical and practical difficulties. This Habermasian perspective sees the functionalist view of organisations as an insufficient basis, serving only the technical interest. What is needed in addition is social science, to service the practical (hermeneutic) interest in achieving communication and consensus, together with critical science to deal with issues of power and domination, serving the emancipatory interest. Critique is applied in a Kantian [9] sense, aiming to: (i) free participants from purely instrumental reason; (ii) enable practical reason, to examine and re-examine assumptions made; and (iii) inform the choice and mix of methodologies in relation to the changing nature of the problem contexts and the strengths and weaknesses of the available methodologies.

Application

The process of TSI is shown in Figure 2 below, and described in summary in the following text.

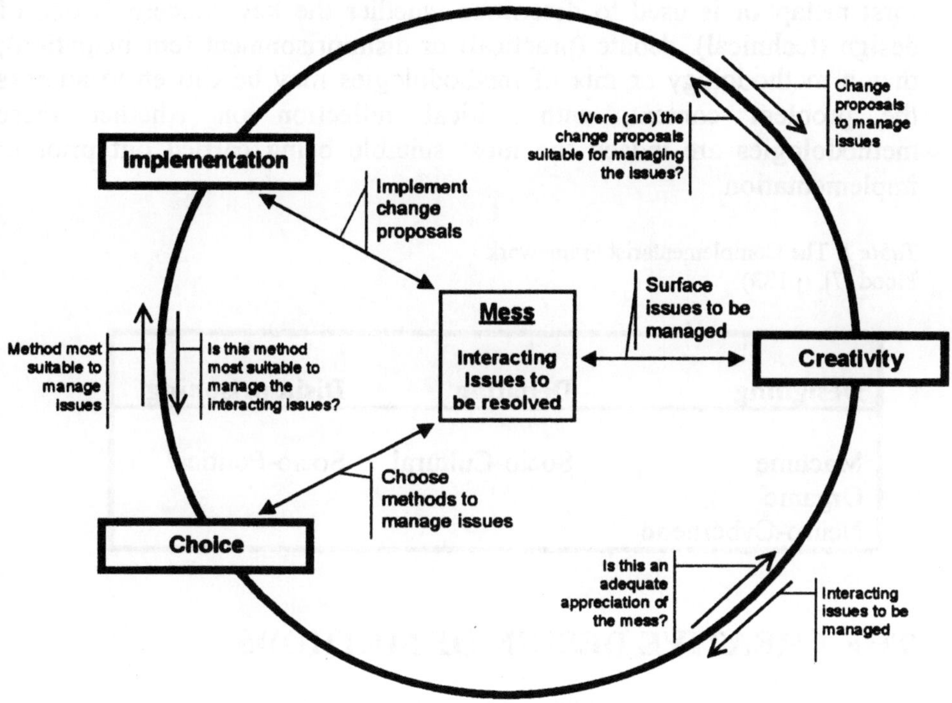

Figure 2. The Process of Total Systems Intervention (TSI) Flood [7]

TSI is iterative and recursive. Iteration implies that the process is continuous, rather than a start-end method. The TSI ideology explicitly recognises the part played by both technical and human activities in organisations, and the extent to which human interpretation may in some instances so distort the so called 'real world' that study of the latter may become meaningless.

TSI provides a critical framework within which choice and implementation of methodologies in an intervention can be managed pluralistically. The problem context is viewed as a 'mess' within which creativity (e.g. brainstorming, metaphor) is used to surface the issues to be managed (Figure 2); reflection on creativity then seeks to critically determine whether an adequate appreciation of the 'mess' has been gained. Originally Flood and Jackson [10], the SOSM was used to inform methodological choice. More recently, it has been recommended Flood [7] that this be replaced by the complementarist framework (Table 1). First metaphor is used to determine whether the key concern is one of design (technical), debate (practical) or disimprisonment (emancipation); then a methodology or mix of methodologies may be chosen to address the problem context, with critical reflection on whether these methodologies are indeed the most suitable being carried out prior to implementation.

Table 1. The Complementarist Framework
Flood [7], (p183)

Designing	**Debating**	**Disimprisoning**
Machine Organic Neuro-Cybernetic	Socio-Cultural	Socio-Political

THE CREATIVE DESIGN OF METHODS

Midgley[12] and Ulrich [11] focus on boundary critique as the key to mixing methods. Boundary critique has a long history, but it is from Ulrich [13, 14, 15] and Midgley [16] that the recommendation to critically challenge what should or should not be considered part of any system is drawn. Midgley's approach is to begin with a boundary definition which is accepted as arbitrary, and progress by " ... looking for grey areas in which marginal elements lie that are neither fully included in, nor excluded from, the system definition."

The critical choices made at the boundary are of truth and rightness: truth being represented by questions of what is, and rightness by questions of what ought to be. Critical assessment of the system boundary should be undertaken by a representative sample of participants in the system. Typically, an arbitrary system definition is presented for discussion in, for example, a brainstorming session, de Bono [17]. Critique can be informed by a combination of Midgley's and Ulrich's approaches to boundary critique: Midgley's [16] approach to examining what is in the margin for elements which support the secondary boundary or the primary boundary; Ulrich's [15] approach to challenging system boundaries through twelve "critically heuristic boundary questions" which address issues of motivation, power, knowledge and legitimisation (see Clarke and Lehaney [18] for an example of the use of boundary critique).

Boundary critique has led to Midgley's promotion of the creative design of methods [12], which was originally conceived as an improvement to SOSM, but is now promoted as addressing issues which SOSM deals with insufficiently. For example, whilst SOSM promotes the idea that there is only one interpretation of each method, creative design of methods sees methods as subject to multiple interpretations. Also, importantly, Midgley argues that SOSM restricts boundary judgement to simple coercive problem contexts, whereas it is a primary concern of creative design of methods to free up boundary judgement for use in all contexts.

Application

Applying the creative design of methods requires that the interventionist maintain a multiplicity of participant viewpoints, together with the potential mix of methods or parts of methods required to address them, within an ongoing critical framework. The boundaries must be critically challenged throughout an intervention, and the approach will be continually changing in response to this and participant feedback.

DIVERSITY MANAGEMENT

Flood and Romm [19] promote diversity management and triple loop learning as an improved way to deal with mixing methods. In essence, triple loop learning is seen as a way to manage the diversity of methodologies and theories available, in addressing the diversity of issues to be found in organisational intervention.

Application

In application, diversity management is about managing design, debate, and might-right issues, and so is a complementarist approach to the perceived hard, soft and critical factors which Flood and Romm see as pervading organisational problem contexts. The overall objective of diversity management might be seen as the enhancement of emancipatory practice.

CRITICAL SYSTEMS PRACTICE

In his most recent work, Jackson [20, 21] continues to promote critical pluralism, but now sees this in terms of developing TSI into critical systems practice. Pluralism in the use of methodology is advocated: "... to make the best use of the methodologies, methods, models and techniques ... to tackle diverse and difficult problem situations while ... ensuring their continual improvement through research" , Jackson [21] (p382). This pluralism must: encourage flexibility in the use of methodologies, enabling practitioners to decompose approaches and tailor them, within a critical framework; encourage paradigm diversity: using methodologies from different paradigms in the same intervention (for a critique of a range of methodologies, see Clarke, Lehaney *et al* [22]).

What is clear in Jackson's recommendations is his view that it is no longer possible to rely on Habermas, but, rather, pluralism calls for a meta-methodology, for which Jackson lays out nine "constitutive rules", Jackson [21] (p393). This "critical systems meta-methodology" is seen by Jackson as a "structured way of thinking which understands and respects the uniqueness of the functionalists, interpretative, emancipatory and post-modern theoretical rationales, and draws upon them to improve real-world problem situations." It is recommended that methods for enhancing creativity are applied, at least, from these perspectives, and that methodologies are used as appropriate.

Critical systems practice, Jackson recommends, should be embedded within a systems and action research approach; should ensure a pluralism of "clients", theoretical and methodological pluralism, pluralism in the modes of representation employed, and pluralism in the facilitation process; and should be sensitive to the organisational context in which it is operating.

Further, the claim to be using a generic system methodology, according to the particular theoretical rationale it is designed to serve, must be justified according to the principles and guidelines established for the use of each generic systems methodology.

Application

In essence, critical systems practice calls for an improved version of TSI, but it is as yet unclear how these ideas are to be applied. In essence, a set of constitutive rules are provided, but a framework within which these might be operationalised is not given.

CRITICAL PLURALISM

In critical pluralism, Mingers [6] promotes what he sees to be missing in critical approaches to the use of a mix of methodologies: multi-paradigm multimethodology. From a discussion of current dilemmas in critical systems thinking, Mingers promotes emphasis on engagement with agents in a social context as the basis for his approach. The focus, he suggests, should be on the relationship between three notional systems seen to form the multimethodological context: the problem content system, or real world situation of concern; the intellectual resources system, or available theories and methodologies; and the intervention system, or agents undertaking the intervention.

In theoretical terms, the work is strongly grounded on Habermas' theory of communicative action, Habermas [23], but with the added consideration of knowledge being linked to power.

Application

Mingers uses this thinking to develop a framework for mapping methodologies against the four phases of appreciation, analysis, assessment and action, based on Habermas' three worlds, Mingers and Gill [6] (p431). The actual process of critical multimethodology, he argues, "will be a continual cycle of reflection, judgement, and action" [6] (p437).

PRAGMATIC PLURALISM

Taket and White [24] offer pragmatic pluralism as a means of mixing methods from an essentially postmodernist perspective. Their approach is strongly grounded theoretically, with the suggestion that guidelines, examples, stories and metaphors are of more value than prescribed frameworks for action. The approach is expressly holistic, and sees pluralism as a means of addressing diversity. Pluralism , they argue, should be applied to the roles of the interventionist, modes of representation, and the nature of the client. It is explicit that work with the disempowered should be seen as fundamental within any intervention context.

Application

In application, it is argued that, in any intervention, there will be multiple rationalities to be managed, and that, whilst guidelines may be offered for addressing these, there is little to be gained from a prescriptive approach. The approach is therefore largely left open to the practitioner, who should follow a strategy of mix and match, operationalising what feels good in accordance with the guidelines provided: the interventionist should recognise differences in methodologies and match these with variety in the local context. Triangulation, the use of parts of methodologies in combination, a flexible and adaptive stance, and critical reflection, are all fundamental to the application of this approach.

This completes the review of perspectives on mixed-mode modelling. In the following section, discussion and critique is conducted, reflecting the issues raised by these theoretical and practical perspectives.

DISCUSSION AND CRITIQUE

All mixed methods have in common the aim of addressing diverse (or 'pluralistic') problem contexts with a diversity of methods, but the outline history given above points to how the domain of mixed-mode modelling has developed to achieve this overall aim.

One of the approaches, however, stands apart from all others in expressly recommending that theory is *not* considered as relevant to the domain: in Ormerod's work, mixing is recommended at a pragmatic level. However, it might be argued that combining different methods in this purely ad hoc or contingent way turns the risk of trying to use a method in a way that actually contradicts the assumptions on which it is based:

> "Different methodologies express different rationalities stemming from alternative theoretical positions which they reflect. These alternative positions must be respected, and methodologies and their appropriate theoretical underpinnings developed in partnership" Flood and Jackson [10] (pp47-48).

The inference to be drawn from the other approaches outlined is that theoretical work in this domain is too important and relevant to be ignored. The system of systems methodologies originally presented an approach to matching problem context to methodologies seen to be applicable to that context, and was expressly based on Habermas' theory of knowledge constitutive interests (KCI). Total systems intervention initially operationalised SOSM into a process for intervention, similarly based on KCI; arguably, diversity management has continued this theme, being essentially an improved application of KCI. With the creative design of methods came an approach which sought to develop the ideas of SOSM and TSI, enabling the use of parts of methodologies, synthesised to address a unique problem context, within an expressly critical framework. The creative design of methods also introduced the idea of a basis in Habermas' theories of communicative action, rather than the theory of knowledge constitutive interests.

The recent critical systems practice advocated by Jackson also moves away from KCI, recommending instead that any claim to be using a methodology according to its theoretical rationale must be justified "according to the principles and guidelines established for the use of each … methodology" Jackson [21] (p393). In this, Jackson might be seen as returning to the need to recognise the distinctive background and theory of each methodology (see, for example, Jackson and Keys [2]; Flood and Jackson [10]; Brocklesby [25]).

Pragmatic pluralism draws on a very broad theoretical range, but much is premised on critical social theory. Finally, critical pluralism provides a framework for intervention grounded on Habermas' theory of communicative action.

If we seek to summarise much of the work in mixed-mode modelling in terms of theoretical development, the primary basis is to be found in critical social theory, with the main theories being applied in determining intervention approaches having been Habermas' theory of knowledge constitutive interests, and his theory of communicative action. Of these, communicative action seems the most promising arena in which to ground future development of the domain. An outline of the arguments in this respect might be as presented below.

A FUTURE FOR MULTIMETHODOLOGY

The ability to communicate by use of language is something that human beings bring to the world by nature of their existence: that is to say, it is not developed empirically, but is *a priori*. To the extent that any theoretical position can be grounded on such an *a priori* ability, then such a position may be seen as fundamental to us as communicative human actors.

In so far as communication, at least partially, may be oriented toward mutual understanding, it might be argued as the foundation of knowledge creation and sharing. In these terms, knowledge is not reducible (as is so often seen in scientific or pseudo-scientific study) to the properties of an objective world, but can be defined both objectively and according to the *a priori* concepts that the knowing subject brings to the act of perception. This knowing subject, being social, mediates all knowledge through social action and experience: subject and object are linked in the acts of cognition and social interaction, and the so-called subjective and objective 'paradigms' may be represented as just a convenient tool for understanding, which has been accorded too much primacy as a form of reality.

Rather, then, than relying on the concept of paradigms, this concept, and particularly the idea of paradigm incommensurability, should be opened up to challenge. Consider the so-called subjective / objective dichotomy. According to the paradigm argument, viewed (say) from an epistemological perspective, one who sees a problem context as positivistic, and seeks, for example, a technological solution, will be unable to communicate and share knowledge with another who views the same problem context as existing in the views and opinions of those participants involved in and affected by the system of concern. There are at least two fundamental difficulties with this:

1. It contradicts common human practice, and, dare it be suggested, common sense. Human participants in social groups commonly combine technical ('positivistic') and interpretative ('anti-positivistic') activity, seemingly denying the paradigm incommensurability thesis from an epistemological standpoint.
2. Theoretically, the paradigm incommensurability view seems to have dubious support. At its most basic level, it derives from the idea that technical, scientific, functionalist activity cannot be conducted together with interpretivistic, subjective activity. But if, theoretically, subjective and objective are inseparable, paradigm incommensurability becomes much less compelling.

In essence, then, it is the argument of this chapter that these difficulties disappear once a scientific basis for our thinking is denied. For example, suppose science (as is suggested by Kant [9] and Habermas [23]) is seen as just *one form of knowledge*, which in any case is simply a convenient human perception of how the world works. Now, all human endeavour becomes mediated through subjective understanding, and the paradigms as impenetrable barriers disappear. So, the problem of interest constitution theory being no longer defensible is resolved, since it is no longer being relied on. However, this problem has been replaced with another, which may be stated as follows:

1. Accepting all human actions as mediated through subjective understanding leads to the possibility of a basis for mixed-mode modelling in the universal characteristics of language.
2. The dichotomy between subject and object has gone, and with it, paradigm incommensurability.
3. Organisational intervention is recast as an entirely communicative issue. For example, the so-called technical interest of knowledge constitution theory becomes instead an question of how technology may further enable human interaction, all within a framework of human intercommunication.
4. The difficulty which now arises is essentially a practical one, of how to incorporate these ideas into management practice.

Work by Habermas [26, 23] on communicative action presents a universal theory of language which suggests that all language is oriented toward three fundamental validity claims: truth, rightness and sincerity.

What is most compelling about this theory, however, is that all three validity claims are *communicatively mediated*. This viewpoint is most radically seen in respect of the truth claim, where it is proposed that such a claim results not from the content of descriptive statements, but from the Wittgenstinian approach casting them as arising in language games which are linked to culture: truth claims are *socially contextual*.

'Truth', can therefore be assessed by reference to communication: truth is what statements, when true, state! Rightness is about norms of behaviour, which are culturally relevant, and are therefore to be determined by reference to that which is acceptable to those involved and affected in the system of concern as a cultural group. Finally, sincerity is about the speaker's internal world: his/her internal subjectivity.

These ideas can now be taken forward to provide a mixed-mode modelling approach, or set of approaches, which are theoretically grounded, and closer to that which is experienced in action. The conclusions below begin this process.

CONCLUSIONS

The review of mixed-mode modelling undertaken in this chapter indicates the potential for approaches explicitly grounded in critical social theory, but raises questions about the success of this project. The arguments of this chapter point to a possible future direction.

Whilst the position taken here is embryonic, and presents many challenges which have not as yet been addressed, it does offer a way forward for mixed-mode modelling, which should be:

1. Grounded in communicative action.
2. Explicitly based on participation.
3. Critically informed.

In terms of *how* this is to be achieved, the aim here is not to develop some new methodology, but rather to offer strategies and guidelines for the use of existing methodologies, methods and techniques. The next part of this project is therefore to apply these ideas to a range of methodologies, and from this develop critically informed guidelines for action.

REFERENCES

[1] Lehaney, B. *Mixed-Mode Modelling*. Annual Conference of the Operational Research Society, Keynote Papers, Warwick, United Kingdom, The Operational Research Society: 150-157, 1996.

[2] Jackson, M. C. and Keys, P. "Towards a System of Systems Methodologies." *Journal of the Operational Research Society* 35(6): 473-486, 1984.

[3] Jackson, M. C. "Beyond a System of Systems Methodologies." *Journal of the Operational Research Society* 41(8): 657-668, 1990.

[4] Jackson, M. C. "Beyond the Fads: Systems Thinking for Managers." *Systems Research* 12(1): 25-42, 1995.

[5] Clarke, S. and B. Lehaney "Organisational Intervention and the Problems of Coercion." *Systemist* 21 (December): 40-52, 1999.

[6] Mingers, J. and A. Gill, Eds. *Multi Methodology*. Chichester, Wiley, 1997.

[7] Flood, R. L. "Total Systems Intervention (TSI): A Reconstitution." *Journal of the Operational Research Society* 46: 174-191, 1995.

[8] Clarke, S. A. and B. Lehaney. *Human-Centred Methods in Information Systems Development: Boundary Setting and Methodological Choice*. Challenges of Information Technology Management in the 21st Century, Anchorage, Alaska, U.S.A., Idea Group Publishing: 605-608, 2000a.

[9] Kant, I. *Critique of Pure Reason*. London , Macmillan, 1929.

[10] Flood, R. L. and M. C. Jackson. *Creative Problem Solving: Total Systems Intervention*. Chichester, Wiley, 1991.

[11] Ulrich, W. *Critical Heuristics of Social Planning: A New Approach to Practical Philosophy*. Berne, Haupt, 1983a.

[12] Midgley, G. "Developing the Methodology of TSI: From the Oblique use of methods to their Creative Design." *Systems Practice* 10(3): 305-319, 1997.

[13] Ulrich, W. *The Itinerary of a Critical Approach*. Berne, Haupt, 1983b.

[14] Ulrich, W. "Systems Thinking, Systems Practice, and Practical Philosophy: A Program of Research." *Systems Practice* 1(2): 137-163, 1988.

[15] Ulrich, W. *A Primer to Critical Systems Heuristics for Action Researchers*. Forum One: Action Research and Critical Systems Thinking, Hull, UK, University of Hull, Centre for Systems Studies, 1996.

[16] Midgley, G. "The Sacred and Profane in Critical Systems Thinking." *Systems Practice* 5(1): 5-16, 1992.

[17] de Bono, E. *Lateral Thinking*. Aylesbury, U.K., Pelican Books, Hazell Watson & Viney Ltd., 1977.

[18] Clarke, S. A. and B. Lehaney "Mixing Methodologies for Information Systems Development and Strategy: A Higher Education Case Study." *Journal of the Operational Research Society* **51**(5): 542-556, 2000b.

[19] Flood, R. L. and N. R. A. Romm *Diversity Management: Triple Loop Learning*. Chichester, Wiley, 1996.

[20] Jackson, M. C. "Towards Coherent Pluralism in Management Science." *Journal of the Operational Research Society* 50(1): 12-22, 1999.

[21] Jackson, M. C. *Systems Approaches to Management*. New York, Kluwer/Plenum, 2000.

[22] Clarke, S. A., B. Lehaney, et al. "A Theoretical Framework for Facilitating Methodological Choice." *Systemic Practice and Action Research* 11(3): 295-318, 1998.

[23] Habermas, J. *Lifeworld and System: A Critique of Functionalist Reason*. Boston, Mass, Beacon Press, 1987.

[24] Taket, A. and White, L. "Pragmatic Pluralism: An Explication." *Systems Practice* 9(6): 571-586, 1996.

[25] Brocklesby, J. "Intervening in the Cultural Constitution of Systems - Methodological Complementarism and other Visions for Systems Research." *Journal of the Operational Research Society* 46 (11): 1285-1298, 1995.

[26] Habermas, J. "On Systematically Distorted Communication." *Inquiry* 13: 205-218, 1976.

2

TOWARDS A GENERAL HOLISTIC FRAMEWORK FOR IMPROVING AND CONTROLLING HUMAN ACTIVITY SYSTEMS

Gary Bell, Jon Warwick and Mike Kennedy
South Bank University, London, UK

Maggie Cooper
City University, London, UK

"I keep six honest serving-men:
(They taught me all I knew)
Their names are What and Where and When
And How and Why and Who."
Rudyard Kipling [1]

ABSTRACT

This chapter introduces the Holon Framework, which aims to improve and control human activity systems. It combines aspects of Soft Systems Thinking and Hard Systems Thinking. We discuss the essence of Hard Systems Thinking and point to a key weakness, which accounts for the emergence of Soft Systems Thinking and soft methodologies such as Soft Systems Methodology. Next, a key weakness of Soft Systems Methodology is highlighted to justify the need to incorporate ideas from representational measurement theory. An overview of the Holon Framework is provided, illustrating what is taken from each approach. The soft part of the framework is associated with improvement, as it addresses basic types of questions *i.e.*

M.G. Nicholls et al. (eds.),
Mixed-Mode Modelling: Mixing Methodologies for Organisational Intervention, 19–62.

'the what', 'the where', and 'the who'. The hard part of the framework is linked with control, as it addresses different questions, *i.e.* 'the how', 'the why', 'the when'. We describe two case studies that have used the soft part of the approach. The first case study (conducted in the *post-mortem* mode) examines a completed software project. The second case study (conducted in the *visioning* mode) investigates a Department within a University. Additionally, we clarify the theoretical assumptions that underwrite the Framework using a one-dimensional scheme based on Burrell and Morgan's work. Finally, we outline future research which is linked by the two objectives of General Systems Theory; firstly to identify common holons and problems which may lead to the discovery of system dynamics archetype structures operating in different disciplines, and secondly to base the maturing framework on a 'spectrum' of theories.

Key Words: Holon Framework, Soft Systems Methodology, Goal/Question/Metrics Methodology, Representational Measurement Theory, System Dynamics.

INTRODUCTION

This chapter describes the development of a new and interdisciplinary planning framework which has emerged from the confluence of two streams of research, each with quite distinct sources. The first stream is management science (viewed from the broad perspective of the systems movement) and the second is software engineering. Although seemingly quite distinct, both are concerned with the management of processes, organisational planning and decision making processes on the one hand, and software development processes on the other. As such they share the twin goals of process improvement and enhanced process control.

From the management science side, there has been a great deal of interest and debate over the last twenty years centred on the nature of structured interventions that might assist organisations with strategic management and planning. In particular, the limitations of the more traditional and quantitative management science models as aids to strategic decision making have been discussed in terms of the factors which characterise strategic problems [2] and which imply 'softness' in the problem domain. These characteristics (which may include multiple and conflicting objectives, stakeholders with differing views and experiences, qualitative issues, poor or non-existent data, *etc.*) have moved the emphasis of such interventions away from quantitative optimisation and goal achievement. Instead, there is an emphasis towards learning about, and exploring, a problem situation so that stakeholders can move in an agreed direction in an attempt to resolve the issues they have identified. Examples here include Strategic Options Development and Analysis, The Strategic Choice Methodology and, perhaps the best known of them all, Checkland's [3] Soft Systems Methodology (SSM). In this chapter, the essence of hard systems thinking (HST) and soft systems thinking (SST) are described, as these key concepts underwrite the systems movement. Indeed, many traditional management science techniques are firmly contained within HST. The chapter describes a key weakness with HST to explain the emergence of soft methodologies and SST. It also points to a key weakness in SSM, which Bell *et al* [4] argues can be alleviated by the incorporation of ideas from representational measurement theory [5].

On the software engineering side, a fundamental area of research has been that of software project management, which subdivides into two areas: software process control (SPC) and software process improvement (SPI). Bell [6] shows that traditional algorithmic cost models produce inaccurate software cost projections and argues that the new goal of cost estimation should be to construct better explanatory algorithmic models to produce more accurate and consistent forecasts. Moreover, Bell contends that the quantitative characterisation of the software development process is historically either inappropriate or inadequate. Bell *et al* [7] shows that the Goal/Question/Metrics (GQM) methodology of Basili and Rombach [8] establishes a way forward in addressing criticisms associated with metrics programmes, but recognises that GQM does not provide guidelines or methods for identifying problems as perceived by key stakeholders. Thus, they contend there is a need to augment GQM with a soft methodology that assists in identifying stakeholder problems, which may require metrication.

This chapter describes the Holon Methodology (originally designed as an informal *post-mortem* SPI approach) as an example of the combination of hard and soft approaches. A case study is described in which the methodology is applied to a major management information system project for a European airline. In the case study, an account is given of the application development, the problems that emerged and the proposed solutions from the perspective of a module leader involved in the project.

The chapter then covers the refinement of the Holon Methodology to produce the Holon Framework (Bell *et al* [4]) which continues the themes of process improvement and control but now applied to the management and planning of Higher Education and, by extension, to human activity systems in general. There is a shift in emphasis from a *post-mortem* approach to a visioning, or soft teleological, approach very much akin to the process adopted by Dearing [9] in producing his vision for Higher Education. System Dynamics (SD) is the primary mathematical technique selected both to explain the behaviour of the human activity system and to identify points of leverage through which motion towards agreed visions can be investigated and controlled. A brief review of the Holon Framework is provided and the research findings of an 'ongoing' case study at a university are described.

Finally, we introduce Burrell and Morgan's [10] framework for exploring social theories and their relationships with different approaches to studying organisations. A number of researchers, *e.g.* Checkland [3] and Lane [11], have applied this intellectual map to link methodologies and practices from their own disciplines with various social theories, in order to clarify the theoretical assumptions underpinning them. Bell *et al* [12] have derived a one-dimensional scheme based on the work of Burrell and Morgan [10] and place the relevant investigations in historical order on this scheme, to guide the positioning of the Holon Framework. This highlights its key characteristics and clarifies the underpinning theoretical assumptions.

We consider mixed-mode modelling to combine both hard and soft concepts. This chapter attempts to show that soft methodologies are associated with improvement for they address certain types of question *i.e.* 'the what', 'the where', 'the who'. Mathematical techniques, *e.g.* SD, are linked with control for they address different questions, *i.e.* 'the how', 'the why', 'the when'. Moreover, it is contended that representational measurement theory can cement hard and soft approaches. The Holon Framework is a mixed-mode modelling approach suited to various disciplines.

SYSTEMS MOVEMENT

The systems movement is concerned with the notions of systemic wholeness and systematic analysis. The systems movement contends that system concepts can provide a source of explanations for many kinds of observed phenomena which are beyond the reach of reductionist science Checkland [3]. Checkland identifies two fundamentally different ways of undertaking an inquiry in which systems ideas are applied. These have been labelled hard systems thinking and soft systems thinking.

Hard Systems Thinking

Checkland considers both systems engineering and RAND systems analysis as hard systems methodologies, because both are systematic in the sense that they proceed in a rational and well-ordered manner. Moreover, he highlights the essence of their approach to real-world problem solving:

> "there is a desired state S_1, and a present state,S_0, and alternative ways of getting from S_0 to S_1. 'Problem solving', according to this view, consists of defining S_1 and S_0 and selecting the best means of reducing the difference between them." Checkland [3]

He argues that the distinguishing characteristic of all hard systems thinking is the belief that real-world problems can be investigated in this way. It is argued that most hard methodologies are goal-centred or goal-orientated in that they assume the problem, *i.e.* 'the what', is given for the goal state S_1. For example, to build a product to meet certain requirements, the usual objective is to find the best way of building the product to meet the requirements *i.e.* 'the how'. Mathematical techniques such as regression analysis can investigate alternative ways to achieve state S_1. It is assumed that there is clarity and no ambiguity in the definitions of S_1 and S_0. We believe that the identification of the problem, *i.e.* 'the what' is a significant weakness of hard systems thinking, and agree that there is a need to combine mathematical techniques with a soft methodology.

Soft Systems Thinking

When investigating social situations, systems theorists realised that the problem, *i.e.* 'the what', could not be assumed as a given. Stakeholders may have different views of what are the most important problems to be solved in order to improve the situation. Over the last 20 years or so, 'soft' methodologies have emerged with the aim of attempting to assist in understanding the perspective of the stakeholder, leading, it is hoped, to relevant improvements in the area of concern.

We argue that some soft methodologies use systems as mental constructs to help the stakeholder and the facilitator make sense of a situation. Note that the frame of reference of the modeller changes from 'observer' to 'facilitator' in order to understand stakeholders' points of view. Most soft methodologies can be associated with soft systems thinking. Bell *et al* [13] argue that the main aim of the soft systems thinker is to identify state S_0 problems, *i.e.* 'the whats', relevant to that social situation which require solving or controlling in order to produce a desired state S_1. A brief overview of SSM is given below, as it is an important methodology, and it has been argued that it should be combined with simulation (see Lehaney *et al* [14]), and more specifically, System Dynamics (see Lane and Oliva [15]).

SSM [3] emerged from systems engineering. It is a systems-based general learning methodology (see Table 1) for investigating, learning about and improving a problem situation.

There are many accounts of successful applications of SSM in a variety of organisations. We would contend, however, that there are weaknesses in the method, and that one of these concerns the way in which system change is controlled. DeMarco [16] states that:

"You cannot control what you cannot measure"

Key stages of SSM Table 1

Stage	Stage Objective
1 and 2	Attempt to build the richest possible picture of the situation.
3	Aims to describe the nature of the chosen relevant system(s).
4	Produces conceptual models of the defined system(s).
5	Compares the conceptual models with the actual situation in order to generate debate with the stakeholders.
6	Outline possible changes that are desirable and feasible.
7	Involves taking action based on stage 6.

Bell *et al* [7, 13] contend that the lack of use of metrics within SSM is a significant methodological limitation. Furthermore, they explain that the identification of relevant problems and their metrication will lead to more informed decision-making. In summary, the mix of SSM as a framework of enquiry and GQM as a process for identifying goals and metrics results in a combined methodology, the Holon Methodology, in which each component enhances the other in a form of symbiosis.

THE HOLON METHODOLOGY

Background: Software Engineering

The software industry has grown and changed rapidly over the last five decades. Computing and software technology has become exponentially more sophisticated and powerful every year, triggering new software markets. Technological advances have enabled the production of complex software applications. As computer hardware costs have decreased, so software costs have increased, since software production is a labour-intensive activity involving skilled professionals. In fact, human costs are the most significant factor in software expenditure.

Unfortunately, the software industry is tarnished by problems such as cost overrun, schedule slippage and poor product quality. Taken together, these problems are known as the 'software crisis', and, despite the emergence of software engineering as a discipline, there are few signs that the crisis is abating. The two fundamental research areas within software engineering are software technology and software project management Thayer [17]; the latter is of interest here. As mentioned earlier, software project management subdivides into two important research areas, Software Process Control (SPC) and Software Process Improvement (SPI).

Software Process Control (SPC) Research

SPC research is underwritten by the notion that a disciplined approach to software production is needed in order to achieve sensible cost, schedule and quality targets. SPC focuses on the software development phases, *i.e.* product design, detailed design, programming/coding and system integration (see Conte *et al* [18]). SPC is attained through establishing a metrics programme, identifying project milestones, use of algorithmic cost models, monitoring differences between actuals and estimated milestones, explaining differences through the use of algorithmic cost models, and deriving strategies to enable milestones to be met. There are two fundamental and interrelated investigation areas associated with SPC research. These are: cost estimation (*e.g.* metrics and algorithmic cost models) and preparation methods (*e.g.* Work Breakdown Structures, Gantt and PERT Charts). SPI frameworks and methodologies are also used when establishing or updating a metrics programme to assist in deriving project goals.

Software Process Improvement (SPI) Research

SPI research is underpinned by the view that all issues of software quality revolve around improving the development process. Additionally, it aims to enhance quantitative understanding through numerical representation of identified problems in order to improve change management decision-making. SPI focuses on 'characterising', *e.g.* establishing and enhancing metric baselines, and 'improving', *e.g.* removing production "bottlenecks", and is underwritten by representational measurement theory [5].

Indeed, both SPC and SPI research are inextricably linked through the use of metrics. Measurement is concerned with capturing information about attributes of entities. A formal definition of measurement is given below.

> "Measurement is the process by which numbers or symbols are assigned to attributes of entities in the real world in such a way as to characterise them according to clearly defined rules. The numerical assignment is called the measure." Fenton *et al* [19]

An entity can be an object, *e.g.* a product, or perhaps an event, *e.g.* a process. The attribute is a feature or property of interest of the entity, *e.g.* effort is an attribute of a process. Refining our focus still further, Bell *et al* [7] suggests that there are three important SPI categories. These are Formal SPI frameworks (*e.g.* Capability Maturity Model [20]) and Informal SPI methodologies (*e.g.* GQM), and Combination SPI frameworks (*e.g.* Application of Metrics in Industry [21]). A Formal SPI framework is a rigid approach that addresses specific issues in order to improve the development process. Informal SPI methodologies, on the other hand, offer flexibility in selecting relevant process problems according to stakeholder viewpoints. A Combination SPI framework integrates a Formal SPI framework and an Informal SPI methodology. An overview of Informal SPI methodologies is now given, as they have been influential in the development of the Holon Methodology.

Informal SPI Methodologies

Many software measurement programmes have failed because they have ill-defined objectives [19]. In addressing this shortcoming, Basili and Rombach [8] developed a goal oriented measurement approach called the Goals/Questions/Metrics (GQM) methodology. They are emphatic in their support for a top-down measurement approach in software engineering, although the process of identifying goals and transforming them into quantifiable questions is complex.

Other researchers have refined the GQM methodology, or incorporated it into larger frameworks. For example, GQM has been incorporated into an evolutionary process improvement approach called Quality Improvement Paradigm (QIP), (see Basili [22]). Mellor [23] developed the GAMMA model, comprising Goal, Attribute, Measure, Means of measure and Action. This latter component is an important contribution to informal SPI methodologies because it emphasises the need to take action. For example, if the cost of effort is likely to exceed the target, then we might reduce the number of staff working on the project and renegotiate the functionality of the application to be delivered.

Goal Driven Software Measurement (GDSM) Park *et al* [24] is a methodology based on the idea that stakeholders use mental models to identify goals. This work emphasises the need to work closely with project teams to ensure that relevant goals are identified. This relates strongly to the work of Senge [25] who identifies methodologies to be used in team settings to elicit and formulate explicit representations of mental models, so that they can become a productive basis for dialogue, discussion and action.

Bell *et al* [7] find the GQM methodology a commendable approach to improving the quantitative visibility of the software development process. However, it does not in itself provide a structure for working with a client group; it does not give guidelines or methods for identifying the problems and goals as perceived by the stakeholders; and it does not encourage stakeholders to take action as part of the process improvement framework. It was felt that these problems could be rectified by the incorporation of GQM within the broader framework of Soft Systems Methodology, thus setting the GQM methodology within a broader system-based enquiry process.

Description: Framing, Enquiry and Metrication

Checkland [3] argues that researchers who apply systems concepts to investigate social situations face difficulties because these situations are never clearly defined. He prefers to use the word 'Holon' rather than 'system' as it highlights a distinctive approach to investigating such situations. Checkland indicates that the word 'Holon' was originally coined by Koestler to express the principle of hierarchical structure. We consider a Holon to be an abstract representation of a social situation that captures all problems. It is used as a framework to discover relevant issues from stakeholders' points of view; these are organised in a layered structure. In accordance with SSM, they are used to enquire into the problem domain by facilitating open dialogue. In its original conception, the Holon Methodology has four modes of working which broadly constitute stages. These are Framing, Enquiry, Metrication and Action.

Framing: this stage has a number of objectives, among which are that the stakeholders are identified and made aware of the methodology being used (it is important that they feel comfortable with this process of enquiry), that the framing Holon and environment Holon are identified and labelled (including sub-Holons where necessary) and that the investigators gain a broad understanding of the problem situation. Outputs from this stage will be the identified stakeholders ('the who') and an agreed Holon structure that can be used subsequently to structure the investigation and any modelling that takes place.

Enquiry: this stage aims to identify the issues and problems as perceived by the stakeholders. The process operates through group meetings with the stakeholders, during which information is placed in the relevant Holons through the use of rich pictures or written notes. The output from this stage is clarification of 'the musts' and 'the wants'. Additionally, the enquiry stage notes suggested links between Holons, the agent enabling the link, and some goals within each Holon which will feed forward to the following stages.

Metrication: this stage attempts to resolve the identified problems to enable metrics to be collected through the use of the GQM methodology, indicating when and where the metrics should be collected and by whom.

Action: this stage uses templates to collect and store metrics internally to the organisation. This increases the quantitative visibility of the situation and should facilitate stakeholder action.

The Holon Methodology is shown in Figure 1. It was originally conceived as a *post-mortem* approach to improve the software development process through examining completed software projects.

Software Engineering Case Study

This section outlines a small case study carried out on a real software project using the Holon Methodology in *post-mortem* mode; this is fully reported by Weetman [26]. The deliverable was a stand-alone client management system for a major European airline. The system was to be used by travelling sales representatives who were frequently away from the office. A client/server application was developed to run on laptop computers so that sales personnel had constant access to customer data from a regularly updated database.

The case study stakeholder was a module leader, responsible to the project manager, and responsible for a number of team members. The stakeholder was involved with design and development and, specifically:

- review of the functional specifications delivered by the client;
- high and low level design of three major modules;
- documentation of design specifications;
- preparation of unit test plans and system test plans;
  unit testing, code walkthroughs and system testing.

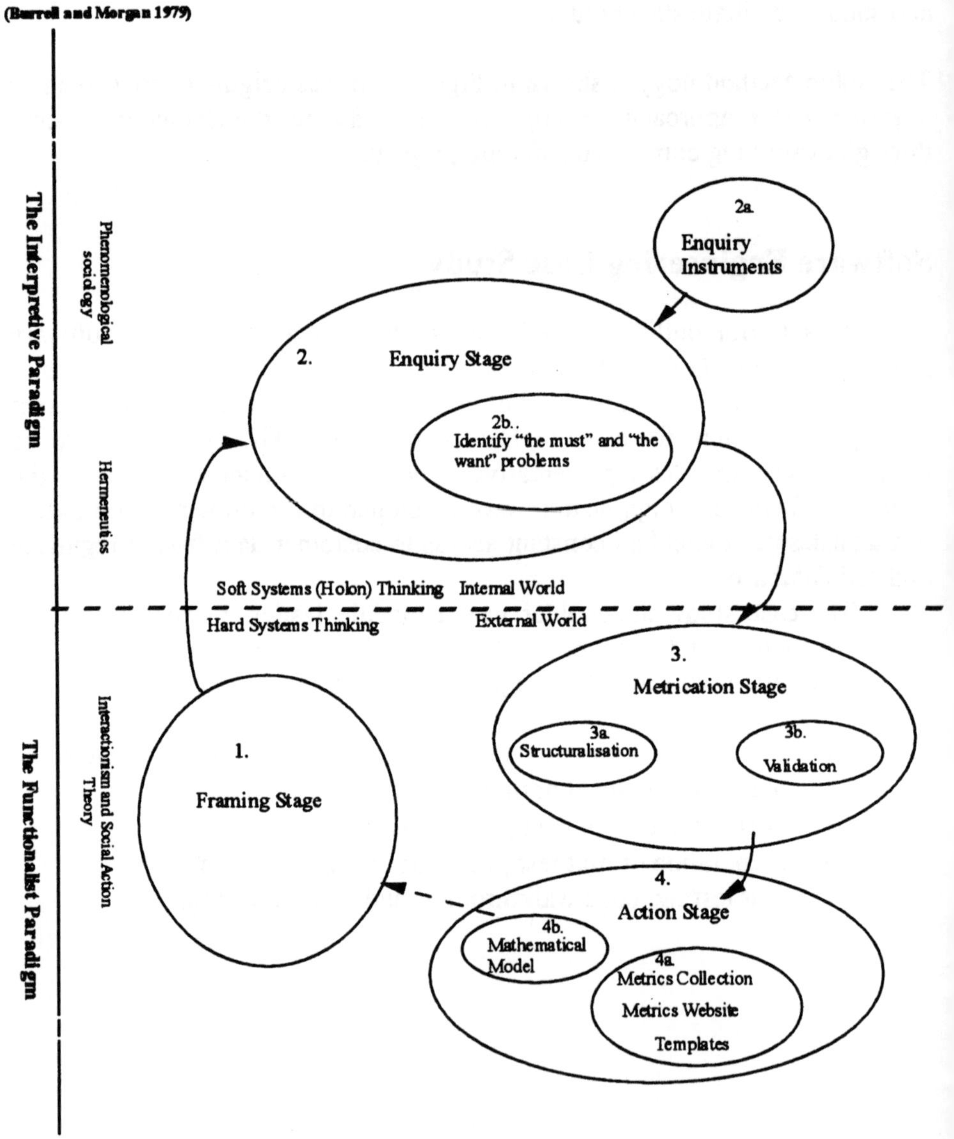

Figure 1. The Holon Methodology (Bell et al, 1999a)

As a module leader, the stakeholder provided information from both the broader management perspective and the more routine daily operations perspective. The approach employed a conceptual model of the development process to frame the sub-Holons within the higher level Holon of the developer organisation. At its highest level, the conceptual model concentrated on the client system in the developer organisation. The system of developing software is seen as a Holon of purposeful activity and the environment of the developer organisation surrounds and impacts on this. The environment must be considered as any changes will naturally effect the framing situation.

There were certain core activities within software development which were carried out as standard over a range of projects. These activities were framed in the conceptual model and represented as sub-Holons. The conceptual model of the development process is shown in Figure 2 below.

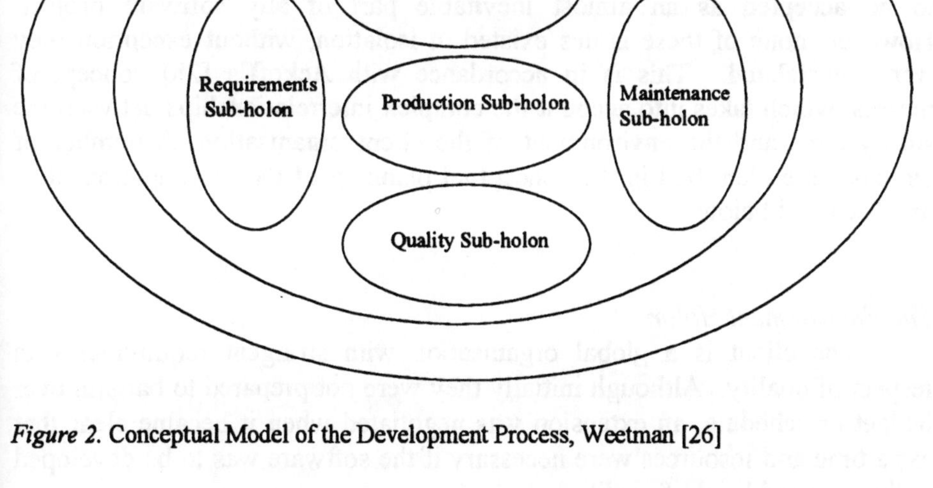

Figure 2. Conceptual Model of the Development Process, Weetman [26]

The conceptual model was used as a starting point in the approach and discussions with the stakeholder ensured the correctness and relevance of the model to the individual software development organisation. This sort of model provides a means of dealing with complexity whilst maintaining a view of the overall area of concern. It both encourages and focuses debate. The framing Holon captures all the problems which existed in the area of software development. It was important to extract those problems that were of relevance to the measurement programme, and these are highlighted by the decomposition of the Holon into sub-Holons.

Enquiry Findings

The first stages of the methodology were conducted through interviews with the stakeholder. The interviews were structured around questionnaires based on those developed by Al-Nakash [27], which were presented in two sections. The first section explored the environment of the developer organisation, seeking information about relatively high level issues. This helped establish a full understanding of the environment and helped build an awareness of any constraints affecting the development process. The second section covered the sub-Holons framed by the development Holon, with the objective of teasing out the main problem areas within the framing system, and determining how these were related to each other and the environment. During the interview process various issues emerged; some were contentious, and instigated debate, while others seemed to be accepted as an almost inevitable part of any software project. However, none of these issues existed in isolation; without exception they were interrelated. This is in accordance with Ackoff's [28] concept of messes, which takes into account the complex interrelationships between the sub-systems and the environment of the client organisation. A number of Holons were identified in the conceptual planning of the investigation; they are discussed below.

The Environment Holon

The client is a global organisation with stringent requirements in respect of quality. Although initially they were not prepared to bargain over budget or schedule, an extension was negotiated when it became clear that extra time and resources were necessary if the software was to be developed to the required level of quality.

The developer organisation is based in India, and has several offices worldwide. It prides itself on the standard of software it produces and at the time of the project was working towards gaining ISO9000 certification (subsequently obtained). Since the organisation operates on a global basis, the management are sensitive about ensuring its reputation beyond the realms of the local Indian software industry. It was therefore essential importance that the client be satisfied with the delivered system.

The project was initiated by the client who approached the development organisation with a set of functional requirements. The two companies had no prior experience of working together, although the developers had previously worked on projects with similar requirements. There was an initial meeting between the client and the stakeholder but, on the whole, the client organisation showed scant interest in issues regarding the software development process.

The Requirements Sub-Holon

At the start of the project, the development team was provided with a rudimentary prototype of the user interface, including a set of screen dumps. The client also provided some test data for the system.

The requirements sub-system was beset with problems from the outset. The main issues relate to the requirements specification provided by the client. This was found to be incomplete and ambiguous in several respects, with the result that new requirements continued to be added throughout the project lifecycle. As the development progressed, non-functional requirements, which had not been made explicit in the requirement specification, were demanded by the client. This raised difficulties not only in having to incorporate new requirements, but also because the development team decided that some of the requirements were not feasible. The situation was worsened by the non-availability of the author of the requirements specification during the project. Developers had access only to other members of the client organisation who could only offer their own interpretations of the original requirements.

The main impact of the requirement deficiencies was to be felt in the resource and production Holons. Slippage was inevitable as further meetings were called to clarify requirements and additional resources were required to compensate for time lost in modifying software to reflect the changes that were called for.

The Resource Sub-Holon

Resource allocation was found to be a critical issue in this project. The initial estimates of resources required were made well in advance and should have been adequate. However, the problems associated with requirements specification placed great pressure on the existing resources. The project team numbered between six and twelve people, increasing in response to slippage. All members of the team had at least three years programming experience, together with knowledge of database and user interface design.

Some difficulties were found in adapting to the introduction of new technology. The screen design required a knowledge of Visual Basic and this was built up over the course of the project. There was little formal training and the team had no access to Visual Basic books or journals. The development proceeded by "trial and error" and, not surprisingly, took longer than anticipated. An additional problem was lack of ownership of the modules. Key personnel were seconded to other projects during the development when management perceived their skills might be better used elsewhere. Module development was passed on to other staff with a resulting lack of motivation and sincerity among some members of the team. The Project Leader had no control over this poaching of staff and was moved off the project herself for a time to work on a system for a more valued client.

The Production Sub-Holon

Software production was inevitably slowed by the issues raised above, in particular the saga of incomplete and changing requirements specifications and the initial steep learning curve for the unfamiliar Visual Basic. Additional factors to do with quality impacted on production; these are discussed below.

The Quality Sub-Holon

The developer organisation was extremely concerned about quality issues. As part of the ISO9000 programme, team members received regular training and adhered to a set of guidelines and checklists to ensure quality. Although this was time consuming it was considered a major asset. Quality control procedures were strictly adhered to throughout the project and the client was satisfied with the delivered system. However, in response to the demands made by the budget and schedule, there were some compromises on the documentation.

The Maintenance Sub-Holon

As the code produced was strong, few problems were identified in the maintenance Holon. This was mainly due to the skill of the project team and the stringent quality control procedures. However, it was felt that maintenance activities were hampered by the poor training received by team members. This could have been rectified by allocating more resources to training, but it was not deemed to be a severe problem. Team members worked on-site for two months following implementation in order to train users of the system. During this time they were also able to remove bugs from the code and accommodate further requirements.

Metrication

From the Framing and Enquiry stages a number of problems emerge, which were developed into a suggested metrics programme through the GQM methodology. Additionally, an appreciation by the stakeholder of the importance of the problem in terms of a simple two valued scale of 'must' or 'want' was appended. A sample of the metrics generated from the requirements sub-Holon is given in Table 2 below.

Findings from the Software Engineering Case Study

Several interrelated problem areas were identified through the case study, many of which stemmed from the requirements specification. The ambiguities and inconsistencies here had major impacts throughout the development process, affecting all the sub-Holons within the framing situation. The methodology was able to identify a range of issues, some of which could be resolved, or at least better understood, through a measurement programme, and some of which required future action by the organisation. For example, a key finding in the Requirements sub-Holon was the need for the introduction of new technology to enable the capture of

Table 2: Identification of Requirement Metrics (amended from Weetman [26])

<table>
<tr><td>Project:
European Airline Case Study</td><td colspan="2">Where
Environmental Holon:
Client Organisation</td><td>Framing Holon:
Software Development</td><td>Sub-Holon:
Requirements</td></tr>
<tr><td colspan="5">Who: Module Leader</td></tr>
<tr><td colspan="5">What: Poor management of requirement changes</td></tr>
<tr><td colspan="5">Goal: Improve management of requirement changes</td></tr>
<tr><td>Problem No.</td><td>Goal</td><td>Sub-Goal</td><td>Question</td><td>Metrics</td></tr>
<tr><td>1</td><td>Improve management of requirement changes</td><td>Improve understanding of requests for requirement changes</td><td>How many requirement changes were requested?</td><td>Number of requirement changes requested</td></tr>
<tr><td></td><td></td><td></td><td>How many requirement changes were implemented?</td><td>Number of changes implemented</td></tr>
<tr><td></td><td></td><td></td><td></td><td>Number of man-hours for each change implemented</td></tr>
</table>

requirements for the system. Metrication alone did not appear to be sufficient to control the requirements specification process. Further iterations of the process would help ensure that the suggested metrics captured the elements of behaviour desired and also help discover more of the complex interactions at work within the software development Holon and its environment. Like SSM, the process should never end as learning and refinement should occur continuously.

Extending the Holon Methodology

The Holon Methodology described in the previous sections contributes to Informal SPI research and was designed as a *post-mortem* approach. However, the notions of process improvement and process control apply equally to organisational processes as they do to software development processes. The methodology has now been revised and is being used to investigate issues of management, quality and resource provision within a technology-based Department in a large University. In summary, it can now be used as a visioning approach, and also allows modelling of the crucial cause/effect relationships in operation so that a better understanding of system dynamics can be attained.

Basic features of the Holon Methodology are retained in the new framework, which combines the methodology with system dynamics (SD). The framework allows close working with a client group in understanding their current situation, in setting goals and asking questions of the current system, and in developing metrics that can be used to monitor performance. When this is coupled with the development of a stakeholder vision of the desired future state, the metrics offer a powerful means of assessing progress towards the vision, and provide reference behaviour modes that can be used to aid model development via SD.

Ultimately, the stakeholder group will be able to use the new framework to update the vision periodically, and to amend or develop new models of behaviour. This should permit the group to take control of the future direction of the Department, through structured debate with the tools available for examining alternative future scenarios in depth.

THE HOLON FRAMEWORK

Background: Higher Education

Higher Education (HE) in the UK has expanded considerably over the last three decades. It is argued that issues of resource management in HE institutions can not be separated from issues of quality and standards. Green [29] stresses that since the mid-1980s, public interest in and concern about quality and standards have been intensified by the increasing attention paid by successive British governments to reforming HE. The reasons for this are:

- Increasing student numbers against a backlog of public expenditure;
- the general quest for better public services;
- increasing competition within the education market for resources and students;
- the tension between efficiency and quality.

Institutional managers have a crucial role to play in relation to quality through:

- finding better ways of using institutional resources and generating new resources;
- being accountable to society by developing the means of assuring academic standards;
- developing improved systems for strategic planning and institutional management.

UK governments have demanded greater accountability in the quality and cost of universities, which should be open to public scrutiny. This has encouraged the emergence of 'managerialism' in their governance and direction. Trow [30] states that hard and soft managerialism concepts are applied to HE institutions. Hard managerialism generally involves people from government and business who are resolved to reshape and redirect universities through funding formulas and other mechanisms, such as criteria to assess teaching quality. Trow contends that business models are central to hard managerialism, as they assist in transforming universities into organisations similar enough to ordinary commercial companies to be assessed and managed in similar ways. The Higher Education Funding Council for England (HEFCE) implements and oversees government policies for the HE system. HEFCE works closely with the Research Assessment Exercise (RAE) team and the Quality Assurance Agency (QAA). The RAE team examines the quality of research within different institutions to guide the distribution of public funds. The QAA investigates aspects of teaching quality, which also affects university funding. We consider these bodies to be an integral part of the hard managerialism concept.

Soft managerialism involves senior administrators and appropriate academics in the universities. The soft concept views managerial effectiveness as an important component in the provision of quality HE at its lowest cost, and is focused around the idea of improving institutional efficiency. We go on to review the dominant approach to HE planning, and highlight weaknesses that question its efficacy in achieving the aims of soft managerialism.

Dominant HE Planning Approach

Galbraith [31] identifies the dominant HE planning approach which is associated with soft managerialism. The key parts of the approach are: a strategic plan, performance indicators (PIs), mathematical models, and artificial structures. A strategic plan usually entails a mission statement and related strategic aims, *e.g.* excellence in teaching and learning, which fulfils it. These strategic aims are treated separately and expressed in terms of goals which are assessed through the use of PIs. Furthermore, regression models and spreadsheets use the collected data for forecasting and budgeting purposes.

A university may be divided into faculties, each containing a number of schools or departments. Galbraith sees these groups as artificial structures used to facilitate competition for resources at the university level. The underpinning argument is that schools in competition will optimise their efforts, thus, optimising the overall performance of the faculties. Maximising faculty performance in turn optimises the total performance of the institution, therefore, meeting government objectives that may lead to further funding.

The use of performance measures within HE has been the focus of much debate. Kennedy and Clare [32] contend that performance measures have evolved for HE which provide some indication of strengths and weaknesses, and can be used as a basis for investigation, discussion and action. However, they point out that the collation of a range of indicators on a regular basis is not standard practice and so does not form part of routine decision-making processes. In addition, they argue that current indicators are formulated in response to perceived managerial issues, given the information available or obtainable. Many are concerned with resource utilisation without reference to the quantity or quality of the output obtained. What is needed is a greater understanding of basic measures so that more complex and meaningful measures can be explored, *e.g.* the 'value added' to student attainment measured against the resource inputs utilised to achieve it. Much of the time, attempts at management and planning result in resource allocations and strategy choices which seem to fail in addressing the educational needs of students, and hinder the academic development of schools. Furthermore, resource allocation often lags significantly behind resource need and these factors all strain at the fabric of academic activity. These issues are caused partly by the tendency to treat faculties and schools as partially under the control of the University and partially as autonomous units within a relatively flat, committee-based management structure.

Ackoff [23] contends that managers are not confronted with problems that are independent of each other, but with situations that consist of dynamic, transient and complex problems that interact with each other. He calls such situations 'messes'. Furthermore, he states:

> "Messes are systems of problems, the sum of the optimal solutions to each component problem taken separately is not an optimal solution to the mess. The behaviour of a mess depends more on how the solutions to its parts interact than on how they act independently of each other." Ackoff [28]

We contend that if every faculty and school has their own mission statement and objectives then dysfunctional behaviour will arise. The notion that dysfunctional behaviour can emerge from well-intentioned actions is associated with the Carnegie school of thought, which recognises that there are severe limitations on the thinking and reasoning power of the human mind. The principle of bounded rationality was formulated by Herbert Simon as the basis for understanding human behaviour in complex systems. It states:

> "The capacity of the human mind for formulating and solving complex problems is very small compared with the size of the problems whose solution is required for objectively rational behaviour in the real world or even for a reasonable approximation to such objective rationality." Simon [33]

This provides a basis for developing a theory of organisational behaviour. Simon later wrote:

> "Organisation theory is centrally concerned with identifying and studying those limits to the achievement of goals that are, in fact, limitations on the flexibility and adaptability of goal striving individuals and groups of individuals themselves." Simon [34]

We contend that the dominant HE planning methodology is inappropriate, and indeed may cause dysfunctional behaviour, as it concentrates on maximising the performance of an individual faculty or school, which may well have an adverse affect on others. An holistic approach is needed.

Emergence of the Holon Framework

Over the last few decades, governments have commissioned major reviews of the HE system in order to address specific challenges. In the latter part of the last century, there was a significant decline in traditional heavy industries, *e.g.* coal and railways, and the notion of a 'job for life' disappeared. In contrast, 'high tech' organisations sprang up, requiring a highly trained and educated workforce to stay competitive (such a workforce is highly mobile, with flexible career opportunities). The shift in employment patterns and rapid technological changes have created new challenges for the HE system.

Dearing [9] was given the opportunity to make recommendations on how the purpose, shape, structure and funding of the HE system should develop over the next 20 years. He investigated the current state of the HE system and its wider context, *i.e.* its relationship with society. Dearing argues that the UK must create a 'Learning Society', committed to learning throughout life. He envisioned HE as making a distinctive contribution to the development of this society through teaching, scholarship and research. He derived 93 recommendations to achieve his vision of a HE system; many of them have been implemented.

Dearing invited a range of senior academics, industrialists and politicians were invited to join the 'National Committee of Inquiry into Higher Education' chaired by Dearing. They investigated the problems, *i.e.* 'the whats', associated with the current state S_0 of the HE system and relevant environmental issues. The committee then constructed a vision of a desired state S_1 for the HE system to meet the needs of a 'learning society', and finally agreed recommendations, *i.e.* 'the hows', to achieve this vision.

The Holon Methodology is extended using Dearing's investigative approach, so that it can be used in a 'visioning' mode (rather than a *post-mortem* mode) and also includes modelling. The resulting Holon Framework is best described as a Soft Teleological Approach (see Figure 3) consisting of four main parts. The first part aims to highlight the problems, as viewed by the stakeholder, associated with the state of the current situation (S_0). The second part encompasses the most important problems to be solved in a vision of a future state (S_1). The third part lists the problems that need to be understood, and a number of goals are identified. Questions are developed to characterise each problem, and the generated metrics are used to assess the problem. The fourth part involves modelling the situation S_0 in order to improve it through informed systemic decision-making, to achieve the vision S_1.

The development of appropriate performance metrics and the use of modelling will allow an understanding of the interrelationships between key variables and a means of monitoring progress towards the vision. Clearly, the form of modelling to be undertaken should reflect the needs of the stakeholder group. However, in previous discussion we have highlighted the complex nature (mess) of interacting forces that many managers face, together with the possible influences of bounded rationality. Ackoff argues that the effective management of messes requires a systemic approach to planning and Morecroft [35, 36] has demonstrated that the concept of bounded rationality is directly represented in feedback structure. It would seem natural then to suggest that System Dynamics (SD) is an appropriate choice of modelling philosophy, as it aims to explain the dynamical behaviour of a system through modelling its structure. Indeed, Galbraith [31, 37] has demonstrated the effectiveness of SD as a core to HE planning and control.

Forrester [38] developed SD as a form of system theory based on a servo-mechanistic perspective (see Richardson [39]). Forrester [40] states that the theory of structure is exemplified in terms of four steps in a hierarchy: closed boundary; feedback loops; levels and rates; goals, observed condition, discrepancy and desired action. The main goal of a SD model is to represent a stakeholder's mental model of a situation, which can be used to explore different assumptions through various scenarios.

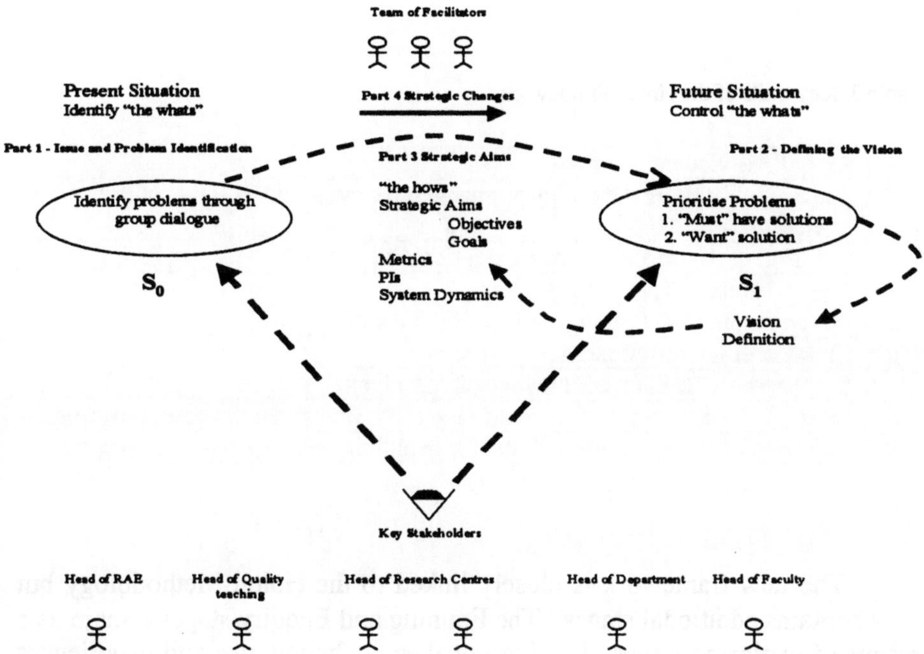

Figure 3. The Soft Teleological Approach, Bell [4]

Description: The Holon Framework

We contend that an informal SPI approach to controlling and improving HE systems complements a systemic view of planning. The underlying principle of the Holon Framework for costing and planning is:

> To identify an agreed future and to design ways of bringing it about within cost constraints

The Holon Framework combines a soft methodology (Holon) and a hard technique (System Dynamics). The Holon Methodology addresses 'the who', 'the what', and 'the where' type questions for the current state S_0 and generates a vision of a desired state S_1. Additionally, this produces a relevant metrics programme, and the collected metrics can be used as dynamic behaviour patterns. The explanatory capability of SD tackles 'the how', 'the why' and 'the when' type questions. Table 3 illustrates the most important traits of this framework.

Table 3: Key traits of the Holon Framework

1	An holistic view of a situation.
2	The use of a soft methodology to enable the capture of the stakeholders' point of view.
3	Controlling the effects of bounded rationality.
4	The researchers' role as facilitator.
5	Development of a desirable and feasible vision.
6	Creation of a relevant metrics programme.
7	Emphasis on the SD model ownership problem.
8	Producing the 'best solution' to achieve the vision given the cost constraints.
9	The continuous use of a SD model for examining various 'what-if' scenarios.

The new framework is closely linked to the Holon Methodology but now contains additional stages. The Framing and Enquiry stages remain as a means of exploring issues, drawing out themes, boundaries and experiences that the stakeholders feel are important within the problem context. These first two stages encourage a thorough examination of the current state, S_0, resulting in its definition. Next we include a new stage – Visioning – in which the client group explore a vision of the future that they feel is achievable and desirable. The vision will be expressed in terms of the Holon structure used throughout the enquiry and may be expressed formally in terms of root definitions. It is important though that the discussion of S_0 and the vision, S_1, are linked through issues and problems. The stakeholder group should identify the critical issues and problems, which require resolution if movement towards the vision is to be achieved. The issues and problems will, as in the previous case study, generate goals, questions and metrics. The Metrication stage allows the stakeholders to learn more about the problems and issues in S_0, and the subsequent Metrics Collection Stage enables them to measure their progress towards S_1. This is followed by the Action stage in which modelling is undertaken to clarify the processes which can effect movement from S_0 to S_1.

Naturally, although the stages are denoted sequentially, it is likely that, for a large project, different modes of working may happen simultaneously. For example, the metric collection process could well be undertaken over a long period of time (a year or more) and during this time modelling might be undertaken, further enquiry might take place, and the vision might change as the environment changes. A diagrammatic representation of the new framework is shown in Figure 4.

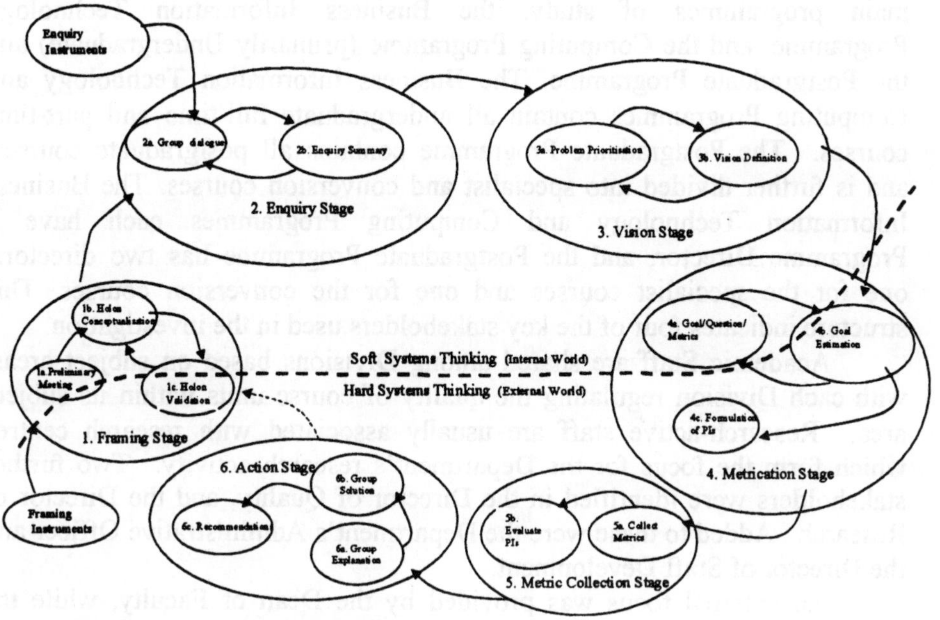

Figure 4: The Holon Framework, Bell [6]

Higher Education Case Study

The Holon Framework is being applied within a technology-based Department in a large University in an exploratory case study. In summary, a review of the QAA and RAE literature assisted in the identification and labelling of the relevant Holons, *i.e.* 'the where'. Relevant academic and administrative staff, *i.e.* 'the who', were identified as participants. Individual and group meetings were held to identify the problems, *i.e.* 'the whats', associated with the current state S_0 of the Department. This led to the formulation of an agreed desired state S_1, *i.e.* the vision, and an appropriate metrics programme, (see Warwick *et al* [41]).

The Framing Stage

It was first necessary to define a basic structure for the investigation in terms of the key stakeholders, *i.e.* 'the who', within the Department and the Holons, *i.e.* 'where', to be used to capture the issues, *i.e* 'the whats'.

The Department is organised so that all courses fall into one of three main programmes of study: the Business Information Technology Programme, and the Computing Programme (primarily Undergraduate) and the Postgraduate Programme. The Business Information Technology and Computing Programmes contain all undergraduate full-time and part-time courses. The Postgraduate Programme contains all postgraduate courses, and is further divided into specialist and conversion courses. The Business Information Technology and Computing Programmes each have a Programme Director, and the Postgraduate Programme has two directors, one for the specialist courses and one for the conversion courses. This structure indicates four of the key stakeholders used in the investigation.

Academic Staff are shared among Divisions based on subject areas, with each Division regulating the quality of course units within its subject area. Research-active staff are usually associated with research centres which form the focus for the Department's research activity. Two further stakeholders were identified in the Director of Quality, and the Director of Research. Added to these were the Department's Administrative Officer and the Director of Staff Development.

An external focus was provided by the Dean of Faculty, while the Head of Department provided an overview of all the Department's activities and external links within the University and with industry. The complete list of stakeholders is shown in Figure 5.

Intervention Structure

In order to structure the discussion of issues and concerns a number of Holons were identified which it was felt would capture the essential structure of the HE problem area. The Holons were identified with reference to the published guidelines for both the QAA. and the RAE. and with reference to the activities undertaken by the Department.

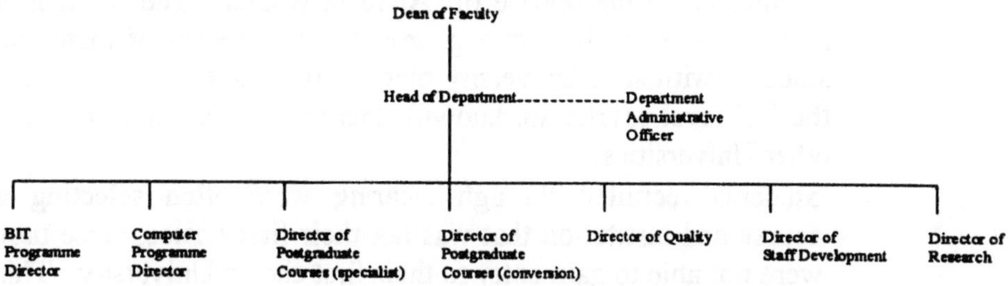

Figure 5. *List of Stakeholders, i.e. 'the who', Participating in the Study*

The Framing Holon was the Department itself and within this there were Holons for Admissions, Research Progression, Resources, Student Progression, Student Support, Quality Management and Cost Management. The Framing Holon itself was within wider Holons representing the University, Government and Industry. A summary of the activities conducted thus far is shown in Figure 6. As part of the Framing Stage, a first round of individual interviews with stakeholders was conducted so that issues and concerns could begin to be drawn out.

The Enquiry Stage

The group meetings that followed the first round of individual meetings began to produce themes within each Holon and to define issues associated with the current situation, S_0. It is not possible to include the entire analysis of all Holons here, so some elements from the Admissions Holon are used as an example of the type of enquiry undertaken and to illustrate the process. A number of particular issues within the Admissions Holon seem to result from general forces and trends. Examples of issues raised within the Enquiry stage for the Admissions Holon:

- The Department has expanded rapidly over the last 10 years, responding to changes in Government policy, market forces and University policy. New and innovative courses have fuelled the growth and provide a diverse computing and IT programme, so increasing choice and appeal to students. However, the pressures of rapid expansion and diversity are now being felt and should be addressed.
- Undergraduate recruitment activity seems to result in relatively few "firm acceptances" that convert into students in the period

running up to the release of 'A' level results. The result is a high reliance on the clearing process (the process of matching students without a University place with course vacancies once the 'A' level results are known); this is in common with many other Universities.

- Students recruited through clearing were often selecting a course and institution that was not their first choice, since they were not able to gain entry to their first choice University. This may impact their motivation and a high reliance on students recruited through clearing may place downward pressure on student retention.

Discussion in both individual and group sessions centred around general issues of the type described above. As an example of the type of feedback structures emerging, it was felt that the reliance on the clearing process for recruitment placed pressure on course retention rates, which in turn (assuming the Department is maintaining its size) increased pressure on the need to recruit new students the following year, which in turn placed greater

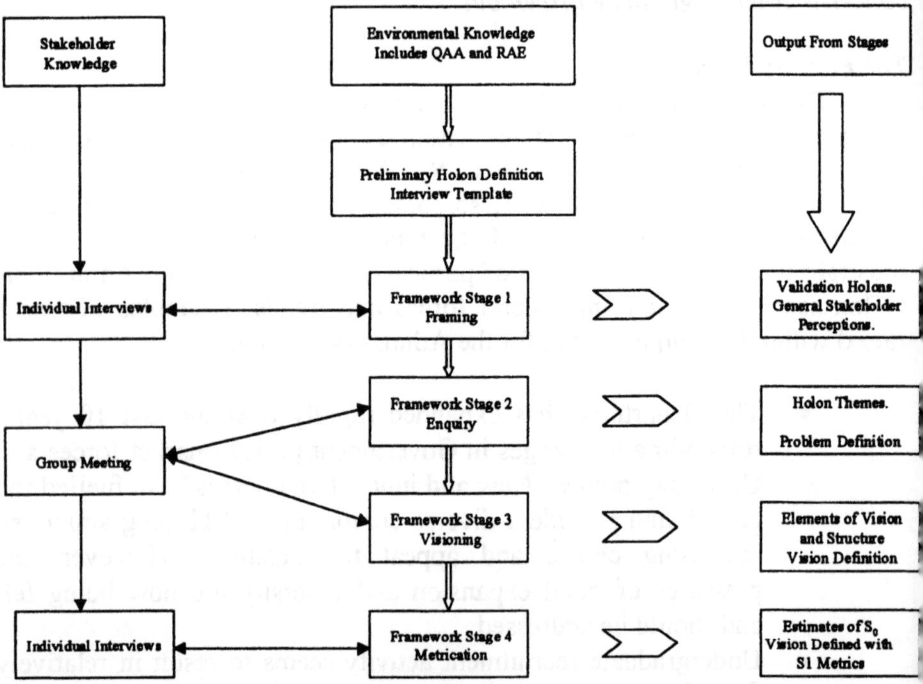

Figure 6: The Intervention Process to Date, Warwick et al [41]

emphasis on the clearing process, and so on. Leverage points for easing the pressure on recruitment would include increasing the retentionof students on courses (with feedforward to the Resources and Student Progression Holons), encouraging more students to accept places prior to clearing, and so on. Larger feedback structures emerged such as the extent to which new students applied as a direct result of hearing about the successful and rewarding experiences of graduating students. This was a feedback mechanism operating strongly at postgraduate level where a high proportion of MSc students apply as a result of word-of-mouth recommendations.

The enquiry stage produced, for each Holon, a number of themes and associated issues. For the Admissions Holon these included, *inter alia*:

- The requirement to maintain greater control over the admissions process.
- The need to recruit only those students who we believe have a reasonable expectation of passing their course (this would include adherence to entry qualifications and the counselling of students as to their choice of course when necessary).
- The need to ensure that all students have realistic expectations of their course, of passing their course, and of University life on entry to full or part-time study. Mismatch of their expectations with those of their tutors and the University often leads to withdrawal or failure.

In thinking about how the future might be, *i.e.* in beginning the visioning process, these themes highlight a number of problems that require addressing, and indicate a possible type of response to each.

The Visioning Stage

In moving towards a vision of the future, the Holon Framework encourages stakeholders to address the problems that have been identified in a number of ways. Ackoff [42] argues that problems can be resolved, solved or dissolved. Resolution requires finding an heuristic, or satisficing, outcome that would normally have a subjective, experiential and qualitative orientation. Solving a problem means to select a means that will produce an optimal, or best possible, outcome, and would normally be quantitatively based, relying on observation and measurement. Problem dissolution requires change to either the entity that has the problem, or to its environment in order to remove the problem.

In much the same way, problems identified by the stakeholders require a response, and these responses were of differing types. Some were for policy definition (or redefinition), some were for further investigation, some called for a metric collection programme and some suggested systemic change within the Department and perhaps the environment (at Faculty or University level). The problems arising were listed and a response suggested. The stakeholders were also asked to decide whether a problem was a 'must' or a 'want', *i.e.* a problem that must be solved or one which they would like to solve. As an example, some problems and responses relating to the theme of Admissions Standards are shown in Table 4.

The vision for each Holon was articulated by the stakeholder group and general descriptions were written in the form of root definitions, a concept borrowed from SSM. It should be emphasised that the vision is not intended as a utopian ideal that stakeholders could only dream of, but a realistic and attainable vision of a way for the Department to develop over the next two or three years.

The Metrication Stage

Some of the problems identified required responses which involved metrication -- a process of observation and measurement. The metrication stage aims to define a protocol for the collection of the metrics, and to obtain estimates from the stakeholder group for each metric for the current position, S_0, and the desired future position, S_1.

Table 5 is given below to illustrate the process of metrication in reference to the problems described in Table 4, where the responses require metrics collection. Using the GQM methodology, themes and problems are re-expressed as goals and sub-goals, from which follow questions and metrics. For example, the third theme outlined above "Ensuring that all students have realistic expectations of their course ..." is expressed as the goal in Table 5 and the first problem associated with this theme listed above "Concern about quality of some students entering our courses via clearing" is formulated as the first sub-goal in Table 4. The table shows some of the metrics suggested in relation to the undergraduate course.

The metrication process has produced a programme of data collection that is already underway. The information provided will be useful in two ways. Firstly, it will provide evidence by which progress towards the Department's vision can be monitored as it progresses from S_0 to S_1.

Secondly the sequences of observations will provide reference behaviour mode for the System Dynamic modelling stages that are to follow.

Higher Education Case Study Findings

This case study has been running for 6 months during which time the framework stages Framing to Metrication have been completed. As a result of this work to date, a total of 30 initiatives have been identified for the academic year 2000-2001, including the collection of identified metrics in preparation for the next academic year. All of the initiatives have been developed as a direct result of either individual and group meetings with stakeholders. The stakeholders have seemed well-motivated in contributing to this research and many have expressed their support for the intervention being undertaken. Clearly, this sort of positive group feeling is important in driving the process and in developing a commitment to act, whatever that action might turn out to be.

The initiatives have been grouped into the following broad areas:

- IS and IT based tool development;
- Quality Management;
- Process Control;
- Student perceptions and motivation;
- Policy development and redevelopment.

It is hoped that significant progress will be made on many of the initiatives during the 2000/2001 academic year. The next stage of the framework involves development of models of cause and effect using the System Dynamics to investigate inherent interrelationships. It is hoped that the models will develop into a management tool so that senior staff within Department can develop a clearer understanding of system behaviour and use the tool in 'what if' mode as a support for policy definition and analysis.

Table 4: Problems and Responses

Project: Admission Standards Issues	**Environmental Holon:** Department	**Framing Holon:** Admissions	**Sub-Holon:** Recruitment	
	Problem	**Who**	**Must/ Want**	**Response**
1	Concern about quality of some students entering our courses via clearing	All course leaders	M	Develop a metrics programme to understand the problem before changes are proposed.
2	Concern about the high number of new students to be recruited each academic year	Course leaders and senior staff	M	Develop a metrics programme to understand the problem before changes are proposed.
3	Concern about the motivation of applicants to our courses	All course leaders	W	Investigate ways of assessing motivation
4	Concern about the high proportion of students recruited through clearing	Course leaders and senior staff	W	Develop a metrics programme to understand the problem before changes are proposed.
5	No data regarding the schools and colleges feeding the Department	Admissions tutors	W	Define a programme for information collection.
6	No policy for course advertising and targeting potential students	Admissions tutors	W	Define policy and budget for advertising.

Table 5: Goals, Sub-goals and Metrics

Where:		**Environment Holon** University		**Framing Holon** Department		**Sub Holon** Admissions
Who: Admissions Tutors						
What: Admissions Standards						
Goal: Admit students with accurate expectations of the course						
			Protocol		**Estimated**	
Sub Goal:	**Question:**	**Metric:**	**When S_0**	**Data Collection**	**S_0**	**S_1**
Maintain clearing entry standards	What proportion of enrolled BSc students offered places during clearing?	Number of places offered in clearing/ total offered	July 2000	Collect metric when enrolment complete	75%	37%
	What proportion of new BSc students have studied HE before and failed?	Number of students in HE before/ total students	July 2000	Collect metric each week over the clearing period and monthly through subsequent application cycle	3%	1%
	What proportion of BSc students are transferring from another University to an equivalent course?	Number of students transferring/ total students	July 2000	Collect metric each week over the clearing period and monthly for subsequent application cycle	5%	5%

BURRELL AND MORGAN'S HEURISTIC SCHEMA

Burrell and Morgan [10] have produced an intellectual map to highlight the meta-theoretical assumptions of social theories and their relationship with different approaches to studying organisations. Several researchers, *e.g.* Lane [11] and Checkland [3] have used the map to link methodologies from their disciplines with different social theories in order to clarify the different meta-theoretical assumptions underpinning them. Bell *et al* [12] have derived a one-dimensional scheme based on Burrell and Morgan's work to show the underpinning assumptions of cost models and this has been extended to include formal and combination SPI frameworks and informal SPI methodologies.

Burrell and Morgan's framework "is a heuristic device rather than ... a set of rigid definitions" (see Burrell and Morgan [10]). It has two principal dimensions: the nature of social science and the nature of society. The first examines the meta-theoretical assumptions that underpin approaches to social science. They conceptualise social science in terms of four sets of assumptions related to ontology, epistemology, human nature and methodology (see Figure 7). Additionally, they highlight the extreme subjective / objective attributes of each key assumption. The second investigates the different theoretical assumptions that underwrite various ways of studying society. The two extremes of this dimension, which are based on the order / conflict debate, are called the sociology of regulation and the sociology of radical change. We believe that the algorithmic cost models and SPI approaches are associated with the sociology of regulation and we are only concerned with the functionalist and interpretive paradigms.

The functionalist and interpretive paradigms can be found at the top of the one-dimensional scheme. The social theories associated with them are positioned above the assumptions on the nature of social science. The arrows pointing up indicate the general meta-theoretical assumptions underpinning that category of thought.

Considering just the informal SPI methodologies, we associate the GQM, QIP and GAMMA methodologies with integrative theory. This seeks to combine aspects of interactionism and social system theory, and occupies the central position within the functionalist paradigm. Work undertaken within this category of thought attempts to take into account the subjective views of stakeholders. There is a significant shift in realism to a more subjective position within the middle ground of functionalism.

Goal Driven Software Measurement (GDSM) Park *et al* [23] is currently the most subjective SPI approach, where opinions are actively sought and discussed. They accept that social situations tend to be unique so that capturing the subjective views of the stakeholders is important. This implies that they take a nominalist ontological perspective, and a voluntarist view of human nature.

Bell *et al* [12] contends that there is a need to use a soft methodology to allow the researcher to understand the stakeholder viewpoint. We selected Soft Systems Methodology (SSM) because it is a system based methodology. The aim of the methodology is to identify relevant problems, *i.e.* 'the whats' as perceived by stakeholders. Checkland [3] believes that SSM is linked with phenomenology. The positioning of SSM would not be too far left of centre of the interpretive paradigm, because the methodology yields a picture of common structures for specific social situations over a period of time.

We believe the Holon Methodology (post mortem mode) to be connected with Hermeneutics. Hermeneutics is concerned with interpreting and understanding the products of the mind, e.g. books and sculptures, which characterise the social and cultural world. The generation of metrics and qualitative modelling enables the link to the functionalist paradigm. Qualitative modelling, e.g. influence diagrams [43], assists in determining the relationships between identified problems. The Holon Framework (extended from the Holon Methodology) in the visioning mode is linked to Phenomenological Sociology. Phenomenological Sociology is concerned with social reality that is reflected through intersubjective shared meanings, which are continually negotiated, sustained and changed through everyday interactions of relevant individuals. We consider our style of SD modelling linked to Interactionism (characterised by the search for regularities found beneath social situations which are extracted through formal analysis) and Social Action Theory (characterised by the investigation of subjective meanings by which individuals direct their actions). This enables the link to the functionalist paradigm.

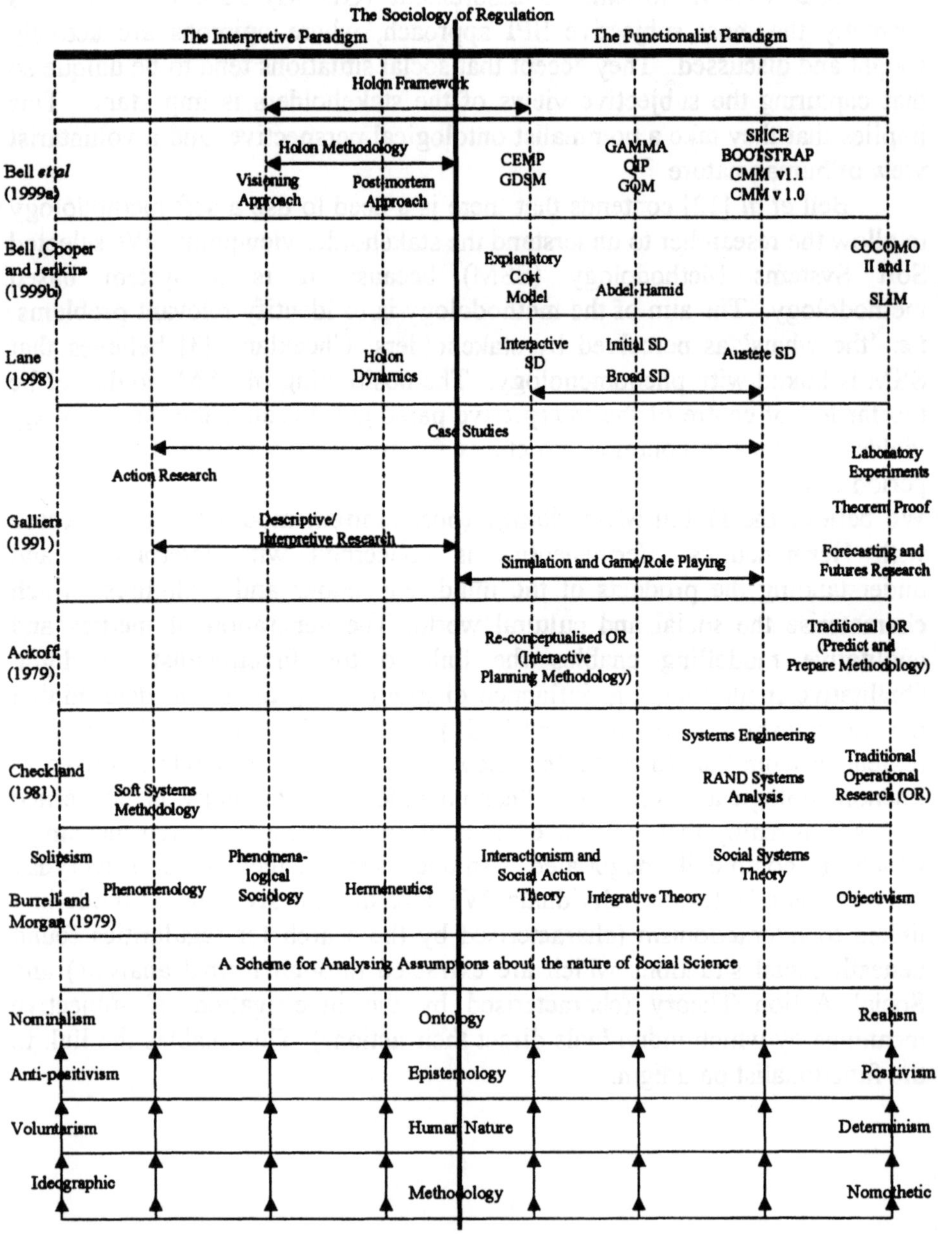

Figure 7. ne-dimensional scheme (amended from Bell et al [7])

CONCLUSION

A detailed account of the manifestation of the Holon Framework has been given. The Kipling quotation at the start of the chapter confirms the view that soft methodologies complement hard techniques. The Holon Framework tackles all the questions identified by Kipling. Soft methodologies address 'the what', 'the where', and 'the who' type questions, which can be related to the process improvement issue. Hard techniques tackle 'the how', 'the why' and 'the when' type questions, which can be linked to the process control issue. Representational measurement theory cements these approaches.

We have described two case studies using the Holon Methodology and the Holon Framework. The first case study, conducted in the *post-mortem* mode, examined a completed software project. The conceptual model (see Figure 2) was found be an effective method for capturing problems associated with the software project. The model was found to act as a stimulus to the module leader, who was able to articulate a clear picture of the relationships between the various Holons. Additionally, metrics were identified to characterise relevant problems, and which could be used to enhance control of future software projects.

The second case study, conducted in the visioning mode, investigated a Department within a university. The conceptual model enabled the stakeholders to identify problems associated with the current state, S_0. The problems that 'must' be addressed influenced the formulation of a future state, S_1. Moreover, the identified metrics (see Table 5) that epitomise the problems will allow the stakeholders to assess whether or not progress towards the agreed vision is being achieved. The collected data may be viewed as reference behaviour mode patterns that can be used to construct an SD model to highlight the interrelationships within the system, *i.e.* the structuralisation of the identified system. Moreover, the SD models can guide the formulation of strategies, through 'what if' scenario planning, to ensure the future state is reached. The Holon Framework contains aspects of both 'soft' and 'hard' systems thinking, although it is not a rigid sequential approach. The strengths of the framework are:

- it is flexible (stages can be revisited or emphasis can be placed on different stages according to stakeholder needs);
- it offers a means of working with the stakeholder group and empowering them to define a viable future and move towards it;

- it provides explanation and understanding of a complex world through the modelling stages.

(see Table 3 for key traits associated with the Holon Framework).

Moreover, a one-dimensional schema, based on Burrell and Morgan [10] is used to highlight the distinctiveness of the Holon approach, which ranges across the Interpretive to the Functionalist paradigm. From our case studies, regularities are beginning to emerge. This type of research may be underpinned by the essence of General Systems Theory (GST); Boulding [44] considers that it has two fundamental objectives:

> "The objectives of General Systems Theory then can be set out with varying degrees of ambition and confidence. At the low level of ambition but with a high degree of confidence it aims to point out similarities in the theoretical constructions of different disciplines, where these exist, and to develop theoretical models having applicability to at least two different fields of study. At a higher level of ambition, but with perhaps a lower degree of confidence it hopes to develop something like a "spectrum" of theories - a system of systems which may perform the function of a "gestalt" in theoretical construction."
>
> Boulding [44]

We have found that some Holons, *e.g.* resource and quality Sub-Holons, were used in both case studies. Additionally, similar problems in these Sub-Holons were identified by the stakeholders, *e.g.* high staff turnover rates, lack of ownership of modules (software or course units), compromising of various quality procedures, *etc*. This finding generates the conjecture that common SD archetypes will be found in Software Engineering and Higher Education case studies. It is likely that future research may fulfil the 'generalisation' objective of GST

The Holon Framework is going through a process of maturation through practical use. We have already identified a number of important areas for improvement. First, the enquiry instruments need enhancement. Second, further grounding in Holism and Gestalt Psychology may help guide the enquiry process. It is thought that the latter finding indicates we are developing a spectrum of theories, fulfilling the second objective of GST.

Finally, stakeholders from both case studies have found the modelling process thought-provoking and enlightening. Moreover, some of the issues raised through the initial stages of the Higher Education case study have already prompted change within the Department concerned. It is to be expected that academic objections may be raised to this type of intervention framework, however the stakeholders will rightly be the ultimate arbiters of the success or otherwise of such an intervention.

REFERENCES

[1] Kipling, R. *Just So Stories*, 2nd Ed., Doubleday, New York, USA, 1912.

[2] Rosenhead, J. *Rational Analysis for a Problematic World. John* Wiley and Sons, Chichester, UK, 1989.

[3] Checkland, P.B. *Systems Thinking, Systems Practice*, John Wiley and Sons, Chichester, UK, 1981.

[4] Bell, G.A., Cooper, M, A., Kennedy, M., and Warwick, J. The Development of the Holon Planning and Costing Framework for Higher Education Management. In *Proceedings of the 18th International Systems Dynamics Conference*, Bergen, Norway, 2000b.

[5] Fenton, N.E. and Pfleeger, S.L. *Software Metrics: A Rigorous And Practical Approach,* International Thomson Computing Press, London, UK, 1996.

[6] Bell, G.A. *An Interdisciplinary Systems Approach to Software Cost Explanation – A Way Forward*? Forthcoming PhD Thesis, 2000a.

[7] Bell, G.A., Cooper, M.A., Jenkins, J.O., Minocha, S. and Weetman, J. SSM + GQM = The Holon Methodology: A Case Study, *10th European Software Control and Metrics Conference, Herstmonceux,* England, 1999a.

[8] Basili, V.R. and Rombach, H.D. Tailoring the Software Process to project Goals and Environments. *Proceedings of the Ninth International Conference on Software Engineering,* Monterey, IEEE Computer Society Press, 1987.

[9] Dearing, R. *Higher Education in the Learning Society*: Report of the National Committee, The National Committee of Inquiry into Higher Education, HMSO, UK, 1997.

[10] Burrell, G. and Morgan, G. *Sociological Paradigms and Organisational Analysis*, Gower, Aldershot, UK, 1979.

[11] Lane, D.C. Social Theory and System Dynamics Practice. *European Journal of Operational Research*, 113 (3), 1998.

[12] Bell, G.A., Cooper, M.A., and Jenkins, J.O. Software Cost Estimation: Where Next? *In Proceedings of the United Kingdom Academy for Information Systems (UKAIS '99)*, York University, UK, pp. 575-587, 1999b.

[13] Bell, G.A., Cooper, M.A., and Kennedy, M. The Emergence of the Holon Methodology, *INCOSE UK Autumn Event*, Malvern (DERA), UK, 1999c.

[14] Lehaney, B, Clark, S.A. and Paul, R.J. A Case of an Intervention in an Outpatients Department. *JORS*, 50, 9:877-891, 1999.

[15] Lane, D.C. and Oliva, R. The Greater Whole: Towards a Synthesis of SD and SSM. *European Journal of Operational Research*, 107: 214-235, 1998.

[16] DeMarco, T. *Controlling Software Projects*, Prentice Hall, New York, USA, 1982.

[17] Thayer, R. H. *et al*, Major Issues in Software Engineering Project Management, *IEEE Transactions on Software Engineering*, 7 (4): 333-342, 1981.

[18] Conte, S.D., Dunsmore, H.E., and Shen, V.Y. *Software Engineering Metrics and Models*, Benjamin Cummings, Menlo Park, CA, USA, 1986.

[19] Fenton, N.E., Whitty, R., and Iizuka, Y. (Eds) *Software Quality Assurance And Measurement A World-Wide Perspective*, International Thomson Computing Press, London, UK, 1995.

[20] Humphrey, W.S. *Managing The Software Process*, Addison-Wesley, Reading, MA, USA, 1989.

[21] AMI, *AMI Handbook: A Quantitative Approach to Software Management,* South Bank University, London, UK, 1992.

[22] Basili, V.R. (1995) "Applying the Goal/Question/Metric Paradigm in the Experience Factory", In *Fenton, N.E., Whitty, R., and Iizuka, Y.* (Eds.), 1995.

[23] Mellor, P. The GAMMA Paradigm, *Private Communication*, City University, London, UK, 1997.

[24] Park, R.E., Goethert, W.G. and Florac, W.A., Goal-Driven Software Measurement - A Guidebook. Tech. Report *SEI*-96-HB-002, Software Engineering Institute, Pittsburgh, USA, 1996.

[25] Senge, P.M. *The Fifth Discipline: The Art and Practice of the Learning Organisation*. Doubleday/Currency, New York, USA, 1990.

[26] Weetman, J. *Enhancing GQM Through SSM: A Case Study*. Unpublished MSc Report, City University, London, UK, 1998.

[27] Al-Nakaash, K.K. *A Tentative Approach to Software Process Improvement.* Unpublished MSc Report, City University, London, UK, 1997.

[28] Ackoff, R.L. The Future of Operational Research is Past. *JORS*, 30:93-104, 1979.

[29] Green, D. *What is Quality in Higher Education?* St. Edmundsbury Press, 1994.

[30] Trow, M. Managerialism and the Academic Profession: The Case of England. *Higher Education Policy*, 7 (2): 11-18, 1994.

[31] Galbraith, P.L. When Strategic Plans are not Enough: Challenges in University Management. *System Dynamics: An International Journal of Policy Modelling*, X (1 and 2): 55-84, 1998a.

[32] Kennedy, M. and Clare, C. Some Issues in Building System Dynamics Models for Improving the Resource Management Process in Higher Education. In *Proceedings of the 18th International Systems Dynamics Conference*, Wellington, New Zealand, 1999.

[33] Simon. H.A. Rationality and Decision Making, *In Models of Man*. John Wiley and Sons, New York. 1957.

[34] Simon, H.A. *Administrative Behaviour*, 3rd Ed. Free Press, New York, USA, 1976.

[35] Morecoft, J.D.W. System Dynamics: Portraying Bounded Rationality, *Omega*, 11 (2): 131-142, 1983.

[36] Morecroft, J.D.W. Rationality in the Analysis of Behavioural Simulation Models. *Management Science*, 31 (7): 900-916, 1985.

[37] Galbraith, P.L. System Dynamics and University Management. *System Dynamics Review*, 14(1): 69-84, 1998b.

[38] Forrester, J.W. *Industrial Dynamics*, Productivity Press, Cambridge, MA, USA, 1961.

[39] Richardson, G.P. *Feedback Thought in Social Science and Social Theory*, University of Pennsylvania Press, Philadelphia, USA, 1991.

[40] Forrester, J.W. Market Growth as Influenced by Capital Investment. *Industrial Management Review*, 9: 83-105, 1968.

[41] Warwick, J., Bell, G.A., Cooper, M.A., and Kennedy, M. Higher Education Planning Using the Holon Planning and Costing Framework: From Framing to Metrication. South Bank University Technical Report, *SBU-CISM*-00-05, London, UK, 2000.

[42] Ackoff, R.L. *Creating the Corporate Future*. John Wiley and Sons, New York, 1981.

[43] Coyle, R.G. *System Dynamics Modelling: A Practical Approach*, Chapman and Hall, London, UK, 1996.

[44] Boulding, K.E. General Systems Theory - the Skeleton of Science, *Management Science*, 2, 197-208, 1956.

3

FRAMING: A META-FRAMEWORK FOR THE USE OF MIXED-MODE MODELLING

John Davies and Vicky Mabin
School of Business and Public Management
Victoria University of Wellington, New Zealand.

ABSTRACT

This chapter looks at framing as a meta-framework for the use of mixed-mode modelling. We outline a variety of problem solving and decision-making approaches that draw implicitly or explicitly on notions of framing, and demonstrate how framing acts not only as a meta-framework, bringing together a range of methodologies under one umbrella, but also helps us to recognise subtleties within and distinctions between approaches. The use of framing is illustrated through a number of mini-cases involving a variety of typical organisational and problematic situations, where framing can be used to develop better understanding of often ill-structured situations. Frames are drawn from a range of complementary fields and disciplines, from the management and social sciences, and spanning the hard and soft spectrum. We discuss general issues of problem identification and organisational problem structuring, make links to aspects of organisational theory and knowledge management, and consider the development of framing as a pedagogical strategy.

This chapter draws together and builds on materials previously presented at IFORS, ORSNZ, ORS and DSI conferences.

M.G. Nicholls et al. (eds.),
Mixed-Mode Modelling: Mixing Methodologies for Organisational Intervention, 63–119.

Keywords: mixed-mode modelling, framing, OR/MS, metaphor, multimethodology, pedagogy,

INTRODUCTION

In this chapter, we explore framing as a meta-framework for the use of mixed-mode modelling. In providing a selective review of related literatures on framing, we outline a variety of problem solving and decision-making approaches developed by the authors and others that can be said to draw implicitly or explicitly on notions of framing. We demonstrate how framing acts not only as a meta-framework, bringing together a range of methodologies under one umbrella, but also helps to recognise subtleties within and distinctions between approaches, highlighting and shadowing various framing effects.

The chapter will thus seek to use framing as a meta-framework to identify commonalities and complementarities in seemingly disparate approaches to the understanding of a variety of problematic situations. The situations addressed will relate, for instance, to typical organisational problems, using specific examples of downsizing and resource allocation. Comment will also be offered on the use of framing in understanding the effective use of rhetoric and rhetorical critique as well on more general issues of problem identification and organisational problem structuring, and the development of framing as a pedagogical strategy.

The use of framing is demonstrated using a number of mini-cases. The frames that are used in illustration are drawn from the management and social sciences, spanning the hard and soft spectrum. Some may be labeled as mathematical frames facilitating 'technical' analysis of highly structured problems where there may be little disagreement of what the problem is or about how to solve it, at one extreme, or as qualitative metaphorical frames facilitating effective problem description and the 'better understanding' of ill-structured problems, at the other. Examples of the latter qualitative frameworks will be drawn from a range of complementary fields and disciplines, encompassing aspects of organisational theory, and demonstrating links to drama theory and fantasy theme analysis.

The chapter starts with a review of the literatures upon which our use of framing is based, after which we will demonstrate how framing can be used as a meta-framework for mixed-mode modelling through a number of mini-cases. Finally we discuss the use of framing and reframing as a pedagogical strategy for teaching OR/MS.

THE NATURE AND ROLE OF FRAMING

Our use of framing as a meta-framework for mixed-mode modelling has been influenced by developments in a number of fields - OR/MS in general, multimethodology, in particular, and framing itself.

Many OR/MS writers, particularly those with an interest in pedagogy, have argued the need to adopt multiple approaches and to develop and adopt multiple perspectives to cope with the richness of 'messy' problem situations. Much of the work in the field of multimethodology has arisen out of need to better understand the complementary use of different approaches, techniques, methods and methodologies. This need is especially marked when these approaches etc are underpinned by different value systems or paradigms, and especially when the different world-views lead to alternative perspectives of problem situations.

However, the framing and metaphor literatures make it explicit that the perceptions, perspectives and choices arising from problem situations are likely to be shaped by the frame or metaphor-in-use.

Our work then can be seen as a conscious attempt to apply framing concepts to better understand problems from the synthesis of multiple perspectives.

Before developing further our particular views on, and uses of, framing, we will review their theoretical underpinnings from the literatures in the above-mentioned fields.

Multimethodology

The development of multimethodology, multimodal approaches and mixed-mode modelling has received considerable attention over the last two decades and such attention has been justified on several grounds. Mingers and Brocklesby [1] have argued for the considered use of multimethodology both on theoretical/philosophical grounds and on the practical grounds that practitioners are increasingly doing so already. They argue that the complexity and multi-dimensionality of real-world problem situations require a multimethodological approach to be able to focus and refocus attention on the many different aspects of any problematic situation and to provide associated multiple perspectives. Indeed, they contend that it is necessary "to go beyond using a single methodology to always combining methodologies, in whole or part, and possibly from different (even incommensurate) paradigms to make the most of dealing with the richness of the real world." This contention accords with the view of Gioia [2] who writes about achieving an increased level of complementarity amongst perspectives, and more comprehensiveness in portraying the complexities facing decision makers concerned with satisfying different stakeholders.

As such, the use of multimethodology or multimodal approaches has been described as an opportunity for researchers/analysts/managers to develop competence in managing complexity [3]. However, whilst the emergence of multimodal approaches presents an opportunity "to see, think and act" in a more systemic way in handling complexity, it has also generated an accompanying debate about the challenges and feasibility of doing so. Indeed, there has been an ongoing debate about the philosophical, theoretical, cultural and psychological feasibility and challenges associated with the use of multimethodology and multimodal approaches [4, 5, 6].

At the practitioner level, the need for clarity about the distinctiveness or complementarity of different methodologies has been addressed by the development of classification systems. Jackson and Keys' system of systems methodologies (SOSM) [7], together with Flood and Jackson's development of TSI [8] linked hard, soft and critical methodologies to particular theoretical rationalities embodying the distinctive concerns of stakeholders, and necessarily focussing on, and making assumptions about different aspects of the reality in which problem situations are embedded. Zhu [3], quoting Midgely [9] has suggested that the problematique confronting practitioners has always been the need to identify an appropriate method choice or methodological intervention. Several frameworks regarding method choice [10, 11, 12, 13] have subsequently emerged. One consequence has been that descriptive frameworks such as SOSM have come to be viewed (and used) uncritically, perhaps unwittingly, as frameworks providing meta-methodological guidelines for method choice [14] - a criticism that, ironically, may also be levelled at Mingers and Brocklesby's framework for mapping methodologies [1]. Nevertheless, we concur with Zhu of the need to make our frameworks, tacit or otherwise, the basis for dialogue and learning.

The development of such frameworks - the so called 'framework' approach - is viewed by some [15] as leading to an uncritical or unwitting limiting of method choice tied to the theorised links between a pre-identified categorisation of problem situations and the appropriateness of pre-specified methods. Both Gregory [15] and Midgely [9] also disavow attempts to, or suggestions that one can, bring about a 'once-and-for-all' theoretical unity to the growing multiplicity of problem solving methods and methodologies through the development of a singular meta-theoretical framework - such as Jackson and Keys' System of Systems Methodologies (SOSM) [7]. They welcome the tension between perspectives that distinct and complementary methodological approaches can give rise to, and they see value in celebrating differences and accepting 'similarities' in perspective and method, as exemplified in the work of Ackermann, Belton, Bennett, Eden and Williams [16, 17].

As a precursor to discussion of our approach, it is perhaps sufficient to state here that we are not espousing the use of framing and meta-framing as a means of achieving paradigm unification or theoretical integration. We suggest that meta-framing is more likely to address issues arising amongst those who use different methodologies but who may share interest or value perspectives [2] or who may wish to better understand the practical implications of operating within a particular methodology or paradigm [1].

Indeed, as Zhu [3] states, there is another particular need - to promote critical discourse between perspectives, to challenge, yet accommodate perspectives, and to instill a methodological acceptance of 'critical appreciation', not just of multiple perspectives but of the methods/methodologies/frameworks that surface them, thus extending the 'discordant pluralism' of Midgely and Gregory. This need, though, reflects a far from recent recognition of the value of addressing these issues, especially that noted in OR/MS, as will be discussed below.

The chapter continues with a brief outline of developments in the fields of OR/MS pedagogy and framing, prior to some case demonstrations of framing as a meta-framework for mixed-mode modelling.

OR/MS Pedagogy

> "Pedagogical advances follow naturally epistemological and methodological advances - and perhaps, premature pedagogical expressions are as natural. We are ever-learning and there is a compulsion to communicate to others that which we learn." Swanson [18]

The early years of Operational Research/Management Science (OR/MS) were characterised by the deliberate use of multi-disciplinary project teams, whose composite strengths, creativity and problem solving abilities were enhanced by the complementarity of the different approaches and perspectives that were brought to bear on a problem. As stated by Ackoff and Sasieni [19] the reason for interdisciplinary teams linked the belief that a problem "may be looked at through the eyes of any discipline" with "the desirability to consider and evaluate as wide a range of approaches to a problem as possible". More recently, the notions of framing, and framing methodology, have gained credence, increasing use and acceptance. This is particularly so in the examination of organisational structures and organisational effectiveness; and more generally, as an aid to problem identification and problem structuring that values and encourages the development of multiple problem representations and multiple perspectives

Simon, Dantzig *et al* [20] have stated that "the OR/MS community has, as its common mission, the development of tools and procedures to improve problem solving and decision making". Indeed, we may reflect that this view has pervaded the academic community since the introduction of OR/MS to management education in the sixties.

However, we may also reflect that our OR/MS education programmes have provided, in the main, a 'traditional' hard systems emphasis on technical analytical skill and the generation of optimal solutions, rather than the development of 'softer' problem identification and problem structuring skills. The hard systems approach deals with how to solve the problem; the soft systems approach seeks to ask what the problem is. It was as if, as Daellenbach [21] contends, our educators assumed that problems had been or could be readily identified, and/or such problems would be amenable to our familiar hard systems analytical approaches. Such assumptions do not fit comfortably with Ackoff's view [22] that "managers do not solve problems in well-ordered mathematical worlds as much as manage messes" which have to be understood. Such assumptions have been similarly critiqued by Grinyer [23] who has stated that whilst effective operational researchers have long recognised the use of models as a means of assisting managers to reframe their understanding of the world, the typical frames-in-use have been mathematical in structure and content, with a prime purpose of specifying a 'best' solution to the problem as 'captured' in its mathematical form, often regardless of the ill-match between model and reality, or of the uncertainty surrounding the problem.

Fortunately, such assumptions are less likely to be typical of twenty-first century educational practice, given the many initiatives gaining momentum in OR/MS education [24]. Recent focus on aspects of pedagogy, especially as they relate to the teaching of OR/MS or decision making, and especially as they relate to the phenomenon of post-experience management education, have been most evident in recent major conferences. Bell [25], for example, has specifically referred to the need for teaching via case studies, and has asserted that the way a business school positions itself helps determine not only the content and pedagogy for its programmes, but also its courses. The implications for OR/MS courses and pedagogy, he suggests, are that they must evolve away from being theoretical, content oriented and analysis driven, towards being practical, skills oriented and decision driven, or be considered irrelevant, a view previously expressed by Olaffson and Hannibalsson [26], and later by Goldratt [27]. In a similar fashion, Gass [28] whilst commenting on the educational requirements of MBA students, has suggested that their need is to be given the opportunity to build an appreciation of OR/MS, not to be trained as analysts - because the analysts will be working for them.

In this vein, several authors have commented directly or indirectly on the pedagogical/computational trade-offs arising from the use of spreadsheets. Plane [29], Hesse [30] and Davis [31] have confronted the question of how we should use spreadsheets in the teaching and learning of OR/MS - whether we should teach OR/MS by providing spreadsheet models to address common situations, in typical black box fashion, or whether we teach students how to construct, or be constructive with spreadsheet models. Powell [32] and Savage [33] both convey the power of spreadsheets as being a platform for intellectual exploration not restricted to analytical problem solving. Clauss [34] has similarly suggested that the essence of good OR/MS teaching relates to students exploring and understanding "what to do with solutions after obtaining them", and understanding whether to change conditions for which "a bad solution is optimal"! Rothkopf [35] too, has emphasised that models must be used as aids to further thought, not substitutes for thinking, stating "It is dangerous to stop thinking once the model is built".

The suggestion is that OR/MS educators should recognise that whilst they have a role to play in helping future users learn the appropriate applications of spreadsheet tools, that they should also recognise the 'languaging' role that spreadsheets implicitly play amongst managers, manifest where managers may often develop a model within a spreadsheet without even acknowledging it [32]. It is not, then, surprising that the intuitive use of spreadsheet models can tend to be more for evaluative and discussive purposes rather than for the prescriptive purpose of say, optimisation. In other words, managers need to know more about how to evaluate and use 'solutions' than how to obtain them, and about how to capture an appropriate representation of the problem if the intent is for any resulting 'optimal solutions' to be meaningful.

Given the need to manage Ackoff's messes which have to be understood, the authors agree with Grinyer [23] and Bryant [36] that the 'quality of discourse' engendered by 'model-building' may often be more important than any direct application or specific solution proposed. Indeed, if we accept the notion of a 'model-as-convention', rather than as a description of reality, then we can accept models as providing the context 'which directs discourses in particular paths' or 'as providing a way of talking about something in a manner that is understandable and useful' [37], that is as communication vehicles. We concur with Thomas [38] that we can/should help managers "less in the form of the provision of technical, algorithmic knowledge which will enable managers to read off solutions to their problems, as ... more ... in the form of sensitising frameworks - ways of seeing and thinking which alert the manager to alternative ways of understanding and hence managing".

As OR/MS practitioners, we are well trained in framing problems as mathematical models, capturing the essence of problems in mathematical form to enable investigation of, analysis of, and to ultimately improve the understanding of the system under investigation. The modelling process underpinning such framing is a reflection of problem solving and decision making as a rational process. The process involves activities ranging across different 'logical' levels - identifying appropriate objectives and criteria at higher levels, generating and evaluating action options, and choosing and implementing preferred options at lower levels.

Usually, there is, at least implicitly, recognition, even intention, to regard the process as an iterative process; and that once one has identified an initial solution, that the 'problem' will be revisited in each of the process stages. In practice, there is always the temptation to refine, expand and develop 'models' with a focus on lower logical levels, that is on ever increasing detailed structure, addition of modules, detailed evaluation etc. However, such attempts to refine structure are often limited by the context within which the problem has been framed. The process of sensitivity analysis, for example, often focuses on changing some content factors [39], but otherwise, leaving the basic form of the model, the nature of the constraints and the objectives unaltered. It is much less usual, much harder and more courageous, to revisit the initial assumptions concerning higher level objectives and criteria, as they may ultimately involve abandoning much of the existing model/frame, and starting from scratch. The authors have argued [40] that often, more expansive, creative options may be generated by re-examining these higher levels components of the problem solving process. It is our contention that effective OR/MS practitioners already do this but that much practice, which is regarded as failure, could be attributed to the restricted framing of such higher level issues.

So, if we believe that "how people construct their world and account for what they do in it necessarily influences how they behave" [41], then providing a framework (indeed a framework encompassing multiple frames) that encourages the construction of multiple perspectives should, hopefully, provide the insights and understanding that lead to better and more 'enlightened' choice in situations of complexity. Whether or not it can be demonstrated that the use of multiple frames and the development of multiple perspectives leads to more effective decision-making outcomes is problematic [42]. However, the cases that we provide suggests that it does.

The chapter continues with a brief outline of developments in framing. We will then illustrate how framing can be used as a meta-framework, by demonstrating the application of a range of frames to fairly typical organisational problems and to a classic OR/MS problem - the product mix problem. Frames will be drawn from the domain of metaphorical framing, traditional OR/MS and from the more recent Theory of Constraints (TOC), and we will put forward a case for the use of framing and reframing as a pedagogical strategy for teaching OR/MS.

Frames, Framing and Metaphors

"Thinking depends upon metaphors." Howard [43]

The next section will provide a brief selective review of literatures on framing and metaphors, drawing particularly on the work of others in the field of organisational analysis and in a variety of complementary fields.

We then describe the use of framing as proposed by Russo and Schoemaker [44], and developed further by the present authors. The latter work has been developed in pedagogical settings with graduate and post-experience students. It has been found to be particularly useful in exploring the structure of Ackoff's messy and problematic situations, leading to a greater understanding of the issues and cognitive structures that are used implicitly or explicitly to identify and describe problematic situations. Metaphors are used to enable problem owners to 'see' their situation through simplifying lenses and interpretative filters. It will be demonstrated how the use of a variety of metaphors can contribute to different phases of the problem solving process, for example, helping generate or extend the range of possible options, or often engendering the creativity to provide breakthrough ideas.

Much of the work undertaken on the framing of organisational problems and situations has been linked to the use of metaphor. The work of Pondy [45], Morgan and others [46, 47, 48] has given much impetus to the use of metaphor in examining organisations, organisational activity, business and management. Morgan claims that our understanding of organisation(s) is based on the 'unwitting' use of metaphor that pervades our life, impacting on how we 'see' and 'think'. The use of metaphor is based on the premise that insight into organisations, the unfamiliar and complex, can accrue by thinking about them as though they were something else, that is the familiar and simple [49]. The importance of framing in business through the use of metaphors has become acknowledged in the past decade [45, 46, 47]. For example, several authors have noted the widespread use of the military metaphor in business. Some claim that it is the cause of many poor decisions [50]. Others advocate the use of yet another specific metaphor, such as the performing arts metaphor, as being superior and generally applicable [51]. However, the use of any one metaphor in isolation is problematic, whatever it may be - for the very nature of metaphor ensures a partial view only.

Flood and Jackson's three phase Total Systems Intervention (TSI) methodology [8] provides an example of an attempt to facilitate creative thinking about problem situations, problem description and problem structuring, through the use of metaphors; and then through the identification and recognition of dominant and dependent metaphors to determine an appropriate intervention methodology or methodologies

Morgan similarly, but implicitly advocates the deliberate and selective use of metaphor to derive deeper understanding of particular facets of organisational life. In a sense, Morgan metaphorically advocates the use of 'horses for courses'!

We take the view that it is not necessary to seek metaphorical matches to organisational or problem situations, nor necessary to find appropriate analogies, nor to draw the 'best' set of parallels. Instead, we state there is considerable value in exposing student managers/analysts to a variety of frames or metaphors in a directed way [52] as a means of drawing out creativity and creatively exploring problem situations. Ohmae, indeed, offers a striking example of 'directed analogy' in his discussion of 'planting for a global harvest'.

> "I have come to think that the culture of an organisation is like the soil; a business is like a tree growing in the soil; and profits are like the fruits of the tree. An effective corporation will have the same kind of soil, with the same pH, in all regions of the world where it operates. And in that soil will grow similar kinds of trees. If you put the wrong seeds in this or that patch, if you try to grow someone else's kind of tree, if you play the mergers and acquisitions game and just want to steal the fruits without planting or fertilising anything - that is, if you do not take the time to grow healthy trees in the spots suitable for them - you will never be able to reap a proper long-term harvest." Ohmae [53]

The notion of framing makes explicit the view that any situation can be seen or explored from a number of perspectives. Frames, wittingly or otherwise, provide a cognitive structure that can be used to build understanding of problems or problem structure, and to simplify complexity. They can be considered as mental windows through which we perceive and structure our understanding of problem situations -

offering multiple perspectives yet often partial views. Rivett describes the notion of problems being 'constructs in our minds', and as such, argues for use of the term problem description as often being more appropriate than terms such as problem definition or problem formulation which perhaps imply a higher level of specificity, closure or objectivity [54]. Given that alternative frames act as sensitising frameworks and interpretative filters helping to generate multiple perspectives on problems, we would regard problem framing as contributing more to Rivett's notion of problem description than to problem formulation.

Framing, Multi-methodology and OR/MS Pedagogy

The purpose of using framing, therefore, is to free the analyst/manager from the implicit or hidden assumptions that s/he may be constrained by, and to surface new insights about the problem, and how to tackle it. It is in keeping with Nutt's view [55] of the importance of identifying what may be included/excluded from the manager's view during the problem-solving/decision-making process. This approach is essentially Kantian in its view that knowledge is limited by "the manner in which our faculties of perception and thinking organize the raw data of experience", and by how we "perceive it through the 'lenses' of our *a priori* categories of though" [56]. It may also be described as Kantian in the manner that we seek to distinguish "the mode in which we intuit ... phenomena ... from the nature that belongs to them in themselves" [57]. However, we acknowledge the paradox of framing - that a single frame may be highly beneficial as a simplifying structure, yet may be limited in providing a partial view. Hence, we encourage the deliberate use of multiple frames, and the development of multiple perspectives to evolve our understanding of problems.

This approach accords with the earlier stated views of Midgely [9] and Gregory [15] who welcome the tension generated by different perspectives, and of Zhu [3] who wishes to promote a critical discourse between perspectives and between the methods/methodologies that give rise to them.

We will now present some case demonstrations of our use of framing as a meta-framework for mixed-mode modelling, starting with metaphorical frames applied in 'ill-defined' settings, and then continuing with OR/MS frames applied to a relatively 'well-defined' problem.

METAPHORICAL FRAMING AS A PROBLEM DESCRIPTION AID

Our use of framing and reframing can be seen as an attempt to demonstrate the extent to which context and the nature of the frame can play a part in the surfacing and identification of problem features, as well as the generation of action options. We propose a process which recognises and makes explicit the frame-in-use. It promotes acceptance of the use of multiple frames and the deliberate change of frame. It has been developed as a reaction to the often asked question - "Which frame/approach/method shall we use?" Our approach is to provoke the decision maker to consider other possible interpretations of the problem, its objectives, prevailing criteria, existing value judgements etc, and to widen the possibilities from which the decision maker can ultimately choose. The major aim of modelling and models is insight not numbers. The process of multiple framing and reframing provides another means for improving insight. Here, as in previous work [40, 58], we attempt to show the power of 'metaphor' framing and reframing as a problem description, problem solving and decision-making tool, and to display the versatility of the approach. The successful outcomes of the framing exercises confirm findings from elsewhere [59].

This section also provides some evidence of how we have attempted to re-orient the delivery of 'Problem Solving and Decision Making' courses in graduate management education programmes, away from the 'traditional' hard-systems emphasis on technical analytical skills and the generation of optimal solutions, towards the development of 'softer' problem identification, problem description and structuring skills, such as framing.

We advocate that decision makers should be encouraged to draw on a range of metaphors not only to enlarge the range of possible decision options open to them, but to develop a better understanding of the problem situation that they are confronted with. By choosing contrasting metaphors, the range of possible options is expanded, allowing the decision maker to reframe the problem and ultimately to improve decisions.

Our approach follows that of Russo and Schoemaker [44] summarised in the guiding questions below:

The essential features of the approach differ from Russo & Schoemaker [44] mainly in respect of not necessarily seeking a best metaphorical fit. The approach also differs from Morgan [45] in that we do not necessarily seek to frame the organisation as a machine, brain, psychic prison etc. Rather we take the problem situation in its most general form, and 'place' it in a series of frames that can be described, for example, as 'setting' or 'action' frames [60]. It is likely that each frame, whether it be a family frame, football team frame or an orchestra frame, for example, will connote different value systems or cultures, connote different preference systems, and that choices be subject to different constraints, bounds or boundaries etc. The purpose of such a framing exercise is to free the analyst/manager from the implicit/hidden assumptions that s/he may be constrained by, and to surface new insights about the problem situation or how to tackle it.

Frame Analysis - Guiding Questions

- What issue or issues does the frame address?
- What boundaries do I (we/they) put on the question?
  In other words, what aspects of the situation are left out of consideration?
- What yardsticks/performance criteria do I (we/they) use to measure success?
- What reference points do I (we/they) use to measure success?
- What metaphors - if any - do I (we/they) use in thinking about this issue
- Why do I (we/they) think about this issue in the way that I (we/they) do?
- What does the frame emphasise or highlight?
- What does the frame minimise or shadow?
- Do other people in the industry think about the problem differently from the way that I (we/they) do?
- Can I (we/they) summarise my (our/their) frame in a slogan or motto?

Adapted from Russo & Schoemaker, [44]

In the next section, we present two examples from the work of graduate student managers which show the power of metaphorical framing and reframing as a problem description, problem-solving and decision-making tool. The variety of such situations (shown in detail elsewhere [58]) highlights the versatility of the method; and the frames chosen show both the creativity of the students, and the value of the reframing exercise to them and their organisations. While each student was asked to take at least two frames, we would expect that if more frames were to be used, the decision-making process would be even less partial.

The examples are fairly typical situations, and readers may well see situations that appear familiar. The first case, concerning a downsizing exercise conducted by a state-owned enterprise, includes a sketch of the analysis, while a second displays more selective extracts.

Our approach, modified from that of Russo and Schoemaker [44], is first, to describe the problem situation and review the way in which the decision was implemented. Secondly, the approach requires the analyst/manager to describe a frame within which to evaluate the implementation of the decision; and, finally, to use an alternative frame to provide a different perspective on the situation.

The evaluation process is very much guided by the cognitive structure of the frames and features of that structure. For example, the notion of considering frames as mental windows or interpretative filters implies that views may be partial, that different perspectives may emerge, and that some ideas or information may be beyond the bounds of the frame, which of course leads to a need for explicit consideration of frame boundaries. Similarly, recognition must also be given to the notion that different value systems may attach themselves to particular frames, impacting on goals, criteria, the attractiveness of action choices and outcomes - in general, what may be called performance yardsticks. Another feature of the cognitive structure of framing emphasised in Russo and Schoemaker's approach is that which relates to reference points as identifiers of what constitutes acceptability, failure, success etc. As such, reference points align with yardsticks.

We note therefore that our approach, like that of Russo and Schoemaker, imposes a cognitive structure on our use of frames which helps make explicit the frame dependency of our analysis, interpretation and insights.

Case A - TooBigCorp♦ - TBC

TBC, formerly a public service organisation, was made a State Owned Enterprise in the late 1980's. After a period of ongoing restructuring, an external review of the organisation suggested downsizing, involving redefining core operations, cutting some operations completely, and restructuring some divisions. Management wanted to implement the decision but wanted to ensure this happened smoothly.

Previous restructuring had not gone smoothly, and the cost to business and staff morale had been high. Employees were told that the proposed changes would cost jobs, but were given no details on who would be made redundant. They were given a period of time to discuss options and come up with suggestions. By the end of this period, no feasible alternatives had emerged, and management enacted the proposed changes, making some 30 or so staff redundant, and dismantling and restructuring some divisions.

The consultative process was apparently used for two reasons. First, it was hoped that by doing so, staff would feel part of the decision, and would accept the decision more readily. Secondly, it was envisaged that this would prevent industrial action. It was believed that both these two were required if the restucturing was to proceed smoothly, so that TBC could continue to provide the service it was in the business of providing. What follows are two frames that were used to evaluate the situation, decision and implementation process in TBC.

Case A - The First Frame: A Dog's Show

The story is based on the New Zealand television programme "A Dog's Show", (similar to the British TV Show with the title "One Man (sic) and His Dog"). It details the events of a typical competition day at the dog trials. It is narrated from the viewpoint of its two main characters, the farmer and one gutsy little *sheep* who belonged to a small flock.

"The farmer knows the competition will be tough today. He has been doing this for years, and the younger competitors get harder and

♦ Names and details have been changed to preserve confidentiality harder to beat. He has won this competition on several occasions including last year, and knows he can do it again. Providing he gets the right combination of events - the dogs perform on the day, he doesn't get a difficult flock of sheep to work with, and all else goes well - then, there's no reason why he won't take the winner's trophy home again. Pressure of competition is in his blood and he loves working under stress: it seems to bring out the best in him. There are many obstacles to overcome, bridges to cross, and gates to go through, all in a tight time frame.

"Today, he has to herd six sheep through the gate, over the bridge, through the stream, split them into two groups of three, and pen both groups within ten minutes. They're a well drilled team, he and his dogs, Blue and Trev. He thinks highly of them and considers them his 'generals'. The team has been through the rigours of competition many times before and have intimate knowledge of the sheep they work with. Push them here, prod them there, point them in the right direction, bring the dogs a little closer and steer them down the course. 'The gold trophy's as good as on the mantelpiece!'

> "Meanwhile for the sheep.... "Oblivious to what the day would bring, we graze peacefully on the lush green pasture. The first sound of the farmer, and Blue and Trev, indicates an interruption to our otherwise peaceful afternoon. Firstly, the farmer, with the aid of his two dogs, rounds us up and brings us together. Then we are taken on a long winding path across the pastures. Blue and Trev stay aloof and the farmer calls them in if one of us happens to stray too far from the rest. The farmer does a lot of shouting and whistling, and Blue and Trev seem to obey all his orders."

> "Then comes that really nerve wracking moment when the farmer, Blue and Trev, stop and bring us all together for another meeting inside the circle. The pressure really goes on. We are all surrounded. The three of them, the farmer, Blue and Trev, move in slowly and eventually we are forced to make a decision which way to go. Stay with the group or make a run for it."

"The farmer couldn't believe how easily the group split today. It was as if they already knew what was required of them. With the split accomplished so easily, his thoughts drifted to the trophy and how good it would look sitting on his mantelpiece.

The first lot penned easily and he still had three minutes to go to get the second group caged. Plenty of time! There was one stubborn one in the second group that really made him sweat. The little blighter would not stay with the rest of the group and refused to go through the open gate. A little nip around the heel from Blue did the trick and he closed the gate with five seconds remaining on the clock. Success!!"

> "Well, another day over and it's time to get back to some serious munching on the nice spring growth. Hold on, what's this? We're not going back! But the other group is. Why not us? I know I'd upset the farmer today when I decided to play a little game with Blue and Trev. Okay, so I wanted to be different from the rest, make them work for the trophy. A little fun and games adds spice to life. But what's that in the distance ... a truck coming into view with the words 'Wairarapa Freezing Works'• painted on the side. Ooh no!"

Interpretation

The farmer in the metaphor represents TBC's CEO. The dogs - Blue and Trev - represent the GM and Director of Finance. The sheep are representative of the employees of the 'O & M' division and the whole scenario is representative of the implementation process.

The CEO's objective was mapped out before the 'consultation' process began, just as the farmer had his eye on the trophy. The course had been laid out in advance for both the sheep-dog trials and for the restructuring exercise. Getting from the starting point (where the O & M division was) to the finish point (the implementation of the consultants' recommendations) is critical to success. The farmer (CEO) is in control of the situation and his dogs (general managers) respond to his directions as they serve him faithfully (depend on him for their well-being).

The sheep (staff) were brought together on two occasions, once at the beginning of the course (restructuring) and once towards the end. In the meantime they were allowed to amble along in a loose knit group. A similar routine was initiated by the CEO when he brought the employees together and briefed them at the start. Later on they were brought

• A southern hemisphere *Freezing Works* is an *abattoir* elsewhere.

together for a conference. An evaluation of employees was carried out at the conference, as was done when the sheep were split and penned. Any employees that didn't make the grade or didn't play the game faced redundancy; the unlucky sheep were rather harshly dealt with and shipped to the freezing works. The lucky ones lived to see another day.

The implications of the frames can be analysed more formally using Russo and Schoemaker's framework [44] of identifying boundaries, yardsticks and reference points, as provided below in outline.

Boundaries

Whilst the consultation process was put in place as a mechanism for employees to put forward ideas and suggestions, the unwritten boundaries limited the scope of those discussions. The employees were allowed some latitude in their discussions with management (the sheep are allowed some latitude as they amble towards the pens), but the ultimate aim of management (the farmer) was to make the changes (pen the sheep).

Although employees could discuss ideas and alternatives, the main event in the consultation process, the conference, was organised and run by management. Management steered the process through to its conclusion and guided staff along the way. Radical ideas were pulled into line and eventually management achieved its goal. Similarly, the sheep had to follow a predetermined path, go through predetermined gates and bridges all under the direction of the farmer and his dogs. Any sheep that left the group were quickly put back in line by a bark or nip from the dogs.

Time was also an important boundary set by management. The CEO agreed to give the employees a set period to work through the consultation process and formulate suggestions and ideas. Similarly, the farmer had ten minutes in which to complete the process. These time frames created pressure on the parties involved to achieve a result within a given deadline - or accept the consequences.

Yardsticks

There is more than one yardstick that can be used by the farmer to measure the success of his day. Having the trophy on his mantelpiece after the event is the most important measure of success but there are other success factors that lead to it. He had to negotiate the course without incurring points deductions for missed gates, wrong splits and breaking the ten minute deadline - strict measures all the way.

There are also several yardsticks to measure the success of the implementation of the changes. First, implementing the changes outlined in the consultants' report with minimal industrial disruption; second, continuing important services for the rest of the TBC business; and third, reducing operating costs of the O & M division and fourth, reducing the amount of money spent on researching and developing new products.

Reference Points

The key reference points for the farmer are his past achievements. He comes into the competition as the reigning champion and has put in a lot of work leading up to the competition. The only way he can be happy with the results is if he wins on the day. Second or third would not do.

The CEO's reference point is the success of the changes he has previously made within the organisation. Some of them have not gone as smoothly as he would have liked. He will only be happy if the implementation process goes better than on previous occasions, preferably like clockwork.

Limitations

The boundaries imposed by the frame can mean that the best solution may not become apparent. For example, we note a narrow vision by management, possibly resulting from total reliance on the consultants' recommendations and a limited listening to the wealth of experience contained within the business. This may have meant that perfectly good suggestions by employees were discarded all too quickly. The mindset of the CEO and his GMs meant the decision was finalised well before the employees were briefed.

Had the employees or the sheep been inclined, they could have caused chaos quite easily. The sheep could have scattered in six different directions leaving the farmer totally impotent. The employees could have created havoc through industrial action and thus would have kept the CEO's marginal record of change.

Reframing the Decision Situation

We now offer a view that had the implementation of the restructuring of the O & M division been viewed with the military metaphor, the scenario and outcomes would have been completely different.

Case A - The Second Frame: A Military Exercise

The Major-General (CEO) would have called his Generals (GMs) into the war room and a 'plan of attack' would have been mapped out. Orders would have been given to the Generals to carry out the changes at 0900 hours on 24 March. No consultation with employees would have been entered into. Time would not have been a consideration. The changes would have been in place by 0900 hours on 1 April.

Redundant employees would have been given an honourable discharge, industrial action would not have been a consideration for the Major-General as this would be viewed as dishonourable amongst the ranks. He could rely on age-old tradition to ensure any dissent was crushed before it began. "Yes, Sir" would have been the motto of the day. Employees would view it as an honour to have worked for the company. Most boundaries would be tightened under the military model and no consideration would be given to an employee's family situation, length of service, good conduct etc. Expediency would be the order of the day. Cyanide tablets may be issued for those who fall into the hands of the business's competitors!!

Boundaries

One boundary that may be relaxed is the boundary relating to funding limits. Operating as a commercial operation, TBC had to consider the profit implication of all decisions it makes. Under the military model, profit would not be a consideration. Therefore, there could be more flexibility in funding.

Yardsticks

A yardstick to measure the success of the implementation would be the constant monitoring, and feedback against the plan of attack designed by the experienced Major-General and his Generals. The plan would identify key battles to be fought, with each battle won bringing them one step closer to winning the war.

Reference Point

The reference point for success or failure of the operation would change. The military personnel would compare the operation to recent wars won and lost and ensure their unit came out on the winning side. Consideration would be given to major battles fought by companies such as Equiticorp and Fortex where rapid change and expansion has been their downfall.

Summary

The consultation process used by management to implement its decision served to ensure the CEO's record of change management improved. Framing the implementation process and comparing it to the 'Dog's Show' metaphor brought out the fact that the employees of the O & M division had little chance to affect events. Their 'destiny' was predetermined. Under the military metaphor's more regimented approach, we see that the decision may have been expedited, but that human factors, such as family and employee loyalty, would have had little bearing on the decision.

At the time, the student involved in the exercise concluded that "The path TBC is following is the right one. It has already lowered the barriers to reframing through the process of ongoing change. That will mean only one outcome for the business in the future - Success!"

Case B - The Ineffective Computer System

The next extract considers the problematic situation of deciding what to do about a computer system that does not meet an organisation's needs.

Case B - The Frame-in-Use: A Construction Site

The frame-in-use being used for this problematic situation was one of extreme negativity, almost one of complete failure and disaster. The picture being painted was one where the current system had not proceeded along the development path according to plan and had failed to deliver many of the benefits that were promised with the introduction of the computer system. Furthermore, it was considered that the likely benefits of open systems architectures then becoming available were in marked contrast to the construction methods of the system-in-use.

The central metaphor being used to describe the decision frame, when thinking about this problem was one of a 'construction site'. This may be considered apt especially with respect to the shared terminology in use. For example, in 'building' an information system, many terms and techniques are synonymous with the building or construction industry. In fact, the design and construction of in-house information systems were then being undertaken by using a methodology referred to as Information Engineering. Similarly, 'fixing up' applications that may have gone astray was referred to as Business Process Re-engineering! The terminology, then, was/is 'heavy' in construction images. The construction metaphor envelops the described problem as fellows.

> "In 1996, construction began with the drawing up of architect's plans that detailed what the building would look like. It was to be a three-storeyed house with solid foundations anchored into the hillside, overlooking Oriental Parade. The ground floor was to consist of a double garage and rumpus room. The next floor was to contain the living areas while the top floor contained the bedrooms.
>
> Unfortunately the owner kept making modifications to the design as fast as the builders tried to erect the house. He

> didn't consult with the designers, simply made ad-hoc changes as the builders hammered away. Prior to moving in, the owner turned up to view the house he found a four-storeyed house, with extra bedrooms bolted onto the external walls of the fourth floor because he had increased the size of his family. The ranch-sliders in the lounge opened onto the cliff face and the garages were on the second floor but could not be reached by a car.
>
> The house which in the planning and early construction stages had promised to be one of high quality, excellent design and high standard of functionality had turned out to be a shoddily constructed, rabbit-warren teetering on the side of a steep Wellington hillside. It would not pass a building inspector's close attention - it would have to be pulled down and started all over again."

This decision frame could be subject to an interpretation that once the architects had designed and planned construction, once the foundations had been laid and the framework established, only cosmetic changes could be allowed. An additional interpretation could be that any radical departure from the plan, any major structural changes incorporated in an ad-hoc manner, would be considered to reduce the robustness of the structure and the likelihood of it meeting the functionality as specified in the initial designs. As such, certain options for change could be considered as out-of-bounds.

Case B - The Second Frame: Buying a Car

We now briefly contrast the frame-in-use with an alternative way of framing the problem using a metaphor of buying a new car.

> "I bought a Fiat Bambina when I first started university. It was really great. I could get to lectures on time and I didn't get wet when it rained. It was economical on petrol and really easy to park in the smallest places imaginable. Well, you do know what parking around the university is like. It gave me such freedom. No longer was I reliant on parents, friends or public transport - I could go wherever I wanted and whenever I wanted.

Of course that was in 1986. My lifestyle was different then. Now I'm married and we're expecting our first child at the end of the year".

"It will be so difficult with this present car. Getting the baby-seat in and out of the back of the car will be a real pain. I just don't see how I can get the pushchair in as well as all those groceries from the supermarket."

"And we've just bought a caravan - goodness knows how we can tow that around the South Island. And what about the dog? He'll want to come on holiday too."

"You know I've recently noticed oil spots on the driveway, and I'm certainly spending more money at the petrol station, filling the thing full of oil as well as petrol. The heater's packed up and it's really cold in the winter."

"The prospect of a bigger and newer car is coming to mind!"

These two frames are markedly different in the attitudes that are evoked and then brought to bear on the situation. Consequently, we may offer the opinion that not only will the options that are to be considered likely to be different but that the options chosen will also be different as well.

Metaphorical Framing and other analytical approaches

The foregoing provides an illustration of the differing nature of problems and problem situations for which framing and reframing can be effectively employed to improve the quality of the decision-making process.

The images evoked by and through metaphorical framing have found resonance in several other approaches that seek to describe and understand the different perspectives and interpretations that emerge amongst managers when faced with a problematic situation. Here, we make specific reference to the method of rhetorical critique developed by Bormann and known as Fantasy Theme Analysis [61].

As indicated by Jackson [60, 62], when people seek to make sense out the situations in which they find themselves, they often find comfort in creative and imaginative representations and in "interpretations of events that fulfil a psychological or rhetorical need". These interpretations, labeled as 'fantasies' by Bormann can often 'speak convincingly to an individual's problems in a dramatic form', and may coalesce or consolidate as 'fantasy themes' to provide a credible and meaningful interpretation of that individual's reality in what has been described as a 'rhetorical vision'.

Conceptualising the rhetorical vision as a 'composite drama' allows us to find meaning in how fantasy themes are organised and scripted. Jackson [60] quotes Bormann [61] as distinguishing between 'setting themes', 'character themes' and 'action themes', as a means of highlighting nuances that may, for example, involve characters' diverse personal attributes acting out specific plotlines in specific action settings.

Jackson uses fantasy theme analysis to seek understanding of the impact that management gurus have on those who become non-discriminating followers, and about how individuals may interpret and empathise with messages constructed by management gurus and conveyed and comunicated in the form of rhetorical vision.

In our modified use of Russo and Schoemaker's approach to framing [44], we acknowledge parallels to Bormann's framework [61], in the sense that each frame can be conceptualised as exhibiting characteristics of action or plot that are played out in dramatistical fashion by characters whose values and behaviour is meaningful in different ways in different settings.

Howard [63, 64] and others [65, 66] also consider characters, together with their values and preference systems, as constituting frames. In Howard's dramatistical approach, however, a frame is to be viewed as a 'situation' seen by characters at one point in time, and as having its own internal 'logic' or rationality that may develop over time or change from frame to frame.

The use of framing illustrated here is underpinned by a similar rationale which legitimates the framing process-in-use whereby the analyst/manager chooses to 'move' his/her problem from one dramatic setting or frame to another. In doing so, the manager is likely to become more aware of the way in which frames and framing impact on values, preferences and action choices, future outcomes or preferred positions, and as a consequence, may develop a deeper understanding of the problematic situation at hand including their own values and beliefs [67].

MULTI-FRAMING IN MANAGEMENT SCIENCE

For the next example of framing, we turn to the OR/MS repertoire as a source of inspiration. We will use a case example to illustrate the deliberate use of multiple framing and reframing in order to encourage the investigation of problem structure. We also demonstrate the diversity of frames implicit in the OR/MS body of knowledge. We will use a familiar resource allocation problem (the classic 'product mix' problem) to explore a variety of traditional OR/MS frames, and also to showcase the use of frames derived from a more recent addition to OR/MS methodology, the Theory of Constraints.

This exposition builds on material presented previously at various national and international OR and decision science conferences. The authors hope that the use of framing outlined in this chapter will provide an additional motivation and means for OR/MS educators to incorporate framing within their teaching.

Illustrative Example - The Goulds Fine Food Case Study

Here we examine a case study [68] developing multiple perspectives of the case through the creation and use of alternative frames. The case has been analysed in Mabin and Gibson [69] and whilst the presentation here derives from that paper, it has a different purpose, namely that of examining aspects of multiple framing.

Just as case material can be collected in different ways, so too can it be delivered to students in different ways, but, most often, material is delivered, presented - or framed - as narrative. The student is then expected through 'analysis' to gain insights by re-working and re-presenting the case material in different ways, that is, in different frames. It is as if reframing is limited to being the outcome of, or pre-determined by some prior analysis within the frame-in-use. The authors contend that this process implicitly creates unnecessary hierarchies of seemingly dependent parent/daughter frames, undermining their value and/or potential use.

In the following sections, the case material is presented or framed in several ways - as narrative, as a table, as a flow chart, as a spreadsheet model, as a set of equations, as matrices and as a graph, and then it is viewed from perspectives developed using frameworks provided by the

Theory of Constraints [70, 71, 72, 73, 74, 75]. The case is one of a kind that typically requires attention be given to resource allocation/product mix issues. It is intended to demonstrate insights and issues that emerge from the 'filling' of the frames and from use of multiple frames.

Frame I - the Frame as Narrative

Goulds Fine Foods is a medium-sized, Wellington-based company manufacturing and selling bacon, ham, smallgoods and other convenience food products. It had experienced significant growth over a two-year period, resulting in the construction of a new plant in Petone in 1994. The machinery was relatively old and was being replaced as the cash position of the firm allowed, with priority being given to areas experiencing the most growth in volume. The case focuses on manufacturing hams for commercial food products and sandwiches, and pre-cooked sausages. The production process and demand environment is described below.

> 'The ingredients for the two products (manufacturing hams and pre-cooked sausages) are mixed separately, but both use the same filling operation. The products are then cooked after filling, taking some 4 hours for the hams, and around one hour per batch of sausages. Each cooker is 2 cubic metres in volume which can take a maximum of 500 kg of product, so hams are cooked in half batches. It is normal practice to cook 350kg of sausage (1 batch) at a time. There are 4 cookers available. After cooking, the batches need to be chilled. Hams take 10 hours to chill, while sausages take only 2 hours. The chillers are quite large, and can handle any quantity made. The packing line has 4 people usually, each working a 40 hour week. However packers are happy to do overtime or work Saturdays if needed. The main time involved on pack and despatch is for sausages, as they need shrink-packaging in small packs for retail sale, while hams are sold in the plastic packs they have been cooked in. Both products require packing in outer cartons, and despatch documentation. Each packer can repack approximately 50 kgs of sausages per hour, so that it takes 7 person-hours to pack and despatch a 350kg batch of sausages. The two separate mixing processes are able to mix a 1000kg batch of ham mix in 5 hours, while sausages take 30 minutes to prepare. Filling takes place at a rate of 125 kg per hour for hams, and 1 hour per batch of sausages.
> The current weekly demand for hams is in the vicinity of 8 batches per week, though that varies by up to 35%. Likewise sausage demand equates to roughly 20 batches per week, plus or minus 100%. The profit margin on a batch of hams is roughly 6 times that of a batch of sausages.'

The original narrative provided more contextual information and then posed the question of whether or not Goulds should purchase more filling and cooking capacity. Management had estimated that this equipment might give perhaps 50% more capacity than presently available. Given that demand was certainly more than they could meet at their levels of production at the time, it appeared the extra equipment would be worthwhile.

The narrative sometimes poses artificial problems for students, some deliberate, some not so deliberate. For example, neither the chilling or packing times for hams is stated clearly in the narrative. In addition, students may not note as readily from the narrative as they would from 'live' data-gathering that the chilling operation is best described by a volume capacity rather than a flow rate, or that the chilling capacity is not stated explicitly - but it would be an issue that they would be expected to confront at some time. For this particular case, de facto chilling capacity is "much in excess of potential requirements", and can be set at any arbitrarily large level for the purpose of analysis (here, we set it to 200 hours of available use). Similarly, since the narrative is vague about the exact time it takes to pack hams, the student will be expected to make an educated guess, and then to be vigilant about the effect that his/her guess might have on analytical outcomes (here, we set the time to pack a batch of hams to be 1hr). For further background to the case, see Mabin [68].

At this stage, it needs to be stated that as far as most students are concerned, the frames that are displayed in the following sections will have seemed to emerge from the narrative, and will appear to be an abstraction from, or dependent upon the narrative, whereas the reverse is probably true. The authors argue that such notions of 'frame dependency' are inappropriate, and may lead to students shying away from the use of frames that could be effectively employed early in the initial problem structuring phase of an investigation.

Frame II - the Frame as a Flow Chart

The use of flow charts to describe work-flow and process is routine. However, it is easy to lead our students into the trap of thinking that the flow chart is used to summarise and represent aspects of case narrative - when we know that, in practice, a flow chart, or other schematic representation, is a often a first frame used by practitioners.

Framing the manufacturing process as a flow chart facilitates understanding of the sequencing logic. The flow chart frame reduces the cognitive load involved by acting as an information filter, highlighting the absence of data, yet allowing for appropriate annotation. It becomes immediately obvious when the practitioner attempts to fill this frame what is missing, and what extra information is needed.

'Filling' the frame is part of the problem structuring process. However, this frame is recognised as being incomplete; it may not convey the richness of the picture painted by the narrative, but it does compensate by providing a more structured platform for further analysis - intuitive or formal.

For some, it will emphasise the stages or sequencing of production. For the more numerate analyst, information is now 'in sight'

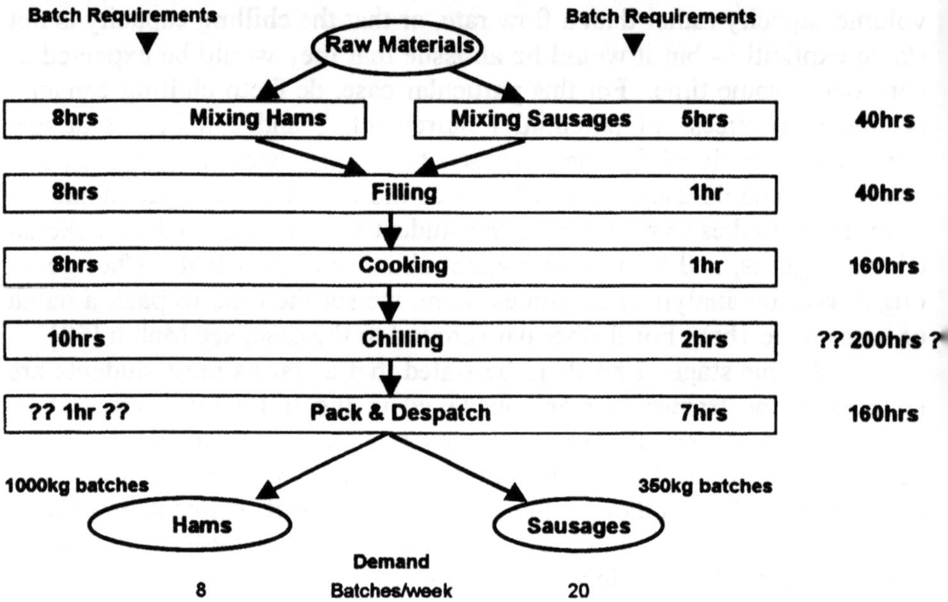

Figure 1. Frame II: The Flow Chart

that can lead quickly to realisation that meeting average demand is not possible, given a lack of Filling machine capacity.

Frame III - the Frame as a Tableau

The building of tables or tableaux is also routine for OR/MS practitioners. For many practitioners, the development of a process flow chart would accompany the placing of data within a table frame, as part of the problem structuring process. However, experience suggests that many students will regard the table frame as just an outcome of 'analysing' the narrative, or as just a stage in some extended analytical activity. Of course, the table frame, below, does summarise the narrative, but the practitioner working in the field will often use a table to frame her initial investigation, and to provide partial, but deliberate, perspectives on the problem. It is important therefore, that educators generate the live case work that provides students with opportunity to use, in a deliberate fashion, a variety of frames that are valuable in the process of problem structuring. However, if as Clauss [34] implies, the advocacy of so-called 'simple' tools is often 'beneath the dignity of our profession and text books', and OR/MS educators choose not to convey the value of such framing, then our graduating students will continue to be unaware of what effective practitioners do when confronted with new situations.

Framing the manufacturing process as a tableau provides similar insights to the flow chart frame, and reduces the case material to an even more parsimonious form.

	Process Times (Hrs / Batch) Hams	Process Times (Hrs / Batch) Sausages	Total Process Time (Hrs / Week) *Available*
Mixing - Hams	**5.0**	**0.0**	**40**
Mixing - Sausages	**0.0**	**0.5**	**40**
Filling	**8.0**	**1.0**	**40**
Cooking	**8.0**	**1.0**	**160**
Chilling	**10.0**	**2.0**	**? 200 ?**
Pack & despatch	**? 1.0 ?**	**7.0**	**160**
Average Demand (Batches/Wk)	**8**	**20**	

Figure 2. Frame III: The Tableau - Process Times, Demands and Capacities

Missing information is readily spotted, a recognition that the table frame is incomplete. The table frame conveys less information than the flow chart frame presented, but its focus is the capture and representation of the numerical data. It provides another example of a frame structured to generate insights from further analysis. Again, the numerate analyst will see that meeting average demand is not possible given the capacities of the Filling machine.

Frame IV - the Frame as a Mathematical Model

The use of a mathematical frame to build understanding of a problem parallels use of a table frame, but requires the analyst to be more precise about how logic, relationships and quantitative data are represented or codified.

We may set the **number of Ham batches per week as H**, the **number of Sausage batches per week as S.**

Then, we may seek to find the values of H and S that will maximise profit, calculated as:

$$6.0\,\mathbf{H} \quad + \quad 1.0\,\mathbf{S} \quad = \quad \text{Profit}$$

subject to various production constraints and demand patterns:

5.0 H			$\leq$	**40**	Mixing Machine - Ham
		0.5 S	$\leq$	**40**	Mixing Machine - Ham
8.0 H	**+**	**1.0 S**	$\leq$	**40**	Filling Capacity
8.0 H	**+**	**1.0 S**	$\leq$	**160**	Cooking Capacity
10.0 H	**+**	**2.0 S**	=	**200**	Chilling Capacity
1.0 H	**+**	**7.0 S**	$\leq$	**160**	Pack and Despatch
1.0 H			$\leq$	**8**	Ham Demand
		1.0 S	$\leq$	**20**	Sausage Demand

Figure 3. Frame IV: The Mathematical Model

In this case, use of the mathematical frame seeks to specify how we assess resource usage, how profits are generated, and what restrictions are placed on resource availability and use. Importantly, it requires us to consider whether production absorbs resources at a uniform rate, and whether profits accumulate at a uniform rate, surfacing such assumptions early in the problem structuring phase. More importantly, filling this frame requires the analyst to determine the objectives of the problem owner. The mathematical frame, then, requires implicit objectives to be surfaced, and implicit assumptions to be made explicit and queried. The frame has additional value in that it provides us with a basis for further analysis and experimentation. We can use the mathematical relationships to test ideas, or we can invoke our traditional analytical processes to identify choices which may be optimal, provided our assumptions, for example about linearity, have been validated.

Frame V - the Frame as a Spreadsheet

	A	B	C	D	E	F
1	Spreadsheet of Goulds' Production Problem					
2			Hams	Sausage		
3	Decision Variables:	No. Produced	8.0	20.0		
4	Constraints:				Required	Available
5	Production:	Mixing (Ham)	5.0	0.0	40.0	40.0
6		Mixing (Saus)	0.0	0.5	10.0	40.0
7		Filling	8.0	1.0	84.0	40.0
8		Cooking	8.0	1.0	84.0	160.0
9		Chilling	10.0	2.0	120.0	200.0
10		Pack & Despatch	1.0	7.0	148.0	160.0
11					Sold	Demand
12	Demands:	Hams per wk			8.0	8.0
13		Sausage per wk			20.0	20.0
14					Total	
15	Objective function:	Profit	6.0	1.0	68.0	

Figure 4. Frame V: The Spreadsheet Model

It would be reasonable to state that most OR/MS practitioners who employ tabular frames as problem structuring devices would also use the electronic analogue - a spreadsheet - to capture the essence of numerical relationships that exist. It is becoming common practice for problem structuring to be initiated via spreadsheet frames, even by practitioners without OR/MS training.

Although for many analysts, use of tabular paper worksheets precede the development of spreadsheet models, the use of spreadsheet frames mirrors, rather than depends upon, a table frame. Here, the spreadsheet frame requires one to understand and specify relationships between action choices, production levels, profitability, and the use and availability of resources. Of course, in filling the frame, we become aware of missing-data issues, just as with the previous frames.

The spreadsheet frame provides a greater capability for analysis and experimentation - providing feedback on feasibility, since the frame makes it clear that we cannot meet average demand, and on the value of alternative decisions. Such experiments are not solely restricted to decisions with product mix, but can extend to consideration of efficiency improvements in processing, changes to processing capacity, and to profit margins. We are therefore capable of going beyond seeking an optimal 'LP' solution to our current problem (The Excel Solver suggests making 2.5 batches of Ham and 20 batches of Sausages per week), and beyond standard sensitivity analysis, although of course, we could build on such analysis [69].

Frame VI - the Frame as a Graph

Many see the graphical model as an alternative representation of, or being based on, the linear mathematical model. Indeed, attempting to use a graphical frame to build an understanding of problem structure requires the analyst to confront the same issues of how resources are used, how profits are generated, whether there are economies of scale or whether linearity exists, and whether and what restrictions are placed on resource use. A benefit of the graphical frame is indeed how it captures and portrays the restrictions and constraints.

Major insights, often quickly gained from the graphical frame, relate to the relative influence of various so-called constraints and restrictions on choice. The graphical frame illustrates, quite surprisingly for some students, that only one capacity constraint, that of the Filling machine, is limiting choice; while there is seemingly excess capacity on other machines, and that the only other limit is the level of sausage demand. Profitability is thus constrained by limits on demand just as much as it is by lack of manufacturing capacity. These insights are available because this frame seeks and filters information in a different way compared to other frames, and provides a different set of perspectives. However, although graphical frames can facilitate further analysis, they do not provide the same computational comforts as, say, a spreadsheet model.

TOC Frame I - the TOC Product Mix Algorithm

The Theory of Constraints (TOC) methodology pioneered by Goldratt [70-74] provides an alternative series of frames with which to seek and filter information. For example, a focus on incremental production scheduling can be guided by examination of constraining resources or activities, especially their most profitable use. In order to establish production priorities between products, Goldratt [71] provides an algorithm, sometimes referred to as the TOC product mix algorithm, which in simple cases produces the best product mix.

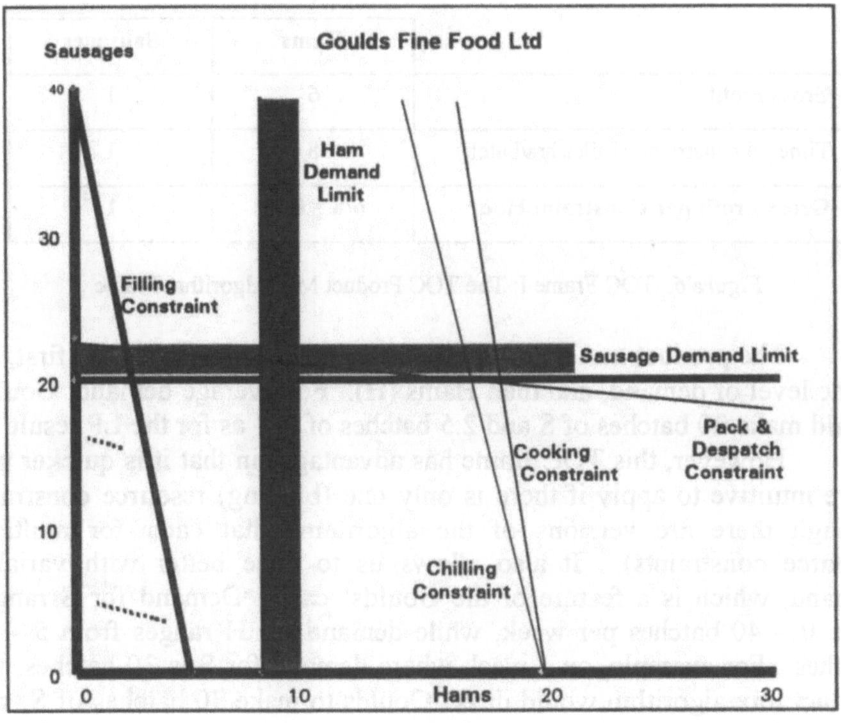

Figure 5. Frame VI: The Graphical Frame

The algorithmic decision rule is based on the ratio of profit to constraint-use for each product, and can be determined as follows:

First, determine the most constrained resource (called the constraint).

Then, calculate, for each product, the ratio of 'gross profit per constraint hour' (GP/CH). Since the Filler is the resource constraint, GP/CH for Hams is 0.75 (= 6 units of profit divided by 8 hours of filling per batch) and for Sausages is 1.0 (=1/1).

Then, rank these products in decreasing order of the GP/CH ratio (for example, Sausages, then Hams) to determine priorities.

This ranking is used, together with resource availabilities and other constraints such as market demand, to determine the actual production quantities of each product.

	Hams	Sausages
Gross Profit	6	1
Time on constraint (Filler hrs/batch)	8	1
Gross Profit per Constraint Hour	6/8 = **0.75**	**1**

Figure 6. TOC Frame I: The TOC Product Mix Algorithm Frame

The product mix algorithm leads to making Sausages (S) first, up to the level of demand, and then Hams (H). For average demand, Goulds would make 20 batches of S and 2.5 batches of H – as for the LP result.

However, this TOC frame has advantages in that it is quicker and more intuitive to apply if there is only one (binding) resource constraint (though there are versions of the algorithms that cater for multiple resource constraints). It also allows us to cope better with variable demand, which is a feature of the Goulds' case. Demand for S ranges from 0 – 40 batches per week, while demand for H ranges from 5 - 11 batches. For example, on a week where demand for S is 30 batches, the product mix algorithm would direct Goulds to make 30 batches of S, and use the 10 hours remaining on the filler to make 1.25 batches of H (if non-integer batches are possible).

TOC Frame II - the Five Focusing Steps (5FS)

A second TOC framework, the TOC Five Focusing Steps of On-going Improvement (5FS), also develops a perspective on constraints - but does so without artificially limiting the view to constraining resources or activities. Indeed, the 5FS process can allow further development of alternative perspectives for this case. A full description of the 5FS is given elsewhere [71, 75, 76, 77]. A brief summary is provided below. Note that when using the 5 Step process, we assume that the goal of the organisation has already been determined, although this is part of the first question addressed by TOC, namely 'What to change?' as discussed elsewhere [71, 76, 77, 78, 79, 80].

Applying the 5FS process to this case, we are encouraged to do all we possibly can to exploit the latent profitability of the over-riding or dominant constraint, seeking if necessary and possible, to subordinate other actions to these exploitative decisions made in 'Step 2'. We seek to do this before adding further capacity.

Five Focusing Steps in the Process of On-Going Improvement
Step 1: IDENTIFY the system constraint(s)
Step 2: Decide how to EXPLOIT the constraint
Step 3: SUBORDINATE other activities to decisions made in Step 2
Step 4: ELEVATE the constraint(s)
Step 5: If anything has changed ... GO BACK to Step 1.

This approach/perspective can be contrasted with the approach or myopic view often implicitly induced by the LP frame. Using the LP lens, one is led to identify the constraints (as in 5FS 'Step 1: Identify'); to exploit the constraint by choosing the right product mix; and then to move immediately to add further capacity (which is the 5FS 'Step 4: Elevate'). We note that using the TOC framework and principles can often lead to considerable improvement before adding new capacity, particularly through Steps 2 & 3. For example, seeking to reduce set-up times and process times on the constraints; and seeking to ensure the filler is never idle, by rescheduling tea breaks, and flows of work, will often resolve the problem without additional capacity.

Sometimes we can proceed through these 5FSteps without difficulty acting at an operational level, but sometimes the constraint is a policy - sometimes explicit, sometimes implicit and unstated, and sometimes all we can see is a seemingly unrelated tangle of symptoms or problems. In such cases, the use of TOC's logic trees is appropriate and can facilitate diagnosis of the nature of the illness (core problems), lead to prescription of appropriate remedies and to the institution of a treatment program, as will be discussed in a later section.

TOC Frame III - Combining LP with a TOC Framework

Using the two frameworks in combination, we can view the LP model results within the TOC 5FS framework. This approach is described by Mabin and Gibson [69], which in turn built on Mabin [81] and Luebbe and Finch [82].

The frame emphasises a stepwise process of problem solving, drawing on the strengths and synergies of the two methods, and fostering a pro-active way of dealing with constraints. Such a combination leads to the following interpretation:

Step1: IDENTIFY the constraint(s)

The first step in using TOC would be to identify the major constraint(s) which are preventing Goulds from reaching their goal. Note, Goldratt's definition of the term 'constraint' is more specific than the LP definition: constraints in TOC equate to binding constraints in LP.

In this case, we note that the goal would be to maximise profit. If we try to make the most profit possible, by meeting market demand, we note that the constraint is the filling process - we need 84 hours of filling to meet market demands, but only 40 hours are available per week.

Step 2: Decide how to EXPLOIT the constraint

Choose the best product mix: one can use the product mix algorithm as before, or LP. Both approaches point to producing Sausages first, then Ham. Make sure every minute of filling is used to advantage. This includes choosing the best product mix as determined above, avoiding idle time through breakdowns, scheduled breaks, or time waiting for materials to work on. Make sure all sausage demand is satisfied.

Using this step, Goulds found that Filler time was not being used to the maximum. They had been giving priority to Hams because of a higher profit margin. They also discovered that by changing personnel on the Filler line, they could increase the production rate. They also reduced set-up times on the constraint.

Step 3: SUBORDINATE other activities to the decisions made in Step 2

Some resources should not be fully utilised, as would be indicated by slacks in LP, eg mixing. Make only 2.5 batches Ham, ie subordinate demand for Hams to Sausage demand.

Subordinate other operations to serve the Filler. For example, mix as required to keep the Filler fully utilised. The TOC scheduling system, Drum-Buffer-Rope, [77] provides a method for this 'subordinate' step.

Step 4: ELEVATE the constraint(s)

If previous steps have not removed the problem, add more Filler Capacity.

In fact, Goulds installed a double nozzle to fill Hams. This action cost a fraction of the expenditure of more filling capacity, but had the effect of doubling the Filling rate for Hams.

Step 5: If anything has changed ... GO BACK to Step 1

If anything has changed, go back. Indeed, in the case of Goulds, the bottleneck had now been substantially relieved due to the changes and improvements in Filling rates for Hams.

We should go back through Steps 1-5. The LP should now be re-solved. At this point, the TOC product mix rule would suggest that Hams should be made first, **then** Sausages! The LP approach confirms this view.

The LP quickly provides a solution and sensitivity analysis information, while the 5FS approach can enhance the use of LP. In the 'textbook' approach, the problem is formulated and solved as an LP, the solution identified, and extra capacity is added if justified by the shadow prices. The 5FS approach would improve on this by applying Steps 2 and 3 before considering adding capacity (Step 4), and often the need for costly extra capacity would be obviated. Step 3 of the 5FS approach also prompts us to consider scheduling aspects which the LP formulation generally ignores and which TOC's Drum-Buffer-Rope method handles well. Once any changes are made to the system, it is easy to modify the LP (if an LP model is still appropriate) and re-solve to see what the new constraints are, so that the process of ongoing improvement continues.

TOC Frame IV - the Conflict Frame

Underlying the Product Mix problem is the dilemma: 'Which product should be given priority in production and sales?' The perspective developed by using Goldratt's exotically named Evaporating Cloud framework [70, 71], is one that draws attention towards the assumptions that underpin or give life to the dilemma.

The frame is constructed as a schematic depiction of the dilemma. The purpose for which the constructed frame is used is perhaps better reflected in the alternative title given by Dettmer [76] - the Conflict Resolution Diagram.

The reason for conflict can be explored by examining assumptions that underlie the relationships depicted by arrows connecting boxes in the diagram. We need to elicit these assumptions, or reasons why the relationships are thought to hold. Some of these assumptions are shown as annotations in the thought bubbles on the diagram.

The view of Production may be that **in order** to have satisfied employees, **we must** get good production bonuses, ... and **in order** to get good production bonuses, **we must** produce Sausages. On the contrary, the view of Sales is likely to be that **in order** to have satisfied employees, **we must** get good sales commissions, ... and, **in order** to get good sales commissions, **we must** make Hams. Hence the conflict!

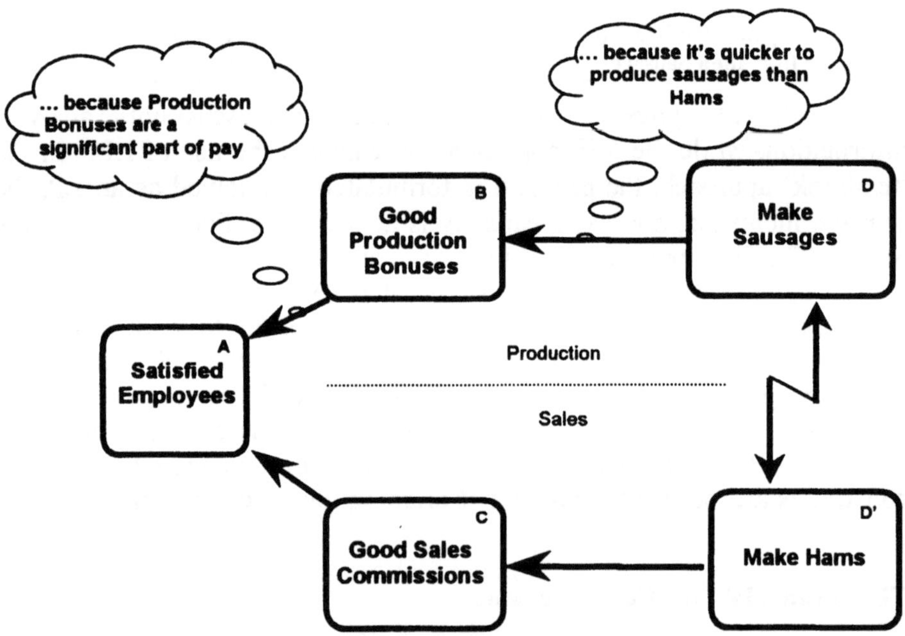

Figure 7. TOC Frame IV - The Conflict Frame

For example, production think that **in order** to have satisfied employees, **they must** get good production bonuses, ... **because** production bonuses are a significant part of their pay.

Similarly, **in order** for staff to get good bonuses **they must** therefore produce Sausages, ... **because** production bonuses are paid according to volume produced, ... and **because** it's quicker to produce Sausages rather than Hams. The rest of the '**because**' assumptions need to be stated in the same way, and then, ways of 'breaking' the assumptions should be sought.

Breaking the conflict arrow denoted by the lightning bolt at the right of the conflict diagram between D and D', that is challenging the fundamental assumption at the real heart of the conflict, is the most effective place to break the conflict. If we could find a way of meeting demand for both Hams and Sausages, then our dilemma would be removed. This may seem an impossible task at first, but as documented in Mabin and Gibson [69] and sketched in TOC Frame III, the application of the 5FS process demonstrates how it can be achieved.

Alternatively, we could resolve the conflict by breaking arrows /challenging assumptions further to the left of the diagram, but this would likely involve challenging some deep-seated beliefs - political, emotional and financial - surrounding, say in this case, the bonus system. Generally speaking, the further to the left the more fundamental will be the nature of issues that are being addressed.

These assumptions can be listed as below or annotated on the Conflict Cloud diagram:

Assumptions:

A - Satisfied employees are what we want
AB - Production bonuses are a big part of wages
Employees motivated by $
BD - Production bonuses are paid on quantity produced
We can make more Sausages than Hams in the time
AC - Sales commission are a significant part of wages
Employees are motivated by $
CD' - Sales commission are based on sales revenue
Hams earn higher revenue
DD' - Can't produce all of both products

Then ways of challenging or 'breaking' each of the assumptions should be found, as the list below illustrates:

Ideas for Solutions

A - Get good work some other way

AB - Remove bonuses

BD	- Change bonus scheme
AC	- Remove commissions
CD'	- Change commission scheme
DD'	- Change operations to make both!

For example, we could change the bonus systems in a way which could impact on arrows between A and B, A and C, B and D, or C and D'. Whichever arrow is broken, it should produce a breakthrough or 'win-win' solution. The authors note that using the cloud often leads to solutions that appear simple in hindsight, with both sides feeling they've benefited. Of course, if conflict is of a chronic nature, then additional steps may be necessary and TOC provides further guidance. However, discussion of such approaches lies outside the scope of this paper. It is worth noting that the conflict frame can prove just as useful in the examination of multi-party conflict as for personal conflict or dilemma.

TOC Frame V - the Logic Tree Frame

Goldratt [70] has also developed a suite of logic trees, which with the Evaporating Cloud are known collectively as the TOC Thinking Processes. The first of these trees is the Current Reality Tree (CRT) which is essentially a map of the cause and effect relationships perceived to underlie the current undesirable situation. Other tree structures within the TOC can be used to map out the desired future and how it can be achieved. Use of these logic trees signals an acknowledgement of other systemic influences that bear upon our decision making, and that need to be understood. Goldratt has provided logic rules (see the Categories of Legitimate Reservation [76, 77, 83] which are used to check the validity of constructed trees. In this discussion we will limit ourselves to the CRT, though readers may find it beneficial to refer to, say, Dettmer [76], Kendall [83] or Scheinkopf [80] for further coverage; to Schragenheim

[84] and Cox and Spencer [75] for an exploration of similar issues; or to Schragenheim [84] for an appreciation of how use of the CRT reflects more generic TOC thinking.

An initial step promoted by use of the CRT frame might be to list symptoms that currently indicate all is not well in the organisation. Such symptoms may include ongoing friction between departments, frequent late orders, the sales force feeling powerless and frustrated dealing with customer complaints, lots of unplanned overtime, and the company not doing as well financially as it would like. The TOC Frame V shows, for illustrative purposes, a logic tree based on our understanding of the situation.

> The tree is read from bottom to top using "**if** ... ... (**and** ...) (**or**...) **then** ... ..." logic. Where arrowheads touch, read the logical **and**, otherwise read the logical **or**.
> For example: "**If** each department has its own goals ... **and** ... rewards are tied to performance, **then** each department will do its best according to its own goals."
> We follow this through to: "**If** performance is impaired ... **or** ... **if** lots of overtime is required ...**then** costs are high."

Our frame then requires that for each symptom, we explore possible cause-effect relationships responsible for their manifestation. Using cause-effect analysis with the logic rules, we attempt to trace these symptoms back to the root cause of the problem, seeking to identify whether a single core problem exists that needs addressing.
A CRT analysis should lead to the identification of the core problem(s) underlying all (or most of) the symptoms, that is the things we normally complain about. If the core problem were to be dealt with properly, these symptoms would disappear. Frequently the core problems are (at least in hindsight) well known to the organisation, but have been avoided or ignored for some time because they are deemed to be 'too hard' to deal with. Kendall [83] describes measurements, policies and training as 'three pillars' of an organisation and asserts that weaknesses in one or more of these areas are often identified as core problems in a CRT analysis.

The core problem(s) is/are the boxes with no arrows leading into them, that lead to the majority of the undesirable symptoms. In this case, we identify measurements that are misaligned with the organisation's goal or with other parts of the system.

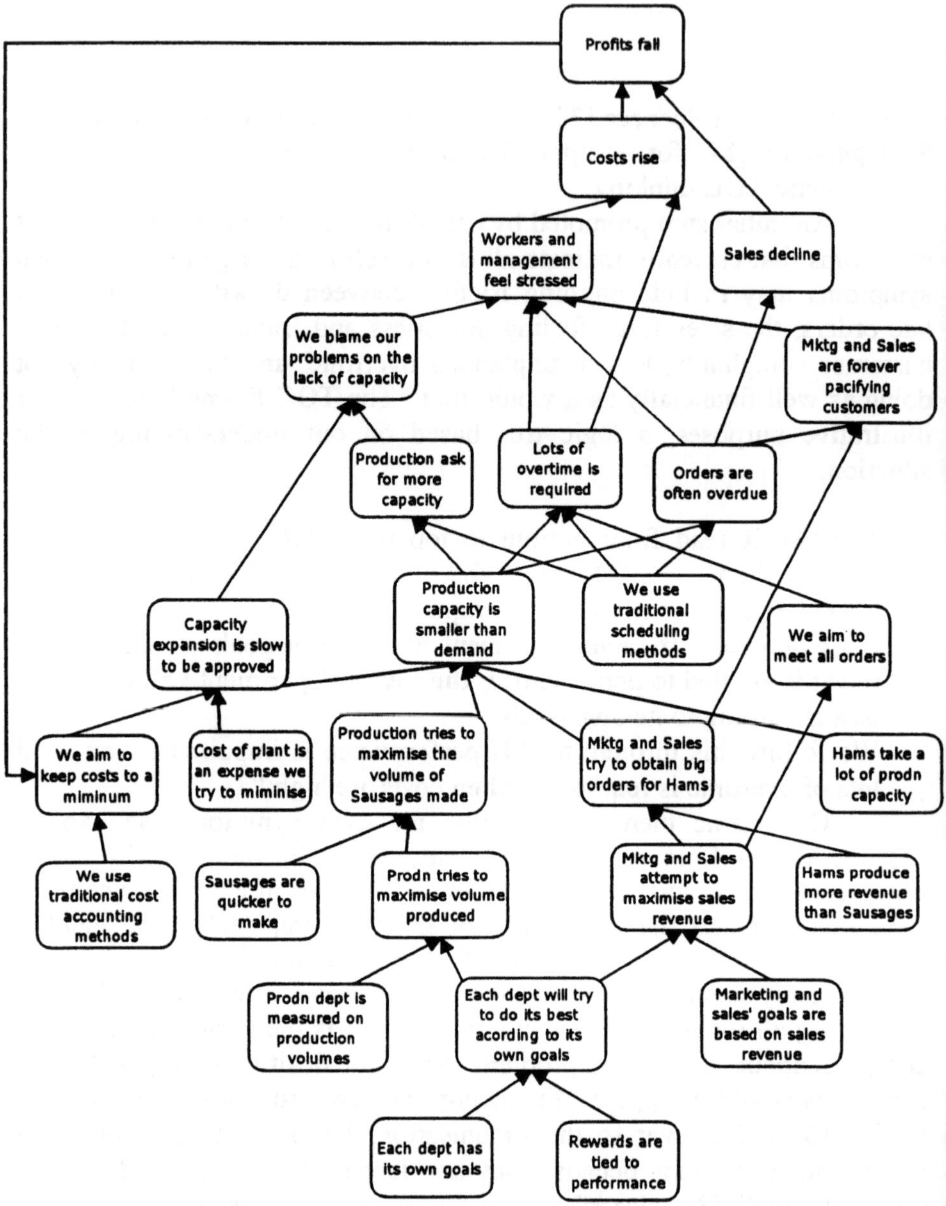

Figure 8. TOC Frame V - The Current Reality Tree Frame

For example, each department might be assessed/measured according to its own goals, with Production trying to maximise output and Sales trying to maximise sales revenue. This may be related to the outdated or erroneous policies involving the bonus system previously identified in the TOC Conflict frame, the use of traditional cost accounting, and to priorities used in the scheduling of jobs. While not shown in this tree, a related issue may be the lack of appropriate training, with, for example, Goulds' staff being unaware of the importance of the filling machine, or not trained to achieve the best production flow.

Framing the problem situation in this way emphasises the acceptance of a systems perspective, and the likely systemic nature of relationships and links between key variables and entities. The frame emphasises the view that there is no point fire-fighting symptoms - it is better to address and eradicate cause(s). It highlights the tangled web of interrelationships between symptoms, policies, measures and behaviours but posits that despite the tangle, it is possible to identify major causes of symptoms and to find ways of dealing with them. This can be achieved through use of the various TOC Thinking Processes tools, starting with the CRT discussed here, and other tools which aim to provide guidance through to the successful implementation of the solution.

Additional frames.

Before leaving this case, it may be useful to demonstrate how we may explore the problem situation further with an extended array of frames from the metaphor and OR/MS domains. As indicated in an earlier section, we may broadly categorise metaphor frames as having character, action or setting themes. We acknowledge the often implicit use of character frames in organisations as individuals take on say, departmental roles expected of them, such as those already portrayed for production and marketing as in the conflict cloud frame, or such as those of the general manager or accountant. A consequence, for example, of adopting the latter frame and perhaps following cost accounting conventions, may be a push for the higher profit product to be given priority, which in this case would lead to inferior overall profit performance. Of course, other character frames may arise from people emulating role models or heroes.

Somewhat differently, action frames often manifest themselves in the workplace as slogans, rules (written and unwritten) or mottoes, exhorting management or workers to particular behaviours or courses of action. For example, "stick to the knitting" may place emphasis on core competencies [85], in this case the standard product, sausages, whilst the exhortation, "quality not quantity" would suggest the reverse. Other action frames like "the squeaky wheel gets the attention", on the other hand provide a different perspective on behaviour, perhaps drawing attention to a reactive fire-fighting mentality, where customers who scream loudest get their orders filled first. Setting frames can be useful in yet other ways, for example, highlighting the dramatic contrast between what is and what could be, and in doing so, often providing a way of creating a shared vision for strategic change. For example, staff may feel caught in a Dickensian time-warp, where to work hard and not complain seems to provide a certain means of survival, yet where any attempt at change bringing improvement would seem a worthwhile but risky prospect [86]. We may then contrast the impact of working within this frame with other setting frames such as a pipeline, sports team or orchestra, which connote maintaining the flow, working as a team, and playing in 'synch'. Of course, many of these frames may exist in an organisation concurrently, each leading to its own preferred course of action but which in combination may lead to some form of chaos/impaired performance. Becoming more conscious of what these frames-in-use are and understanding their impact is often then a first step to constructive change.

We have also found value in using other standard OR/MS frames that on the surface might seem to have little relevance to the problem at hand. For example, using a multi-criteria decision analysis (MCDA) frame would prompt us to identify the various criteria that are important when judging the relative merits of different products. This frame prompts us to consider criterion trade-offs and subsequent weightings of the various criteria; whether excellent performance on some criteria can compensate for poor performance on others, or whether good performance on all criteria is necessary. Such a frame can lead to a broadening of views from previous frames, highlighting, in this instance, important attributes of current and future products. Many important criteria - such as customer service, or product range, which could have been overlooked in previous frames may well be surfaced using an MCDA approach.

Other frames, such as simulation or decision trees, may be overlooked or dismissed in a product mix situation, yet are natural and useful frames to consider. Simulation would focus on the flow of product throughout the production process. Consideration and emphasis would be focused on sequential operations, variability in process times, scheduling aspects and their impact on expected throughput (normally lower than that predicted from average process times). A decision tree frame, by contrast, might surface the impact that the production decision has on subsequent decisions in other functional areas such as distribution and sales.

This brief review should demonstrate that a quick scan of a number of diverse frames can yield many valuable insights that are often missed in our natural tendency to seek a best method to fit a problem. The decisions that should result from this broader view of the problem will be more robust to the criticism that essential aspects have been overlooked.

DISCUSSION AND CONCLUSIONS

The cases outlined here illustrate how framing and reframing can be effectively employed to improve the quality of understanding of problems we face, and of the decision-making processes in which we can engage.

Our first two examples provided opportunity to examine the use and usefulness of metaphorical framing. Although we may conclude from our review of these cases that the use of metaphorical framing, involving 'directed analogy', has offered a structure within which to examine and analyse any problem situation, we find that such 'structure' does not limit the decision maker's creativity in selecting and crafting a frame. On the one hand, whilst the choice of metaphor here has been seemingly unlimited in scope, the deliberate use of selected metaphors has generated striking insights.

In particular, the cases highlight the extent to which analyses, interpretations and choices are often value laden, dependent on the frame-in-use, implicit or otherwise. Indeed, the strength or power of many of the images evoked through the use of metaphor can be so strong that choices that become transparent and clear-cut in one frame, may be subject to reversal in another. The end result can be the creation of 'richer pictures', a greater recognition of implicit frames-in-use, a better understanding of what may be the 'real driving forces' behind decision-making behaviour, and hopefully, better informed decision makers.

Consequently, we have been encouraged to extend the use of framing as a problem-solving and pedagogical device.

The product mix case explored the diversity of insights that arise from multiple framing and reframing. Use has been made of a sample of 'hard' frames that are employed routinely by OR/MS practitioners and educators for 'modelling' purposes, as well as 'softer' frames that also guide problem identification and problem structuring processes as much as solution processes. The latter repertoire of 'softer' frames include TOC framing devices such as the current reality tree, the conflict resolution diagram, the focusing process and the product mix algorithm. These 'soft' frames not only illustrate additional insights that can be derived from their use, they draw attention to how the chosen 'hard' frames also operate from and reflect different perspectives. Indeed, reframing draws attention to how each of the different frames 'promote' the gathering, filtering and structuring of information in deliberate and distinct ways, often allowing a wider, deeper scope of analysis, and generating different insights about problems and how to tackle them.

We may summarise the nature and impact of such frames as follows:

The ... ... frame ...	emphasises or highlights ...
Narrative	contextual detail
Flowchart	sequencing
Tableau	missing data
Mathematical model	linearity
Spreadsheet	constraints
Graphical	spare capacity
Product Mix Rule	value of constraints
Five focusing steps - 2&3	exploiting constraints
LP plus 5FS	hard & soft approaches
Conflict Cloud	win-win situations
Logic Tree	core drivers
Simulation	variability
MCDA	hierarchy of criteria
Decision Tree	sequenced decisions

All of these frames require the modeler to describe the problem using the language or concepts of the frame - that is to use common codification - and all require the modeler to make assumptions in order to represent or structure relationships. The management of these assumptions appears to be one major difference between the traditional

OR/MS methods, TOC and metaphorical framing. The TOC frames, for instance, require not merely a statement of assumptions and of preconceived views, but also a questioning of their validity. They thus tend to be demanding of decision makers in different ways, requiring them to dig below the stated problem to make explicit core issues, often presenting a challenge to preconceived views. Indeed, TOC solutions arise in the main from the surfacing, questioning and breaking of assumptions - that is from unlocking tacit knowledge.

A purpose of this chapter has been to show the practicalities and benefits of using a variety of frames to tackle any given problem. One of our chosen problems is of a form commonly used in introductory OR/MS courses, but also one most often tackled using a limited subset of quantitative frames. Here we have demonstrated the range of effects and insights that arise from using a small set of disparate frames even with a 'simple' problem. The frames used here have been employed because they codify knowledge in different ways, because they tend to emphasise different aspects of the case, and because they provide different insights, shadowing some features, and revealing others that may remain unseen if only one frame were used. The TOC frames add to these effects and contribute new knowledge by providing additional devices for the externalisation of tacit knowledge.

One of the main differences between the OR/MS and TOC frames is that the former ask, "What is the best product mix?" whereas the TOC frames ask, "How can we improve the performance of the system?" The TOC frames suggest, for example, that the usual 'product mix' frame is addressing the wrong question! The latter frame seems to accept that a trade-off has to be made, and in doing so yields an inferior solution to that found using the TOC frames. These differences suggest that the problem-solving processes associated with TOC frames are redolent of Hall and Andriani's 'discontinuous learning' [87] and of the 'double loop learning' of Argyris and Schon [88].

We agree with Rothkopf [35] that "the essence of modeling is deciding what to include and what to omit", but whilst Rothkopf urges the modeler to use his/her model as an aid to further thought and exploration, we suggest the use of *multiple* frames or models to aid this process. We see such use, for example, as a way of generating a better set of action choices, avoiding Rothkopf's trap of "selecting from the impoverished list of options" that may emerge from only one frame. Furthermore, in as much as each frame is partial, harbouring implicit assumptions and potential biases, the multiple framing exercises performed here demonstrate the value of using a variety of disparate frames to reduce such bias, to surface hidden assumptions and to generate new insights about the problem situation.

We thus see that applying these frames in succession reveals the different shadows and highlights of each particular frame, leading both to an acknowledgement of the differences between frames as well as an appreciation of common themes, issues and solutions that arise from the frames taken collectively. Our experience shows where such benefits are recognised, the positive impact on the subsequent behaviour of decision makers is that they are more likely to be tolerant of other perspectives; to seek other possible interpretations of the problem; to search for and examine unstated, implicit objectives, prevailing criteria, existing value judgements etc., and therefore to improve their understanding of problems.

We acknowledge that framing shares the Kantian view that our knowledge is limited by how our perceptual 'lenses' and mental frameworks filter and organise the 'the raw data of experience'. However, the process of framing and reframing goes beyond providing us with a reminder of the limits of our knowledge, our perspectives and our frames-in-use. It provides us with the means of developing multiple perspectives in a directed way to broaden our understanding of problem situations and to aid problem description and problem structuring. As such, framing and reframing can be especially valuable in the early problem description/structuring phase of an investigation in facilitating the development of multiple representations and perspectives.

We also note the impact of framing and reframing as facilitating the externalisation of knowledge [87, 89] and promoting the sharing of experiences and the development of shared insights through use of a common conceptual language and analytical framework. As an obverse, we regard the use of framing and reframing as being a potential remedy to the often 'unconscious codification' or internalisation that so often creates a barrier between the academic/skilled practitioner and his/her student or client.

Additionally, and in the pragmatic and critical sense offered by Zhu, we agree that "introducing methods through frameworks" is essential if we want managers and students to have information and expertise to take part in discourse about decision making; and that being introduced to, or informed about diverse methods and methodologies without the assistance of pedagogical frameworks of one kind or another, our managers and students will have no other choice but to "hit everything with the hammer at hand" [3]

We note other similar positive effects of the use of framing as a meta-framework in the pedagogical setting can be the greater recognition of the implicit frames that we already use, how we make use of them, and how we can extend the contribution of framing from the analytical setting to problem identification and to the problem structuring domain. In the latter respect, we have highlighted the role of 'filling the frame' in helping to recognise, for example, when data is missing, relationships unspecified or overlooked. Additionally, our approach to framing acknowledges that there may not necessarily be any one best method or frame, and that the benefits of framing often relate to insights gained from the complementary effects of frames having differing strengths and highlighting or shadowing problem features.

As such, the development of a meta-framework to provide appropriate guidance to students in the development of problem identification and problem structuring skills, is worthwhile. In this, we conclude that framing as an integrating or synthesising meta-framework may not only provide a powerful means of facilitating and augmenting the complementary use of a variety of typical frames-in-use to develop insights from the creation of multiple perspectives, but also prove useful in generating insights at a theoretical level about the links between various methodologies.

REFERENCES

[1] Mingers, J. and Brocklesby, J. Multimethodology: towards a framework for mixing methodologies. *Systemist*, 18: 101-131, 1996.

[2] Gioia, D. Practicability, paradigms and problems in stakeholder theorising. *Academy of Management Review*, 23 (2): 228-232, 1999.

[3] Zhu, Z. The practice of multimodal approaches, the challenge of cross-cultural communication, and the search for responses. *Human Relations*, May 1999.

[4] Brocklesby, J. Methodological Complementarism or Separate Development - Examining the Options for Enhanced Operational Research. *Australian Journal of Management*, (18) 2: 133-158, 1993.

[5] Brocklesby, J. and Cummings, S. Combining hard, soft and critical methodologies in systems research: The cultural constraints. *Systems research*, 12: 239-245, 1995.

[6] Zhu, Z. Method choice in action research and systems practice: context driven or process oriented? In J Wilby (Ed.), *Forum one: Action research and critical systems thinking*, England: University of Hull, pp 107-112, 1996.

[7] Jackson, M. and Keys, P. Towards a systems of systems methodologies. *Journal of Operational Research Society*, 35: 473-486, 1984.

[8] Flood, R. and Jackson, M.C. *Creative Problem Solving: Total Systems Intervention*. Chichester: Wiley, 1991.

[9] Midgely, G. Mixing Methods: Developing Systemic Intervention. Research Memorandum No. 9, University of Hull, England, 1995.

[10] Flood, R.L. *Solving problem solving*. Chichester: Wiley, 1995.

[11] Flood, R.L. and Romm, N. *Diversity management: Triple loop learning*. Chichester: Wiley, 1996.

[12] Gu, J. and Zhu, Z. Tasks and methods in the WSR process. In J Wilby (ed.) *Systems Methodology II: Possibilities for cross-cultural learning and integration*. England: University of Hull, pp 15-22, 1996.

[13] Mingers, J. Towards a Critical Pluralism. In J Mingers and A Gill (eds) *Multimethodology: The Theory and Practice of Combining Management Science Methodologies*, Chichester: Wiley, pp 407-440, 1997.

[14] Brocklesby, J. Intvervening in the cultural constitution of systems-methodological complementarism and other visions for systems research. *Journal of the Operational Research Society* 46: 1285-1296, 1995.

[15] Gregory, W.J. Discordant pluralism: A new strategy for critical systems thinking. *Systems Practice*, 9: 605-625, 1996.

[16] Ackermann , F. and Belton, V. Strathclyde Business School Working Paper Series, Glasgow: University of Strathclyde, 1997.

[17] Bennett, P., Ackermann, F., Eden, C. and Williams, T. Analysing Litigation and Negotiation: Using a Combined Methodology. In J Mingers J and A Gill A (eds) *Multimethodology: The Theory and Practice of Combining Management Science Methodologies.* Chichester: Wiley, pp 59-88, 1997.

[18] Swanson, G.A. Building ISSS Success - One Failure at a Time. *General Systems Bulletin*, 26: 3, Fall 1997.

[19] Ackoff, R.L. and Sasieni, M.W. *Fundamentals of Operations Research*. Wiley: London, 1967.

[20] Simon, H.A., Dantzig, G. et al.. Decision Making and Problem Solving. *Interfaces*, 17, 11-31, 1987.

[21] Daellenbach, H. *Systems and Decision Making*, Wiley: Sydney, p 522, 1994.

[22] Ackoff, R.L. The Future of OR is Past. *Journal of the Operational Research Society*, 30: 93-104, 1979.

[23] Grinyer, P. Potential Relevance for OR of Perceiving Relevance as Socially Constructed, *ORSNZ Newsletter*, p 4, July 1994.

[24] Bailey, T. and Weal, S. Introducing Undergraduates to the Spirit of OR whilst imparting Substantive Skills. *Journal of the Operational Research Society*, 44: 897-908, 1993.

[25] Bell, P. Positioning the OR/MS Core Course. *OR/MS Today*, 8-10, June 1997

[26] Olafsson, S. and Hannibalsson , I. Improving OR/MS Courses. *OR/MS Today*, 8-10, February 1996.

[27] Goldratt, E. M. *Critical Chain*. North River Press: Great Barrington, 1997.

[28] Gass, S. Necessary components for OR/MS education in the 21st century. Panel Discussion, Joint International Meeting of EURO XV and INFORMS XXXIV. July 1997, Barcelona, Spain, 1997.

[29] Plane, D.R. Spreadsheet Power. *OR/MS Today*, 32-38, December 1994.

[30] Hesse, R. Excel and Statistics: Teaching Templates or Decision Analysis Tools. Proceedings of the 29th Annual Meeting of the DSI. November 1998, Las Vegas, pp 256-258, 1998.

[31] Davis, C.H. Teaching MS/OR with Spreadsheets: Retain the algebra. Proceedings of the 29th Annual Meeting of the DSI, Las Vegas, pp 253-255, November 1998.

[32] Powell, S.G. Innovative approaches to management science: from modelling to multimedia: how to teach difficult technical skills to skeptical students. *OR/MS Today*, 40-45, October 1996.

[33] Savage, S. Innovative use of spreadsheets in teaching. Presented at the 14th IFORS Conference, Vancouver, July 1996.

[34] Clauss, F.J. The trouble with optimal, *OR/MS Today*, 32-35, June 1997.

[35] Rothkopf, M.H. Editorial: Models as Aids to Thought. *Interfaces*, 26: 64-67, 1996.

[36] Bryant, J. OR Enactment: Theatrical Metaphor as an Analytical Framework. *Journal of the Operational Research Society*, 44: 551-562, 1993.

[37] Espejo, R. and Harnden, R. The VSM: An Ongoing Conversation. In Espejo R and Harnden R (eds). *The VSM: Interpretations and Applications of Stafford Beer's VSM.* Chichester: Wiley, p 445, 1989.

[38] Thomas, A.B. *Controversies in Management*. London: Routledge, p 210, 1993.

[39] Ackoff, R.L. *The Art of Problem Solving*, New York: Wiley, 1978.

[40] Mabin, V.J. and Davies, J. Framing and reframing as a creative problem structuring aid. Proceedings of the 30th Annual ORSNZ Conference. September 1995, Wellington, NZ, 1995.

[41] Watson, A.J. *In Search of Management*. London: Routledge, p 40, 1994.

[42] Dunford, R. and Palmer, I. Conflicting views of Metaphors: reconceptualising their use in the field of organisational change. *Academy of Management Review*, 21: 691:717, 1998.

[43] Howard, N. Negotiation as Drama: How Games Become Dramatic, *International negotiation*, 1: 125-152, 1996.

[44] Russo, J. and Shoemaker, P. J. H. *Decision Traps*. New York: Simon and Schuster, 1989.

[45] Pondy, L.R. The Role of Metaphors and Myths in Organisation and in the Facilitation of Change. In Pondy LR et al (eds). *Organisational Symbolism*. London: JAI Press, 1983.

[46] Morgan, G. *Images of Organisation*. California: Sage, 1986.

[47] Clancy, J.J. *The Invisible Powers: The language of business*. Lexington, MA: Lexington Books, 1989.

[48] Kendall, J.E. and Kendall, K.E. Metaphors and their meaning for information systems. *European Journal of Information Systems*, 3(1): 37-47, 1994.

[49] Brocklesby, R.J. The New Operational Research and Management Science: Integrating Hard, Soft and Critical Perspectives. GSBGM Monograph, Victoria University of Wellington: Wellington, 1993.

[50] Monin, N. and Monin, D.J. Rhetoric and action: when a literary drama tells the organization's story. *Journal of Organizational Change Management*, 10(1): 47-60, 1996.

[51] Marsh, N. *The All Star Company: people, performance, profit*. Auckland, NZ: Random House, 1993.

[52] Evans, J.R. *Creative Thinking in the Management Sciences*. Cincinnati: South-Western, 1991.

[53] Ohmae, Kenichi. *The Borderless World*. New York: Harper Business, p 105, 1990.

[54] Rivett, P. *The Craft of Decision Modelling*, Chichester: Wiley, 1996.

[55] Nutt, P.C. Formulation tactics and the success of organizational decision making. *Decision Sciences*, 23 (3): 519-540, 1992.

[56] Stumpf, S.E. *Socrates to Sartre: a history of philosophy*. New York: McGraw-Hill, 1996.

[57] Kemp Smith, N. *Immanuel Kant's Critique of Pure Reason*. London: Macmillan, 1934.

[58] Mabin, V.J. and Davies, J. The Power of Framing. Presented at the 8th Annual Australia and New Zealand Academy of Management Conference. December 1994 Wellington, NZ, 1994.

[59] Harris, M. and Payne, M. A Profound Appreciation of the Whole Orchestra. *Bulletin of Psychological Type*, 17:2, 1994.

[60] Jackson, B.G. The Goose that laid the Golden Egg?: A Rhetorical Critique of Stephen Covey and the Effectiveness movement. *Journal of Management Studies*, 36 (3): 353-378, 1999.

[61] Bormann, E.G. Fantasy and rhetorical vision: the rhetorical critisicism of social reality. *Quarterly Journal of Speech*, 58: 396-407, 1972.

[62] Jackson, B.G. A fantasy theme analysis of Peter Senge's learning organization. 3rd International Conference on Organizational Discourse, London, UK, 1998.

[63] Howard, N. Drama Theory and its Relation to Game Theory. Part 1: Dramatic Resolution versus Rational Solution 3: 187-206.

[64] Howard, N. Drama Theory and its Relation to Game Theory. Part 2: Formal Model of the Resolution Process 3: 207-235, 1994.

[65] Bennett, P. and Howard, N. Rationality, emotion and preference change - Drama-theoretic models of choice, *European Journal of Operational Research,* 603-614, 1996.

[66] Bryant, J. The Plot Thickens: Understanding Interaction through the Metaphor of Drama. *Omega, International Journal of Management Science*, 25(3): 255-266, 1997.

[67] Howard, N., Bennett, P., Bryant, J. and Bradley, M. Manifesto for a Theory of Drama and Irrational Choice. *Systems Practice*, 6(4): 429-437, 1993.

[68] Mabin, V.J. Case: Goulds Fine Food Ltd, Petone, Wellington. Presented to the 8th Annual Australia and New Zealand Academy of Management Conference. December 1994, Wellington, NZ, 1994.

[69] Mabin, V.J. and Gibson, J. Synergies from Spreadsheet LP used with the Theory of Constraints: a case study. *Journal of the Operational Research Society*, 49: 918-927, 1998.

[70] Goldratt, E.M. *It's Not Luck.* Great Barrington: North River Press, 1994

[71] Goldratt, E.M. *What is this thing called the Theory of Constraints and how should it be implemented?* Croton-on-Hudson: North River Press, 1990.

[72] Goldratt, E.M. *The Haystack Syndrome*. Croton-on-Hudson: North River Press, 1990.

[73] Goldratt, E.M and Cox, J. *The Goal: A Process of Ongoing Improvement*. 2nd Rev. Edition. Croton-on-Hudson: North River Press, 1992.

[74] Goldratt, E.M and Fox, R.E. *The Race*. Croton-on-Hudson: North River Press, 1986.

[75] Cox, J.F. and Spencer, M.S. *The Constraints Management Handbook*. Boca Raton: St Lucie Press/APICS Series on Constraints Management, 1998.

[76] Dettmer, H.W. *Goldratt's Theory of Constraints: A Systems Approach to Continuous Improvement*. Milwaukee: ASQC Quality Press, 1997.

[77] Noreen, E., Smith, D. and Mackey, J. *The Theory of Constraints and its Implications for Management Accounting*. Great Barrington: North River Press, 1995.

[78] Coman, A., Koller, A.G. and Ronen, B. The application of focussed management in the electronics industry. *Production and Inventory Management Journal*, 37: 65-70, 1996

[79] Mabin, V.J. and Balderstone, S.J. *The World of the Theory of Constraints: A Review of the International Literature*. Boca Raton: St. Lucie Press/APICS Series on Constraints Management, 2000.

[80] Scheinkopf, L. *Thinking for a Change: Putting the TOC Thinking Processes to Use*. Boca Raton: St. Lucie Press/APICS Series on Constraints Management, 1999.

[81] Mabin, V.J. Using spreadsheet optimisation facilities as a decision aid within the Theory of Constraints framework, Report 9/95 GSBGM Working Paper Series, Wellington, NZ: Victoria University of Wellington, 1995.

[82] Luebbe, R. and Finch, B. Theory of Constraints and Linear Programming: A Comparison. *Int J of Prod Res*, 30: 1471-1478, 1992.

[83] Kendall, G.I. *Securing the Future: Strategies for Exponential Growth using the Theory of Constraints*. Boca Raton: St. Lucie Press/APICS Series on Constraints Management, 1998.

[84] Schragenheim, E. *Management Dilemmas: The Theory of Constraints Approach to Problem Identification and Solution*. Boca Raton: St. Lucie Press/APICS Series on Constraints Management, 1999.

[85] Peters, T.J. and Waterman, R.H. *In Search of Excellence*. New York: Harper & Row, 1982.

[86] Bazerman, M.H. *Judgement in Managerial Decision Making*, New York: Wiley, 1990.

[87] Hall, R. and Andriani, P. . *The theory and practice of knowledge management. Bristol: Constructing Tomorrow*, 1998

[88] Argyris, C. and Schon, D.A. *Organizational Learning: a Theory of Action perspective*.:Reading, MA: Addison-Wesley, 1978.

[89] Nonaka, I. and Takeuchi, H. . *The Knowledge Creating Company*. Oxford: OUP, 1995.

4

INTRODUCING FORECASTING AND MONITORING METHODS TO AN SME: THE ROLE OF SOFT SYSTEMS METHODOLOGY

John E Boylan
Buckinghamshire Chilterns University College
Buckinghamshire, England

Mark A Williams
MRC Business Information Group, Oxford, England

ABSTRACT

In this case-study, we discuss how a company identified a need for a sharper analytical focus to its business and proceeded to introduce such an approach. Soft Systems Methodology was used to define the scope of forecasting and monitoring applications and to encourage debate about the purpose of planning. Questions of system ownership and of forecast monitoring were also addressed. It is concluded that systems thinking helped to reconceptualise the role of forecasting from an adjunct activity to an integral part of the company's planning systems.

Keywords:

Forecasting, monitoring, Soft Systems Methodology

M.G. Nicholls et al. (eds.),
Mixed-Mode Modelling: Mixing Methodologies for Organisational Intervention, 121–135.

INTRODUCTION

This chapter will discuss the introduction of forecasting and monitoring methods to a Small/Medium sized Enterprise (SME). The choice of forecasting method is often the focus of accounts of such interventions but here the emphasis is on the planning systems in which the forecasts are to be embedded. It is shown how mixing methodologies from systems thinking and soft systems methodology, helped the company to focus on how forecasts should be used and who should be responsible for forecasting and monitoring. The methodology provided a structured approach to addressing the human issues that were central to implementation.

ORGANISATIONAL BACKGROUND

MRC Business Information Group (henceforth MRC) was formed in 1984 in response to a perceived need in the international shipping and energy markets for well researched, clearly presented credit analysis and rating. MRC offered a range of reports, from short 'update reports' to in-depth 'consultancy reports'. Recognising the widely varying urgency behind clients' requests, reports could be made available within twenty-four hours, two to five days or three weeks. MRC also offered a 'databank service', whereby clients could access recent reports on a very large number of oil and shipping companies.

In 1996 the company moved to a team-based structure, based on geographical markets. The board envisaged that, through managing their own targets, budgets and staffing, the teams would become more motivated and therefore more productive. Teams needed to have information at their fingertips about targets, budgets, income, productivity and other performance measures.

PROJECT TO ESTABLISH A FORECASTING AND MONITORING SYSTEM

It was recognised by the MRC board that a more analytical approach was needed to address a wide range of questions facing the company. In response to this need, it was agreed that a two-year company-university programme would be established, the aim of which was summarised as follows:

> "The company aims to develop its business by becoming more efficient. It will do this through the Teaching Company Scheme programme, 'Project Clarity', by the development of a range of analytical tools which will improve both the understanding and organisation of its sales and production processes." Boylan and Kenner [1].

The project proposal was agreed and joint funding was secured from the Department for Trade and Industry and from the company itself. The project remit was broad and covered the following areas:

1. Analysis of current operational and planning processes.
2. Investigation of the old and new databases used within MRC.
3. Identification of what needed to be forecasted and monitored.
4. Analysis of forecasting methods and accuracy.
5. Examination of alternative policies of updating reports for the MRC databank (e.g. writing reports not in direct response to a client request, but in anticipation of future requests).
6. Analysis of quality systems.
7. Embedding forecasting and monitoring within the culture of the organisation.

Detailed investigations of the company database were conducted and mathematical analyses of forecasting accuracy were carried out. It was concluded that a form of discounted regression could be employed for forecasting order volumes in the medium term (up to 12-18 months). It was soon apparent that identifying suitable forecasting methods was quite straightforward; implementing them so that the company would obtain real benefits would be much harder. This chapter concentrates on the third and seventh objectives. Williams [2] gives a detailed account of the achievement of the other five objectives.

THEORETICAL BACKGROUND

Makridakis *et al* [3] comment that:

> "The definition of the problem is sometimes the most difficult aspect of the forecaster's task. It involves developing a deep understanding of how the forecasts will be used, who requires the forecasts, and how the forecasting function fits within the organization".

Some authors have proposed forecasting process guidelines. Broad recommendations were made by Barron and Targett [4], based on the work of Jenkins [5]. More detailed guidelines are given by Armstrong [6]. However, little guidance is available in the forecasting literature on how a 'deep understanding' of the organisational context can be cultivated.

Some authors in the 'soft OR' tradition have recognised the need for forecasting to be incorporated within their approaches. Ackoff [7] recommended the use of 'reference projections', so that planners would be able to anticipate the consequences if there were no change to the organisation or its environment. Friend and Hickling [8] recommend that 'uncertainty in the environment' may be reduced by forecasting. However, possibly since forecasting is perceived as a 'hard OR' activity, it has received somewhat scant attention in the 'soft OR' literature.

In practice, forecasting and monitoring go hand in hand. Monitors are continually revisited to check progress against targets. Targets may be changed if forecasts demonstrate their need for revision. Forecasts themselves are monitored to ensure that their accuracy remains acceptable to the organisation. One soft approach that includes monitors as an integral component is soft systems methodology, Checkland [9], Checkland and Scholes [10], Checkland and Holwell [11]. Consultation of the indexes of these three books shows no mention of forecasting. Of course, forecasting could easily be included as an activity in the conceptual model, but this hardly does justice to its importance. In this chapter, it is argued that soft systems methodology can be used to inform the linkages between forecasting, monitoring and operational activities, and can act as a useful catalyst for debate about the human issues in implementing a forecasting and monitoring system.

SITUATION AT THE BEGINNING OF THE STUDY

The company had grown quite substantially in the period 1994-97, owing to its steadily growing reputation for high quality reports and the general health of the shipping market. Relatively little market segmentation analysis had taken place. The most significant segmentation was perceived to be geographical. Four teams had been established in 1996, based on the location of geographical market sectors: Europe, Mediterranean, Asia and the Americas.

John Boylan had conducted a forecasting study for MRC in 1994 in a consulting capacity. The work was prompted by the realisation that, even with some efficiency gains, demand for MRC's reports was likely to outstrip the capacity of the company's production capacity. A series of forecasts was generated, based on the assumption that growth for each of the main product groups would continue at current rates for the next year. On this basis, it was recommended that a small number of additional analysts be recruited. In 1995, another consulting report was commissioned, reviewing the accuracy of the initial forecasts and updating them for the year to come. The review showed that, with few exceptions, all product groups had continued to grow as expected, and the forecasts were remarkably accurate. By the following year, 1996, the rate of increase in demand had slowed down. At the beginning of the study, in January 1997, the four geographical teams were well established and further growth in the staff base was not envisaged in the short term.

A direct marketing manager had been appointed twelve months before the beginning of the study. A review of his activities revealed that it was impossible to *demonstrate* any benefit from his work. This worrying situation pointed to a significant weakness in the monitoring of sales and activities to promote sales. Furthermore, it became clear that the marketing activities of the company were disparate and required integration.

The financial systems of MRC were much more fully developed. Regular reports were generated, showing the financial health of each of the major products and of each of the four geographical market sectors. Revenue was, therefore, well understood. It became apparent later in the study that there was some scope for improving the analysis of costs. Although total costs were closely monitored, it was not so easy to attribute costs to products or to markets.

IDENTIFICATION OF RELEVANT SYSTEMS

The original stimulus for improved forecasting and monitoring arose from under-staffing, resulting from unanticipated growth in orders. Thus, 'human resource planning' was a natural first choice of system in which forecasts should be introduced. As the project progressed, the need for better planning and monitoring of marketing initiatives became apparent; 'marketing planning' became the second arena in which systematic forecasting was introduced. Analyses of the 'financial contribution' of different products focused top management's attention on the need for sharper financial modelling. Therefore, 'financial planning' became the third relevant system of enquiry.

Thus we had an initial view of the relationship between the systems under consideration, reflecting the model of Checkland and Holwell [11] of a 'system that serves' supporting a 'system that is served':

System that serves	***Systems that are served***
Forecasting and monitoring System	HR planning system Financial planning system Marketing planning system

As the project gained a clear direction, this was a helpful overview for managers at the company, who began to appreciate the scope of the programme and the practical applications of the new Forecasting and Monitoring System.

FORECASTING AND MONITORING FOR HUMAN RESOURCE PLANNING

The need for periodic forecasts of human resource requirements was well understood within the company, following the successful use of forecasts in 1994/95. There had been a number of changes in the company since that time. Firstly, teams were expected to take a greater responsibility for planning their own staff needs. Secondly, the company was developing its own analytical capability and did not want to be reliant on an outside consultant for the production of forecasts. Other factors had not changed. The timing of new staff recruitment remained crucial, since previous studies had shown that it may take a new analyst between six and nine months before he/she would be generating reports at the rate and quality expected.

A workshop involving board members and team leaders led to the following root definition:

> *A system, owned by the board of MRC and operated out of Corporate Services, which delivers information about production and productivity to team leaders, so that new employees can be started at the right time to absorb forecast extra business.*

A CATWOE analysis showed the following:

Customers	Directors, team leaders.
Actors	Corporate Services Team Leader.
Transformation	Non-staff become employees when right for MRC.
Weltanschauung	Aim of Teaching Company Programme.
Owner	Board.
Environment	Team leader experience, unforeseen market activities (e.g. crisis in the Asian shipping market), interactions with other systems, such as team organisations.

There was broad agreement on these elements of the CATWOE analysis amongst workshop participants. There was some debate about the 'actors': would it be better for these forecasts to be generated by the team leaders themselves? The team leaders were keen to keep themselves away from as many non-core functions as possible. In many ways, this was quite understandable, since they needed to keep the percentage of time devoted to core business as high as possible in order to meet ambitious targets. Since the directors were also 'customers' of this planning system, it was agreed that Corporate Services should take the responsibility for generating forecasts of order volume and productivity, by team, thereby allowing HR requirements to be gauged.

FORECASTING AND MONITORING FOR MARKETING PLANNING

Early meetings with the sales and marketing team had met with an enthusiastic response. The team members recognised that an inability to demonstrate the efficiency and effectiveness of their own activities was simply untenable. They began to question the geographical split as the only valid segmentation and proposed that sector analyses (e.g. energy, shipyards, engineering, commodities etc) be conducted. They also saw the need for monitors of the larger customers as essential to client retention.

The enthusiasm of the sales and marketing team for acquiring a greater analytical capability is reflected in the following root definition, arising from a workshop:

> *A system, owned by the board of MRC and the sales and marketing team, who operate it, which delivers information about the effectiveness of promotions, and market conditions, so that the sales team can perform its tasks with greater clarity and therefore more effectively.*

A CATWOE analysis showed the following:

Customers	Directors, sales and marketing team.
Actors	Sales and marketing team.
Transformation	Sales and marketing team manages promotions better and measures results.
Weltanschauung	Aim of Teaching Company Programme.
Owner	Board, sales and marketing team.
Environment	Sales team organisation, sales staff training, 'MAGIC' database development for marketing purposes.

It is interesting to note that the sales and marketing team agreed to be 'co-owners' of this system with the board members. At first, the authors regarded this as inaccurate, but did not challenge it, since the continued motivation and commitment of the sales and marketing team were essential to the success of marketing planning. We thought of it as incorrect since 'ownership' was being used by the participants in the general managerial sense of 'commitment', rather than the technical sense of "those who could stop T", where 'T' denotes the transformation [10]. On further reflection, however, we realised that the workshop participants may be right. If a transformation within a system can wither through passive resistance by a team, as well as through a conscious decision by the board, then it may be more accurate to include the team as co-owners of the system.

This reflection led to a realisation that it might be beneficial to recast the definition of 'ownership' within soft systems methodology. Checkland [9] defines ownership as "some agency having a prime concern for the system and the ultimate power to cause the system to cease to exist". He summarises this as "those who could stop T". The 'emblematic model of purposeful activity' [10], shows those who can stop the transformation in stick-people form, with a word-bubble saying 'No!'. These descriptions suggest that 'ownership' is exercised by a conscious decision (saying no) by those with authority (ultimate power). However, transformational activities may simply fall into disuse, possibly because of passive resistance by those who lack ultimate power. We would therefore suggest that the definition "those who could stop T" be amended to "those who could stop T or allow T to fall into disuse".

The following monitors were agreed for the forecasting and monitoring system to support marketing planning:

Efficacy	System is used in advance of marketing and sales campaigns. Results are checked.
Efficiency	Ease of use of the system to provide benchmarks of order volume and income against which campaigns may be scored.
Effectiveness	Growth in knowledge of the market and effective marketing of commercial information (especially when campaign results deviate from forecast).

Marketing planning is now more firmly embedded within the company. An annual plan is submitted to the board, summarising achievements in the previous year (backed up by sound data) and outlining plans for the coming year. One area in which market knowledge has developed is in segmenting clients by frequency of orders and classifying them as 'frequent', 'occasional' and 'passive'. This has led to focussed campaigns to increase the volume and value of orders from occasional users and to initiatives to re-activate passive users.

FORECASTING AND MONITORING FOR FINANCIAL PLANNING

As indicated previously, 1994-97 had been a period of growth in revenue and the company was in a healthy financial position. However, from early 1997, there were signs that the market was becoming less buoyant, and the order volume forecasts were flattening out. This led to a greater emphasis on the controlling of costs within the company.

A proposal was made to develop a 'contribution model' as part of the Teaching Company programme. Such a model would show the contribution to profits from each of the major product groups. It would take into account discount structures, production costs (based on estimates of production time), materials and telecommunication costs. Such a model would allow the product portfolio to be reviewed and pricing levels assessed.

The prototype model was well received and this led to a debate about the wider needs for financial planning. A workshop generated the following root definition:

> *A system, owned by the directors of MRC and produced out of Corporate Services and the Finance Department, aimed at shaping corporate financial policy through quantitative modelling, in order to improve profitability and shareholder value.*

A CATWOE analysis showed the following:

Customers	Directors.
Actors	Corporate Services Team Leader.
Transformation	Directors avoid happenstance profitability by becoming profit planners.
Weltanschauung	Aim of Teaching Company Programme.
Owner	Board.
Environment	Synergy with Management Accounts, targets determined by parent company.

In this case, the root definition debate led to a reconsideration of the purpose of financial planning. The phrase "to shape corporate financial policy through quantitative modelling" reflected a more ambitious aim than had been previously considered. The 'what if' capability of contribution analysis had led to a re-appraisal of what financial modelling could offer the company. The root definition reflected a view of financial modelling informing such decisions as the rationalisation of the product portfolio and changing price and discount structures.

CONCEPTUAL MODELS

A broad conceptual model was generated, that could be applied to each of the three systems. It is shown in Figure 1.

The conceptual model contains sub-systems of data collection, forecasting, interpretation and planning. The sub-systems of 'forecasting' and 'planning' contain their own monitors to reflect the need to check on 'actual versus forecast' and 'actual versus plan'. In the above model, it is assumed that the forecast informs the plan but that the two are distinct.

The conceptual model revealed little that was surprising, but it led to a re-conceptualisation of forecasting *as a part of* the planning system, rather than a system to serve the planning system, as shown earlier in the chapter. In practice, this reconceptualisation was strongest in the sales and marketing team, since:

- Sales and marketing had taken over responsibility for generating forecast and monitors themselves (although they still drew on the expertise of corporate services where appropriate). In the terminology of soft systems methodology, the sales and marketing team had become the 'actors'.
- Sales and marketing's view of the forecasting and monitoring system as being useful to them had changed to a view that it was essential for them. In the language of soft systems methodology, their weltanschauung had changed (although this was not modelled explicitly).

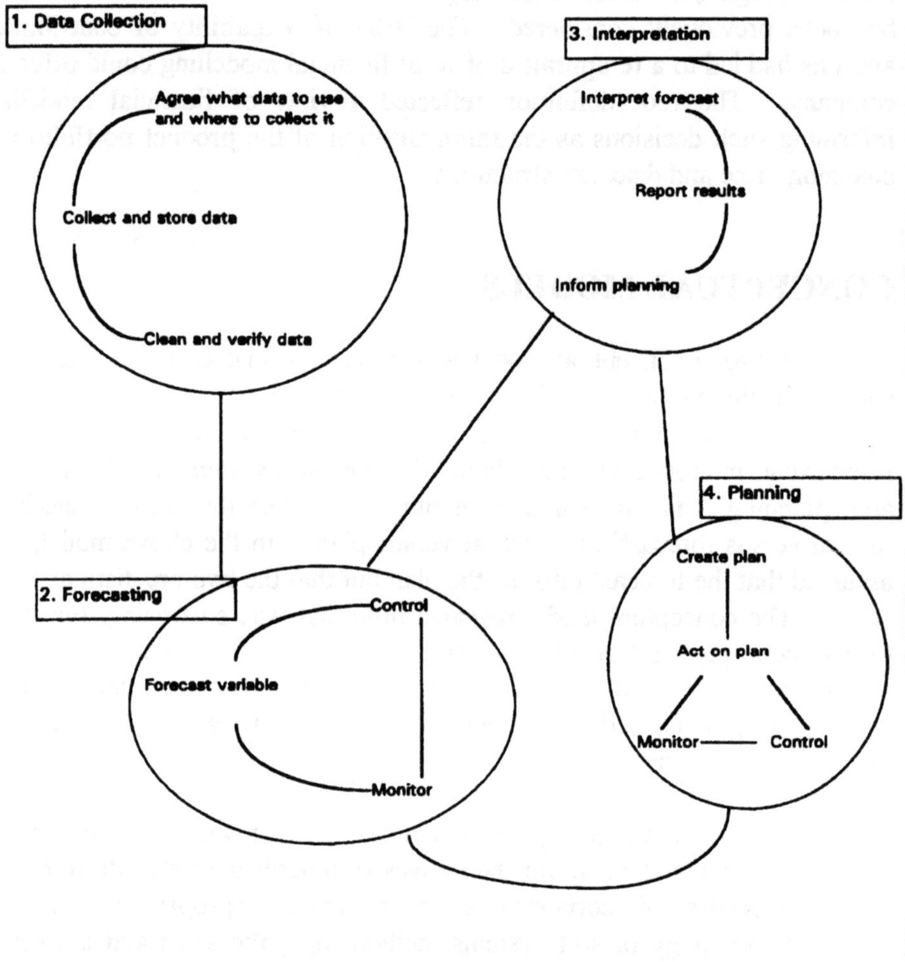

Figure 1: The Broad Conceptual Model.

- Sales and marketing no longer viewed the MRC Board as the sole owners of the system. They came to see themselves as co-owners and included this explicitly in the CATWOE analysis, with agreement from the MRC directors.

The integrated view of forecasting and planning was also adopted by the finance department. The financial controller took more responsibility for financial modelling within the company, gradually reducing his dependence on corporate services for support.

The case of human resource planning shows the pitfalls of not integrating the forecasting and planning systems as closely as one should. Since 1997, the market had been relatively flat and there had been no need for any recruitment drives, although some new staff had been hired as a result of departures. In 1999, the markets picked up and new staff were needed. However, by this time, the corporate services manager and the personnel manager roles had new incumbents and there was a reduced organisational memory of the last major recruitment drive when decisions had been informed by forecasts of order volumes, by team. Therefore, decisions were made without the forecasts that could so easily have been generated. The lack of an immediate need at the time when the system was installed combined with the departure of the corporate services manager resulted in the process not being embedded.

The form of the conceptual model given above may have wider applicability. In systems where forecasting would not be regarded as an 'operational activity', it would be logical to place it outside the main sub-systems boundary. However, it should be considered as distinct from monitoring, since it has its own monitors. The 'forecasting sub-system' would lie outside of the main 'operational activities' and distinct from 'monitoring' but would be linked to both. Within the forecasting sub-system, 'forecast variable', 'monitor' and 'control' are the bare minimum set of activities required but could be expanded upon as necessary.

CONCLUSIONS

In this case study, it has been shown how soft systems methodology has assisted an SME in:

1. Defining the scope of applications of forecasting and monitoring,
2. Considering the purpose of their planning systems and who should take responsibility for their operation. In HR planning, the responsibility for the generation of forecasts and monitors was resolved. In marketing planning, the members of the sales and marketing team put themselves forward as co-owners of the system and took on the responsibility for forecasting and monitoring themselves. In financial planning, discussion

of the root definition led to a more ambitious purpose than had been previously considered.

3. Re-conceptualising the role of forecasting from an adjunct activity to an integral part of planning systems.

Two issues have emerged from the case study, which may have more general implications for systems practice. Firstly, 'ownership' may be usefully extended from 'those who can stop a transformation' to 'those who can stop a transformation or allow it to fall into disuse'. Inclusion of those who could allow a system to fall into disuse as co-owners of the system recognises their power and may serve to motivate them to take responsibility for making desirable and feasible changes within the organisation. Secondly, in systems where forecasts play an important role, but are considered a support activity rather than an operational activity, it may be helpful to consider 'forecasting' as a sub-system in its own right and include its own monitor of forecast accuracy.

In summary, it is not argued that SSM was indispensable. It would have been possible to proceed without SSM, but its use sharpened the analysis of the issues discussed in this chapter and promoted debate between board members and team leaders on the purpose and scope of forecasting and monitoring and the responsibilities entailed.

ACKNOWLEDGEMENTS

The authors would like to thank the board of MRC for permission to publish this case study. The views expressed are those of the authors and not necessarily those of the company; any errors are likewise attributable to the authors.

REFERENCES

[1] Boylan, J.E. and Kenner, S.A. *Teaching Company Programme Proposal, MRC Business Information Group and Buckinghamshire University College,* 1996.

[2] Williams, M.A. Reports submitted for the award of MSc in *Industrial and Business Studies*, Buckinghamshire Chilterns University College, 1999.

[3] Makridakis, S., Wheelwright, S.C. and Hyndman, R.J. *Forecasting, Methods and Applications, 3rd Edition*, Wiley, New York, 1998.

[4] Barron, M. and Targett, D. *The Manager's Guide to Business Forecasting*. Basil Blackwell, Oxford, 1985.

[5] Jenkins, G.M. *Practical Experiences in Business Forecasting*. GM Jenkins and Partners, 1976.

[6] Armstrong, J.S. [Ed] *Principles of Forecasting: a Handbook for Researchers and Practitioners*. Kluwer Academic Publishers, 2001.

[7] Ackoff, R.L. *Redesigning the Future*. Wiley, New York, 1974.

[8] Friend, J. and Hickling, A. *Planning under Pressure, 2nd edition*. Butterworth-Heinemann, Oxford, 1997.

[9] Checkland, P. *Systems Thinking, Systems Practice*. Wiley, Chichester, 1981.

[10] Checkland, P. and Scholes, J. *Soft Systems Methodology in Action*. Wiley, Chichester, 1990.

[11] Checkland, P. and Holwell, S. *Information, Systems and Information Systems*. Wiley, Chichester, 1998.

5

ASSESSMENT OF THE VALUE OF KNOWLEDGE TRANSFERRED: A MIXED-MODE APPROACH

Krishna S. Dhir
Berry College, Mount Berry, Georgia, USA

ABSTRACT

This chapter presents a mixed-mode approach to the assessment of the value of knowledge developed and transferred within an organization by its knowledge experts in the course of its technology portfolio development. Knowledge transferred by experts has value to the extent that it enhances the technology portfolio of a unit. The assessment of such value is a matter of individual judgment, which may be subjective in nature. For such assessment, the application of conventional hard models, based on firm-specific human capital theory and human resource accounting theory, may not be effective by themselves. A mixed-mode approach that links soft psychometric models based on social psychology with the conventional hard econometric models offer greater promise. The mixed-mode approach described here first develops a soft model of managerial judgment, which is then interfaced with hard econometric models to determine the value of knowledge transferred.

Keywords: mixed-mode modelling, knowledge transfer, technology transfer, product development, knowledge management, value of knowledge, valuation, human judgment analysis, social judgment theory.

M.G. Nicholls et al. (eds.),
Mixed-Mode Modelling: Mixing Methodologies for Organisational Intervention, 137–169.

INTRODUCTION

Value assessment is crucial to effective and efficient management of resources. In the emergent knowledge-based economy, a business organization's assets are often in the form of know-how created by the knowledge experts within the organization. The know-how created is transferred within the organization, to its business or engineering unit, for application to business or engineering problem solving. In this chapter the issue of assessment of the value of knowledge created and transferred by the knowledge experts is addressed. This issue is an essential element of the Human Resource Management effort in many knowledge-based, technologically oriented companies. The chapter offers a mixed-mode approach to valuation of knowledge. The approach described here first develops a soft model of managerial judgment, which is then interfaced with hard econometric models to determine the value of knowledge transferred. It includes methodologies of brainstorming, scenario building, judgmental analysis, non-linear multiple regression analyses, econometric model building, and consensus building.

THE NATURE OF INTELLECTUAL CAPITAL

Value is the amount buyers are willing to pay for products or services provided. Porter [1] offers the concept of *value chain* for systematic investigation of all activities a firm performs to create value. This concept desegregates a firm into its strategically relevant activities. Competitive advantage is derived through performance of these activities more cheaply or better than those performed by the competitors. The role of the knowledge experts within the organization may be seen as contributing to improved performance of these activities.

The valuation of knowledge transferred entails integrating of information about employees, products, processes, research, patents, publications, professional expertise shared among employees, and outcomes of business strategies. The intellectual capital created through the transfer of knowledge, when scrutinized minutely, turns out to be complex. Intellectual capacity grows with sharing and dissemination of knowledge. Intellectual capital may be viewed as this capacity, when it is in a state of deployment; that is, when the specific know-how pertaining to the knowledge is in use. Capital *is* assets in use. For intellectual capital to be created from a transfer of knowledge, there has to exist a relationship between the members of a business or an engineering unit and the technology that is based on the particular knowledge of interest. This relationship is of a subjective nature. It depends on what is the business or the engineering unit at the receiving end of the transfer going to do with the knowledge. It depends on how the unit relates to the knowledge transferred. Consider the following scenario presented by Berle [2] (p25)

> "A piece of rock has an owner. If the owner is a sculptor, the rock is in passage toward becoming a work of art. The subjective element is the chief element. A piece of Chinese jade has an owner - perhaps a collector. It is thing in being, objective, lying quietly on a display shelf. The owner neither adds nor subtracts; he enjoys. The less a thing is susceptible to being worked with or upon, the [more] objective it becomes."
>
> "But then property turns a corner. At the extreme of objectivity -- for example, hoarded gold -- it can become, not a thing in itself, but a claim on the goods, the services, or the labor of other men at the will of its owner. At this point, surprisingly, its significance once more becomes almost entirely subjective. Its owner can cause events to happen by selling this purely objective property, or perhaps by drawing and spending the dividends or interest realized from it, but he cannot otherwise affect the property whose prime characteristic is 'liquidity.' To accomplish this liquidity, it is necessary that the property (thing or claim...) have no relation whatever to its owner except that relation arising from the owner's capacity to transfer it. Nothing can be liquid if any value assigned to it depends upon the capacity of effort or will of the owner. Marble would stop being readily salable if its value depended on having the sculptor transfer along with it."

In presenting the above example, Berle was arguing that the value of a property to its owner depends on the relationship the owner has with the property. However, this example also effectively illustrates the value of technology or the knowledge on which it is based. This value would depend on the relationship that a business or an engineering unit could potentially develop with the technology. It also illustrates that to be of value to a business or an engineering unit within the business organization, the technology developed should be transferable.

Why would a business or an engineering unit develop a relationship with a technology, or with the knowledge on which the technology is based? The need of the business and engineering unit managers is for a *technology portfolio*, consisting of products, services, and the processes that produce them, that is better than that of their competitors. The assessment of this need is subjective. Knowledge, and the work of the knowledge experts, has value to the extent that it helps the unit managers obtain a superior technology portfolio. The assessment of the degree to which a particular technology might help unit managers obtain such superiority is subjective. Intellectual capital must, nevertheless, be available and deployed in order for the physical assets to be productive, and for a firm to realize competitive advantage from its business opportunities. It would be appropriate, then, to emphasize the technology content of the expertise shared by a knowledge expert in determining the intellectual capital value, not just the manufacturing costs or market potential to be exploited. This view is consistent with those of Kendrick [3] and Kopelman [4], who suggest that the economic value of personnel activities is defined through their capacity to enhance the economic value of the firm. A knowledge expert's activities may be seen as deriving its value through its capacity to enhance the firm's technology portfolio, and hence its economic impact.

The works of Joll *et al* [5] and Thurow [6] suggest that the activities of the knowledge experts would be considered productive if the expenses incurred by them, individually and/or collectively, during a base period, translates into revenue flows such that a firm's total investment in salaries and mix of personnel activities results in a rate of return equal to or exceeding some desired rate of interest. Akerlof [7], Flamholtz [8], Thurow [9], and Viren [10], point to the labor economists, accounting theorists, and compensation theorists, who suggest that economic value attaches principally to jobs, not individuals. Individual performance drives the productivity of the firm. But the economic value is not embodied solely in individual performance. Instead, economic value is determined by a complex interaction of the market, the institution, and the individual variables. Individual characteristics are an indirect source of value because employers desire a particular profile of skills, knowledge, and abilities that they think will lead to successful job performance [9]. Mahoney [11] suggests that the firms value what he refers to as the standardized unit of labor, which is necessary to obtain a desired level of job performance. Joll *et al* [5] and Thurow [9] present the idea that the value assigned to the standard unit of labor is defined by that unit's *marginal physical product* which, when multiplied by the sales value of the output produced, defines that unit's *marginal revenue product* or its *relative contribution* or *use value* to the firm.

Those subscribing to the marginal revenue product theory often assume that a single productivity value exists for a job. In fact, employees are not homogeneous in terms of the relative contribution. We refer to an individual's relative contribution as that individual's *use value*. Since individuals perform with different motivations and abilities, it is reasonable to expect a distribution of possible levels of output from their performance [9]. Personnel activities positively influence the distribution of individual *use values*. They are economically productive if they lead to increases in the quantity and quality of employee services, and if the revenues associated with this incremental increase exceed the variable costs associated with the change.

While the measurement of value is generally attempted in terms of financial measures, often based on cost figures or market transaction figures, different individuals may in fact, receive different value from delivered functions. Therefore, the conventional hard econometric models, by themselves, may not be adequate for the valuation of these functions. The unit managers in a business organization may regard a technology or knowledge being transferred to them as meeting their specific needs to various degrees of satisfaction. They may deem the transferred knowledge or technology to enhance their respective technology portfolio to different degrees. It is imperative that the assessed value account for not only the properties and qualities of the knowledge transferred, but also the emotional regard the user of the technology has for it. Assessment of such value is a matter of individual judgment, which may be subjective in nature. For this reason, a mixed-mode approach to valuation that accounts for the subjective elements of human judgment is needed.

PHASES OF KNOWLEDGE TRANSFER

The approach needed to assess the value of the knowledge depends on whether the transfer of the technology in question takes place during (a) the *strategic* phase, or (b) the *implementation* phase of a product, process or service development. During the *strategic* phase, issues such as what *attributes* of the knowledge transferred contribute to the functional value; what are their *respective importance* relative to each other; and how are their respective contributions to value to be *measured*, must be determined. In this phase, the 'sculptor' can give whatever shape or form to the 'rock [which] is in passage toward becoming a work of art.' In this phase the knowledge expert can greatly influence the attributes assigned to the technology that is being transferred. As stated in Berle's quotation above, "The subjective element is the chief element." The assessment of value, in this phase, depends on the subjectivity of the assessor's judgment. As such, in this phase, it is appropriate to explore the development of soft psychometric components within a mixed-mode approach to the assessment of value. In contrast, during the *implementation* phase the decision as to which alternative knowledge yields the greatest value is made. This is accomplished by evaluating each alternative technology with a model or a set of criteria that accounts for the contribution of each of its attribute. These evaluations may then be compared with each other to identify the alternative that yields the greatest value. The predominant quality of the evaluation process is its objectivity. Conventional hard approaches to the development of econometric models have been applied to such assessments with considerable success.

This chapter proposes a mixed-mode methodology for the assessment of the value of knowledge or technology, which is transferred during the strategic phase of the product, process or service development. A model may be formulated to describe the hierarchical relationship between activities performed, capabilities of the knowledge or the technology transferred, and value created through the transfer of knowledge. The premise here is that the activities are implemented through deployment of abilities in order to create value. One could, for instance, describe how value may be assessed based on the propensity of the transferred knowledge to be shared, to provide creative solutions to critical business needs, to expand the knowledge base of the business unit receiving the knowledge, and to develop into future innovations. The model may then be extended further to relate these propensities to the activities through which value is created.

Various methods for human resource value assessment that would apply to the implementation phase of the knowledge transfer process are discussed in the literature [12], [13]. These include approaches based on (a) the firm-specific human capital theory [14], (b) human resource value theory [8], and (c) utility theory [15]. However, our interest is in developing a valuation approach for the *strategic* phase of the knowledge transfer process. It is in this context that the mixed-mode approaches, such as the one described here, proves useful.

In a firm, the knowledge transferred by a knowledge expert to a business or engineering unit becomes valuable if a relationship is established with the technology in question by the unit's manager and other members -- *in the manner of the relationship established by the sculptor with the rock in passage toward becoming a work of art*. This relationship would be realized to the extent that the technology transferred enhances the business or engineering unit manager's technology portfolio. In the strategic phase, therefore, value is attributed to the technology by the business or the engineering unit manager. The technology, and the knowledge on which it is based must, of course, be transferable. To be transferable, the knowledge transferred must be independent of the knowledge expert; that is, it must not require the transfer the knowledge expert along with the technology -- *in the manner of the marble*, which may be transferred independently of the sculptor.

The impact of this knowledge transfer, in the strategic phase of a product, process or service development, is, of course, of a probabilistic nature. The future earnings to a firm arising from the knowledge expert's activities in this phase are uncertain. These activities may or may not yield a marketable output, but nevertheless, offer promise. It is also not clear, in this phase of development, how long an economic value arising from the knowledge expert's activities is to accrue. The schedule of payoff, too, is uncertain. It is not known, for instance, whether the economic value would appreciate or depreciate over time.

The considerations explored above suggest that in the strategic phase, the application of the conventional hard approaches to value assessment based on the firm-specific human capital theory and the human resource accounting theory may be wrought with difficulties. Soft approaches, relying on psychometric analyses, and drawing from social and industrial psychology, offer greater promise. Different value may be assigned by different business or engineering managers to the knowledge developed by a knowledge expert, depending on the *fit* or the *niche* of the technology in question relative to the technology portfolio available to the manager. As stated earlier, "the subjective element is the chief element" [2] (p25). In this context, the task of assessing value requires an exercise of human judgment. Let us, therefore, first briefly review the nature of human judgment.

THE HUMAN JUDGMENT PROCESS

The human judgment may be described as a process through which an individual uses social information to make decisions [16] [17]. The social information is obtained from an individual's environment and is interpreted through the individual's *cognitive image* of the environment. The cognitive image provides a representation of the environment based on past experiences and training, and essentially predisposes the person to respond to the social information in predictable ways. These patterns are represented by an individual's *policies* or beliefs about the environment. Human judgments are based then upon one's interpretation of available information. This leads to judgments considered as probability statements about one's environment and how one reacts to it. This condition causes the human judgment process to be inherently limited. It is fundamentally a *covert* process. It is seldom possible for an individual to accurately describe his or her judgment process accurately. Ordinarily, the only means of actually explaining judgments are introspection and guessing at the reasons for the observed judgments. These explanations are generally incomplete and misleading. Subjective reporting is fallible. Judgments are thus *inaccurately reported*. Judgments are also generally observed to be *inconsistent*. Identical circumstances do not always lead to identical judgments. Observations of inconsistent judgment often sets an observer in search for hidden motives or conclusions of incompetence on the part of the decision maker. Psychological theory of human behavior, however, finds such assumption unnecessary. Judgment is inconsistent because its process is not fully analytical and controlled. Inconsistency is, therefore, an inherent characteristic. Consistent judgment requires a degree of mental skill that often exceeds human intuitive capabilities [18]. While *covertness*, *inaccuracy of reporting*, and *inconsistency* may not completely describe the human judgment process, these characteristics make clear that decision aids would prove enormously useful in overcoming the limitations of human judgment. To find means to uncover the covert process of judgment, let us examine its parameters.

Parameters of Human Judgment

If the parameters of one's judgmental policy orientations could be identified, then it would become possible to model the process of that person's judgment, and develop valuation aids. This process may be explored by posing the following questions:

(a) What is the *criterion* being assessed? This may be the decision or the economic criterion variable being assessed. In this particular case, the criterion variable is the value of the technology transferred, or the knowledge on which it is based.

(b) What *factors* influence the individual's judgments? This is to identify the variables that influence the business or engineering unit manager's assessment of the value of the technology or knowledge of interest. These factors would usually be the attributes of the knowledge transferred, or of the contribution the technology makes to the technology portfolio of the unit relative to improving the unit's competitive edge. These factors should have mutually exclusive characteristics or properties.

(c) What relative emphasis or weight does the individual put on each of the factors considered by him or her? This refers to the *relative weights* assigned to the factors in question. One source of disagreement between managers arises from the fact that different weights are likely to be attached by different managers to the factors.

(d) How does the individual utilize the information regarding each factor to arrive at an overall judgment? Since our primary purpose here is to model the judgment process, we may seek to identify the mathematical relationship that describes the dependence of the overall judgment about the criterion variable on the factors considered. The relationship between each factor and the overall judgment may be linear or nonlinear, and the contribution of each factor to the overall judgment may be positive or negative. The nature of dependence of the overall judgment on each factor is referred to as that factor's *function-form*. Our interest in a mathematical description does not imply that the actual judgment process works mathematically. We recognize that different models, analytical or otherwise, could represent the actual process. However, numerous studies demonstrate that the mathematical representation described above is useful in predicting and understanding human judgment [16], [17], [19]. For a detailed discussion of the use of mathematical descriptions of cognitive integration, see [20]. For examples of function-forms, see Figure 1.

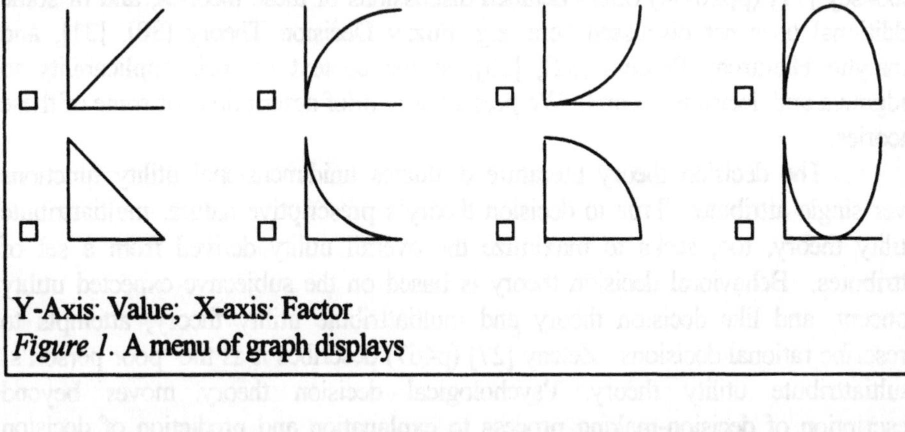

Y-Axis: Value; X-axis: Factor
Figure 1. A menu of graph displays

(e) What is the *consistency* with which the individual is able to make judgments? An individual may make different judgments about the same situation on different occasions. At least two characteristics of the judgment task are known to affect consistency: task complexity and task uncertainty. Studies have shown that consistency is lower when the judgment task is complex, i.e., involving more factors, rather than less; and also lower when the task requires use of nonlinear function forms rather than linear function forms [16], [17]. Even when a decision maker intends to use a specific judgment rule as defined by specific set of factors, relative weights and function forms, his or her judgments or assessments may deviate from those suggested by that rule. Wanting to execute a particular stroke in tennis does not necessarily produce that stroke, or wanting to hit a bull's-eye in target practice does not automatically result in that. Errors may creep into the process of execution. In tennis and target practice, feedback on the result is immediate. In absence of such explicit and immediate feedback on judgment, the decision maker may be unaware of the degree to which the actual judgment or assessment deviates from that intended.

Alternative Theories

There are a number of alternative theories available for application to the assessment of value of knowledge. These include decision theory and multiattribute utility theory [21], behavioral decision theory [22], psychological decision theory [23], information integration theory [24], attribution theory [25], policy capturing [26], [27] (pp452-454), and social judgment theory [16], [17], [28]. For detailed discussion of these theories, and for an attempt at their integration, see [29]. Cooksey [17] (pp26-54) offers detailed discussions of these theories, and of some additional ones not discussed here, e.g. Fuzzy Decision Theory [30], [31], and Analytic Hierarchy Process [32], [33], in the context of their applicability to judgment and decision research. We present very brief descriptions of some of these theories.

The decision theory literature evaluates unidimensional utility functions over single attributes. True to decision theory's prescriptive nature, multiattribute utility theory, too, seeks to maximize the overall utility derived from a set of attributes. Behavioral decision theory is based on the subjective expected utility concept, and like decision theory and multiattribute utility theory, attempts to prescribe rational decisions. Zeleny [27] (p467) describes it as the 'poor person's' multiattribute utility theory. Psychological decision theory moves beyond description of decision-making process to explanation and prediction of decision behavior. It seeks the cognitive sources of departure from the criteria of rationality. It attempts to make decision makers aware of their own errors and biases.

The goal of information integration theory is to discover the metric form of cognitive algebra employed in cognitive activities, e.g., is the information integrated in one situation by one algebraic principle, and in another situation by another algebraic principle? Attribution theory draws from Gestalt psychology. It views people as observing events in their environment and seeking causes of events by evaluating available information. It does not seek models of individual judgment or decision, and offers no relatives weights or component functions.

Policy capturing [26], [27] (pp452-454) uses Brunswik's lens model [34], to make an individual's judgmental orientations explicit through multiple regression analysis. Like policy capturing, social judgment theory, too, evolved from Brunswik's lens model, shown in Figure 2. This figure represents a situation in which a decision maker attempts to make judgments on a distal variable, Y_s. The variable is perceived through a set of proximal variables, X_i's. Using the information of X_i's, the decision maker arrives at a judgment, Y_a. The emerging body of literature on social judgment theory explores interpersonal conflict arising from different judgments and lends itself to applications in policy analysis. The 'social' element in social judgment theory is derived from the interaction it affords among two or more individuals through improved communication.

While policy capturing uses the lens model to make an individual's judgmental orientations explicit through multiple regression analysis, social judgment theory extends policy capturing to *communication* of the judgmental orientations, and facilitates social interaction. While policy capturing applies to single-person systems, social judgment theory applies to systems consisting of two or more decision makers. Not only does the social judgment theory communicate overt judgment differences among decision makers, as, for instance, in the DELPHI technique [35], it also communicates the covert policy differences in terms of its parameters, such as relative weights and function-forms, unlike the DELPHI technique. For comparison of a social judgment theory based approach and the DELPHI technique, see [36].

A major difference between policy capturing and social judgment theory is that the application of social judgment theory requires the separation of relative weights from function-forms. This separation is not necessary in policy capturing. Through this separation, however, social judgment theory allows identification of the *sources* of differences among decision makers, e.g., whether their policy differences arise due to differences in weights assigned to specific factors (i.e., relative weights), or differences in the manner in which the information on specific factors is utilized (i.e., function-forms). Availability of such information facilitates the development of alternative approaches to social interaction. Exchange of such information may or may not require face-to-face interaction among decision makers.

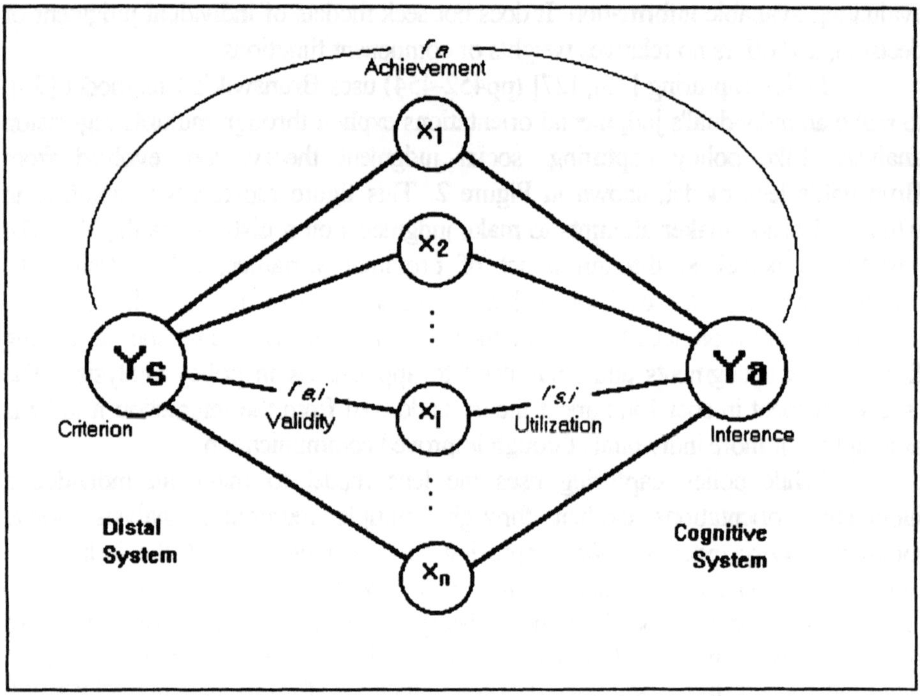

Figure 2. Brunswik's lens model of cognition

The mixed-mode approach described in this chapter incorporates a formal application of the social judgment theory. Soft, psychometric modeling based on this theory is preferred here over others because of the following considerations: Decision theory and multiattribute utility theory are prescriptive, and indicate how rational decisions *should* be made. Behavioral decision theory and psychological decision theory explores *why* decision makers depart from rational prescriptions. To study assessment of value, however, we seek to analyse judgment. The objective here is not to define a prescriptive approach to assessment of value. It is also not to compare observed decision behavior against a rational prescription. It is to *describe* the judgment process involved in the assessment of value of knowledge transferred, as observed. Social judgment theory applies well to such description. It does not prescribe, nor does it seek to explain deviations from 'rational' behavior. In these respects, social judgment theory is preferred over decision theory and multiattribute utility theory, behavioral decision theory, and psychological decision theory.

It should be noted that multiattribute utility theory elicits the relative weights used in making judgments through a direct interrogation of the decision maker. The highly influential work of Nisbett and Wilson [37], however, give reason to suspect verbal elicitation. They take the position that decision makers' accounts do not explain or clarify judgments and decisions actually made by them. It should be acknowledged, however, that certain social psychologists do not accept their claim. Ericsson and Simon [38] argue that useful verbal data *can* be obtained from decision makers' verbal accounts of their subjective thoughts if investigators do so in the right way. More recently, Wiederman and Dubois [39] suggest that self-reported weights may be prone to bias. In contrast to the approach of the multiattribute utility theory, the social judgment theory seeks these relative weights indirectly, and separately from function-forms, through analysis of the decision maker's judgments on a set of alternative scenarios.

Social judgment theory is also preferred over attribution theory, and information integration theory because of the following reasons: Social judgment theory offers means of obtaining a soft model of individual judgment process, which may then be used to develop judgment and decision aids. Attribution theory does not do this. It generally assumes that the person making the judgment does not influence cognitive processes underlying causal judgments. The information integration theory has generally stayed away from applications. For additional discussion, see [17] and [29].

Social judgment theory is also easy to use. The methodology involved in the application of the social judgment theory yields relatively straightforward and mathematically clean results that are easily understood by decision makers. Further, literature reports that the simple additive models of decision-making based on regression analysis seem to be at least as accurate as the more complex models, and are preferred by many users with respect to most criteria of desirability [27].

Social judgment theory has had considerable success in developing soft models for use as decision and judgment aids. For instance, analyses based on this theory have proved quite efficient in reducing conflict, and increasing agreement among decision makers. Such analyses have been found superior in these respects to the DELPHI technique [36]. Social judgment theory has been applied to many problem areas, including assessment of value [40], [41], [42]. For additional examples, see [16], [17], [19], [28], and [43].

AN ILLUSTRATIVE APPLICATION

Consider a situation in which a business manager is faced with transfer of knowledge to his or her unit through a knowledge expert. The business manager must rely on his or her own judgment process to assess the value of the technology in question. Figure 2 shows an environmental system of the knowledge transferred and the business manager's cognitive system. Each system is composed of one distal variable, Y_s for the environmental system, and Y_a for the cognitive system, respectively. Each system also shares a group of proximal variables, X_i, called *factors*, common to both systems. In the context of this chapter, Y_s represents the actual value of the technology transferred, Y_a represents the judgment made by the business manager in regard its value, and X_i 's are the factors taken into account by the business manager to arrive at Y_a, the judgment.

The lens model shown in Figures 2 facilitates the measurement of the degree to which a decision maker perceives a criterion, Y_s, as it is, using cues or attribute, X_i, that are valid. The degree to which the decision maker is able to do so, r_a, is measurable. It also allows measurement of the degree of such validity, $r_{e,i}$, and the degree to which a cue or an attribute is actually utilized in making an assessment about the criterion, $r_{s,i}$.

The relationship between the cognitive models of two individuals may be analyzed through the lens model equation [17] (p212):

$$r_{1,2} = G \cdot R_1 \cdot R_2 + C \cdot \{(1 - R_1^2) \cdot (1 - R_2^2)\}^{0.5} \qquad (1)$$

where $r_{1,2}$ is the correlation between two variables, say, Y_1 and Y_2 (the variables may be two individuals' judgments, or an individual's judgment and an environmental criterion); G is the correlation between the components of Y_1 and Y_2 that are predicted from a linear regression on the factors; R_1 and R_2 are the linear multiple correlations between the factors and Y_1 and Y_2, respectively; and C is the correlation between the residuals from the linear regressions of Y_1 and Y_2.

The term, R_i, may be interpreted as a measure of the fit of the specific model for the ith decision maker. G is the correlation between predictions based on two models. C measures the relation between the components of Y_1 and Y_2 that is not accounted for by the regression analysis. If the regression analysis were based on a linear model, then a high value of C would suggest presence of nonlinear variation shared by the two systems. In such cases, inclusion of nonlinear terms in the model may be considered. If two individuals have identical policies, which are represented by linear models, then G becomes 1. If no shared nonlinearity exists, then $r_{1,2}$ would become a measure of agreement between two individuals, ($R_1 \cdot R_2$).

THE VALUE ASSESSMENT PROCEDURE

We now present a narrative based on actual experience to illustrate the psychometric approach to valuation presented in this chapter. Consider a business organization manufacturing electronic components that are utilized in the assembly of computer systems. An engineering unit within this organization develops new products. This unit is considering alternative technologies, developed by knowledge experts within the business organization of which it a part, for inclusion into its set of technology portfolio. This unit consists of a leader and a deputy leader, both members of the management cadre. Additionally, the unit is staffed with 13 design engineers, 5 factory information specialists, and 6 technicians. Thus, the total number of staff is 26. The leader must assess the value of the alternative technologies to select the one that is most valuable to the unit. The leader decides that he would like to have inputs from all members of the unit to aid him in arriving at a determination. He calls in consultant to help him. The consultant sets about his job, and administers the method described here.

The assessment of the value of knowledge transferred, in the method proposed here, requires the following steps: (A) determination of the valuation policy; (B) application of the valuation policy to the specific knowledge of interest; and (C) conversion of the value rating into an economic value.

(A) Determination of the valuation policy

This step involves the development of a soft model capturing the judgmental policy of a manager. The following steps are involved in determining the parameters of a manager's judgmental policy for assessing the value of an knowledge: (1) Define the criteria to be assessed; (2) Choose or identify the factors influencing the manager's assessment of value; (3) Obtain the manager's *a priori* policy for value assessment; (4) Design profiles of a set of alternative intellectual technologies; (5) Test these profiles for orthogonality; (6) Have the manager assess each profile for value; (7) From these value ratings, obtain the manager's judgmental policy for value assessment through nonlinear regression analysis.

(1) The Criteria

In this study the criteria selected is the relative value of the technology in terms of the degree to which it enhances the engineering unit's technology portfolio.

(2) Choice of Factors

The proposed model is required to describe how value may be assessed based on the attributes of the alternative technologies. The consultant calls for a brainstorming session. At this session, with all 26 members of the engineering unit participating, a number of attributes are cited. Many of these are related to each other. The related attributes are lumped together, and the resulting factors are so defined as to capture all related attributes in a single definition. In this manner, ultimately, a total of 6 factors are identified as being pertinent to the assessment of the relative value of a technology, for their purposes of this unit. These, listed in no particular order, were as follows:

(i) *Customer Responsiveness*: This factor refers to the degree to which the technology improves the response time to customer requests through agile, flexible manufacturing. This method of manufacturing is established through such features as modular product designs, rapid automated machine tooling and process set-up and changeover, and reconfigurable tooling. This factor is represented in this study on a scale from 1 to 10, where 1 represents an extremely low degree of customer responsiveness, and 10 represents an extremely high degree of customer responsiveness.

(ii) *Information and Communication Accessibility*: This factor refers to the degree to which the technology provides the ability for easy access to information and communication by providing an environment, internal and external, including linkages with suppliers and customers, for integrated computer-aided design, computer-aided manufacturing, and computer-aided engineering, high speed networking, intelligent machine interfaces, and wireless communications. This factor is represented in this study on a scale from 1 to 10, where 1 represents an extremely low degree of accessibility, and 10 represents an extremely high degree of accessibility.

(iii) *Quality Enhancement*: This factor refers to the degree to which the technology provides the ability to improve or enhance product quality through the use of process control technology. Process modeling and simulation, real time adjustable tooling and automatic process diagnostics are examples of methods to improve manufacturing quality levels. This factor is represented in this study on a scale from 1 to 10, where 1 represents an extremely low degree of quality improvement or enhancement, and 10 represents an extremely high degree of improvement or enhancement.

(iv) *Environment Friendliness*: This factor refers to the degree to which the technology conserves and protects the environment, with the involvement of the suppliers and vendors, by minimizing adverse impact minimal scrap, effluents and undesirable by-products, and recycling or reuse of materials. This factor is represented in this study on a scale from 1 to 10, where 1 represents an extremely low degree of environment friendliness, and 10 represents an extremely high degree of friendliness.

(v) *Cost Effectiveness*: This factor refers to the degree to which the technology maximizes the unit's manufacturing capability in a cost effective manner, minimizing the cost of manufacture with the objective of being the lowest selling price producer of products. This factor is represented in this study on a scale from 1 to 10, where 1 represents an extremely low degree of cost effectiveness, and 10 represents an extremely high degree of effectiveness.

(vi) *Personnel Productivity*: This factor refers to the degree to which the technology maximizes the output per unit man-hour of direct labor for the entire human resources. This factor is represented in this study on a scale from 1 to 10, where 1 represents an extremely low degree of personnel productivity, and 10 represents an extremely high degree of productivity.

The reader should consider the 6 factors listed above as exemplary of the set of factors that influence judgments in assessing value of the knowledge transferred. A different group of managers and staff, in a different business organization, within the same or different industry, may consider a different set of technology attributes when assessing its value in terms of the degree to which it enhances their technology portfolio. For instance, some managers may wish to consider a set of attributes of the knowledge itself. Others may wish to consider the set of or the range of technological functionalities that facilitate the unit's implementation of business strategies. A manager may prefer such technology-portfolio-related factors as *strategic fit* of the proposed technology with the unit's existing technology portfolio, *transferability* of the technology, its *processability*, *reliability*, *maintainability*, *ease of use*, *safety*, etc. The manager may also wish to account for *profitability*, *manufacturability*, *marketability*, *product life*, *product image*, etc. The primary purpose here is to provide an example that can be helpful to the managers in investigating the role of the preferred cognitive variables in value assessment of the knowledge or technology of interest.

(3) Obtaining the A Priori Policies

Each manager participating in this study is asked to indicate the relative emphasis he or she places on each factor, respectively. To indicate this, the manager is asked to distribute 100 points among the 6 factors listed, i.e., *customer responsiveness*, *information and communication accessibility*, *quality enhancement*, *environment friendliness*, *cost effectiveness*, and *personnel productivity*, in such a way that the points assigned to each factor indicate the relative importance of that factor in the manager's assessment of value. Each individual is also asked to indicate the functional relationship between each factor and the value. They do this by selecting out of a menu of graph displays shown in Figure 1, one that in his or her respective judgment best represents the relationship between each factor and the value. The options include: linear positive function, linear negative function, J-function, reverse J-function, inverted J-function, inverted reverse J-function, U-function, inverted U-function. Thus, with the relative weights for each factor described and their respective relationship with the value assessment criterion indicated, we will obtain the *a priori* description of each individual's policy regarding assessment of value of technologies transferred.

(4) Design of Alternative Technology Profiles

A total of 25 different profiles are now designed, each representing a different hypothetical alternative technology. A sample profile, describing a technology profile in terms of technology-portfolio-based factors selected by the 26 members of the engineering unit, is shown in Figure 3. To generate these, random values are assigned to each factor on a scale from 1 to 10. A value of 1 represents very low levels of measure for the factor, and a value of 10 represents very high levels of measure.

It is important to check the profiles thus designed for inter-correlations among the factors. Their presence confounds the efforts to attribute variations in the judgment of value to the respective factors.

(5) Testing for Orthogonality

The profiles designed are tested for orthogonality to minimize the effect of inter-correlation among the factors, as follows: The objective is to establish the absence of significance among *all* correlations. The Pearson product-moment

TECHNOLOGY PROFILE 16

Factors	***Value*** (On a scale from 1: very low, to 10: very high.)	
Customer Responsiveness	5	XXXXX
Information and Communication Accessibility	8	XXXXXXXX
Quality Enhancement	3	XXX
Environment Friendliness	6	XXXXXX
Cost Effectiveness	2	XX
Personnel Productivity	10	XXXXXXXXXX

What is the relative value of this technology in terms of the degree to which it enhances your unit's technology portfolio? Please indicate your value rating on a scale from 1 (very low value rating) to 100 (very high value rating): ☐

Figure 3. A sample profile of technology transferred

correlation coefficient may be used to estimate the population correlation coefficient. If the highest correlation coefficient thus found were established not to be significantly different from zero, then it would be fair to conclude that none of the correlation coefficients are significantly different from zero. The significance test is performed on the highest correlation coefficient observed, by computing the t-statistic as follows:

$$t \quad = \quad r_{ij} \cdot [\{(n-2)/(1-r_{ij}^2)\}^{0.5}]$$

where r_{ij} is the sample correlation coefficient, i.e., the Pearson product-moment coefficient, for variables i and j, and n is the number of observations.

In the present case, the highest correlation the consultant observes is 0.32. The corresponding t-statistics, for degrees of freedom of 23, is 1.62, well below the critical t-statistic of 1.71 for 10 percent level of significance.

(6) Exercise of Judgments

Each member of the engineering unit is now asked to assess all 25 technology profiles described above for their respective values. This rating is on a scale from 1 to 100, where 1 suggested a very low, and 100 a very high, value rating. When all profiles has been so assessed, the each participant is given the opportunity to review the 25 profiles and make whatever revisions in their assessments he or she deems appropriate, until satisfied with the ratings.

(7) Obtaining the Judgmental Policies

After the participants express satisfaction with their respective value ratings, the next step is to extract from these ratings the description of the policy orientations deployed by them. This is accomplished through nonlinear multiple regression analyses. These regression analyses are performed with the ratings given to the different profiles by the managers as dependent variable and the 6 factors as the independent variables. These analyses yield the parameters of the participants' respective judgmental policies. Nonlinear, additive models of polynomial form presented below have been found useful in several studies of human judgment:

$$y_{ij} = \sum_{k=1}^{m} (b_{ik} \bullet x_{jk} + b_{i\,(k+m)} \bullet x_{jk}^{2}) + c_i + e_{ij} \qquad (2)$$

where y_{ij} is the judgment of the individual i for a profile of a situation j, m is the number of factors, b_{ik} is the raw score regression weight for individual i on factor k's linear term $b_{i\,(k+m)}$ is the regression weight for individual i on the quadratic term of factor k, x_{jk} is the value of factor k on profile j, c_i is the constant term for individual i, and e_{ij} is the residual error from the model of individual i for profile j.

Equation (2) presents a problem in that the weights and the function-forms for each factor are not separately available. If separated, however, they would allow feedback to individuals making judgments. An algebraic transformation of Equation (2), described by Cooksey [17] (pp178-180), accomplishes this separation easily. Thus, the relative weights as measures of emphasis given to the different factors, and the function-forms for the different factors are obtained in a format that facilitates communication. An example of weights and function-forms obtained by the consultant from one of the participants is shown in Figure 4.

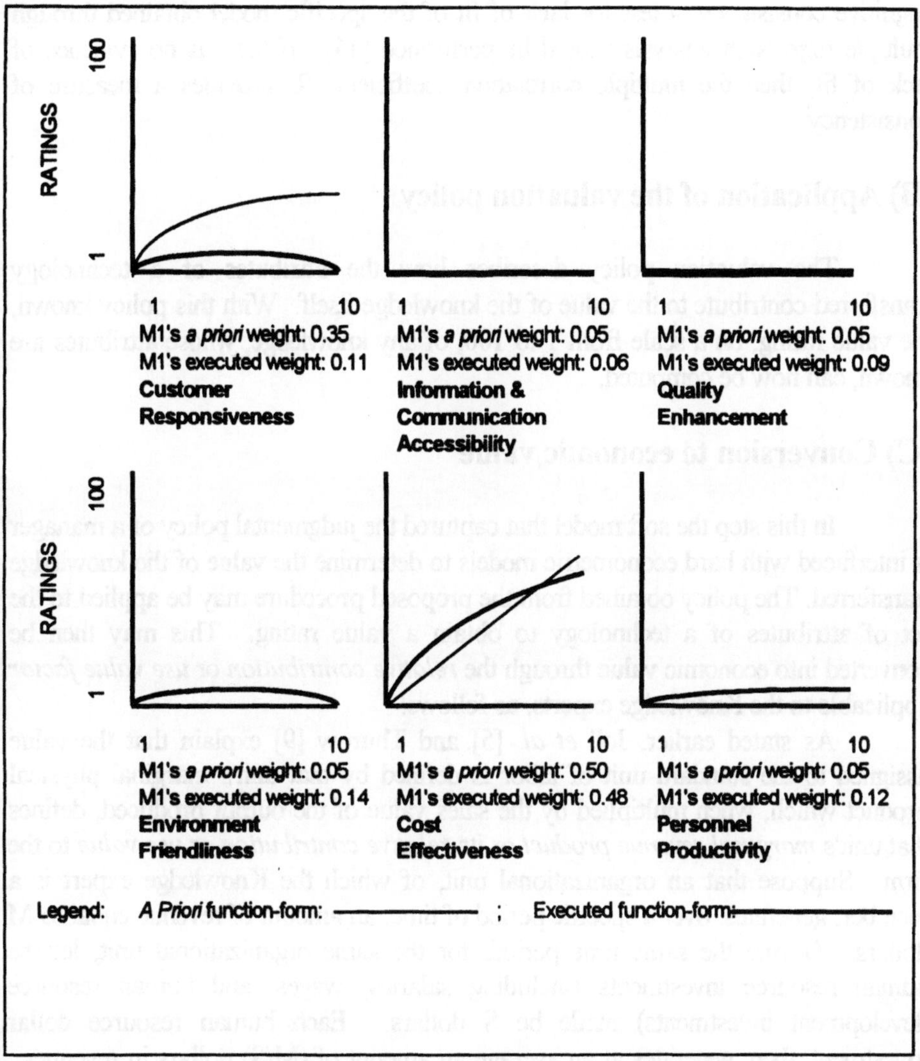

Figure 4. A sample of weights and function-forms obtained from a Participant

Cognitive consistency exercised by a participant with respect to the particular model obtained through nonlinear multiple regression analysis is measured in terms of the multiple correlation coefficient, R. To determine whether in a specific case the multiple correlation coefficient will provide a measure of cognitive consistency, a test for lack of fit of the specific model obtained through multiple regression analysis should be performed [44]. If there is no evidence of lack of fit, then the multiple correlation coefficient, R, provides a measure of consistency.

(B) Application of the valuation policy

The valuation policy describes how the attributes of a technology transferred contribute to the value of the knowledge itself. With this policy known, the value rating, on a scale from 1 to 100, of any knowledge, whose attributes are known, can now be computed.

(C) Conversion to economic value

In this step the soft model that captured the judgmental policy of a manager is interfaced with hard econometric models to determine the value of the knowledge transferred. The policy obtained from the proposed procedure may be applied to the set of attributes of a technology to obtain a value rating. This may then be converted into economic value through the *relative contribution* or *use value factor* applicable to the Knowledge experts, as follows:

As stated earlier, Joll *et al.* [5] and Thurow [9] explain that the value assigned to the standard unit of labor is defined by that unit's marginal physical product which, when multiplied by the sales value of the output produced, defines that unit's *marginal revenue product* or its *relative contribution* or *use value* to the firm. Suppose that an organizational unit, of which the Knowledge expert is a member, generates, over a specific period of time, an amount of revenue equal to M dollars. During the same time period, for the same organizational unit, let the human resource investments (including salaries, wages, and human resource development investments) made be S dollars. Each human resource dollar investment, then, generates at an average an amount of (M/S) dollars in revenues. If the human resource investment made on each member of the organization is s_i, then it follows that:

$$S = \sum_{i=1}^{N} s_i$$

Also the amount of revenue attributable to individual members, m_i, may be computed as:

$$m_i = (M / S) \cdot (s_i / S)$$

This computation assumes that all members of the organization unit in question contribute at an equal rate. In order to adjust for the differences among the contribution rate of the members of the organization, and among Knowledge expert and other professional or non-professional members of the unit, an adjustment factor, k_i, may be deployed for each organizational member, subject to the following condition:

$$\sum_{i=1}^{N} (k_i \cdot s_i) = S$$

This factor may be assessed from the past performance evaluations of the organizational members relative to other members of the unit. The amount of revenue attributable to an individual member, r, who is, say, a knowledge expert, now becomes:

$$m_r = [(M / S) \cdot \{(k_r \cdot s_r)/ S\}]$$

The *relative contribution* of the knowledge expert, L_r, may be measured as:

$$L_r = (m_r / M)$$

Now, suppose that the Knowledge expert makes a contribution of an knowledge to a Business unit in the development of a process. Let us suppose also that the total market size that could realistically be claimed by a firm through this knowledge, with an appropriately effective process in this context, is P dollars. A value rating of Y, on a scale from 1 to 100, for an knowledge transferred by the Knowledge expert, may then be converted into the economic value of the knowledge transferred, EV, as follows:

$$EV = (Y/100) \cdot L_r \cdot P$$

COMPUTATIONAL OPTIONS

Let us now review some of the various computational analyses that were carried out.

Relative Weights and Function-Forms

For each participant, the consultant in this case obtained the relative weights associated with each factor from the judgments exercised by them, through nonlinear regression analyses. The consultant could have obtained these anonymously, if the goal was to accomplish a general diagnosis of the variations in the policies among participants. However, in this case, the consultant's goal is to develop a unit-wide consensus. To work toward this consensus, he provided feedback to each individual members of the unit on their own policies along with anonymous feedback on their colleagues. Thus, while each participant is told which set of relative weights and function-forms are obtained from his or her own set of judgments on profiles, the identity of the participants associated with the remaining sets of relative weights and function-forms (i.e., those obtained from the judgments of other participants) are reported collectively, without the identification of source. Each participant is thus be able to compare his or her own set of weights and function-forms with those of others. Each participant is also able to compare these weights and function-forms with the *a priori* weights and function-forms he or she had expected to use. See Figure 4 for a sample of the format used for these feedbacks. Each participant is also provided feedback regarding his or her own cognitive control as measured by the multiple correlation coefficient.

Notice that prior to actually rating the various technology profiles, the participant described in Figure 4 had expected to place relatively higher weights on *customer responsiveness* (at 0.35), and *cost effectiveness* (at 0.50). When making judgments, however, this participant did not actually emphasize *customer responsiveness* to the degree he had expected (at 0.11 instead of 0.35). Also, he placed slightly greater emphasis on *environmental friendliness* (at 0.14 instead of the expected 0.05), and *personnel productivity* (at 0.12 instead of 0.05) aspects of the technologies when assessing their relative value to the unit.

Developing a consensus

The staff of the engineering unit could now be asked to revise their respective *a priori* estimates of the relative weights and the function-forms associated with each factor so that the revised estimates would indicate those weights and function-forms which the participant now felt *ought* to be assigned to each factor for the assessment of value. They could then be presented with a new set of randomly generate profiles of intellectual technologies. However, this time the participants could also be provided one additional set of information with each profile to be rated for value: For each new technology profile, value rating could be computed based on the revisions made by each participant in the *a priori* policy. These value ratings could be presented to each participant, prior to the participant making value assessments for the new set of profiles. While each participant could be told which ratings were computed from his or her own revised *a priori* policy, the rest of the computed ratings (i.e., those computed from the revised policies of other participants) would be reported anonymously. Prior research indicates that this procedure usually results in a shift in individual judgmental policies towards a consensus. For instance, Harmon and Rohrbaugh [45] conclude that "... individual learning in tasks of cognitive conflict derives from direct access to graphic representations of members' judgment policies that explicitly communicate the key differences in their use of available information." According to Jaeger [46], an iterative use feedback reduces the variability among the policies of the respondents and leads to a reasonable degree of consensus around a collective policy.

Each participant would then be asked to once again assess the value of all new twenty-five technology profiles. As before, this assessment would be on a scale from 1 to 100. Again as before, when all profiles have been assessed, each participant would be given the opportunity to review and revise any or all of the twenty-five assessments to his or her satisfaction.

As before, the ratings given to the 25 technology profiles would be analyzed to obtain the final judgmental policies. Also, as before, the relative weights, function-forms, and cognitive control measures would be obtained for each participant. The cognitive control measures would also be measured. These would likely be higher than those obtained in the previous iteration, indicating an improved degree of consistency in exercise of judgment.

Other alternative procedures could also be devised. Consider the case at hand. On receiving feedback on their respective policies, the staff members of the engineering unit engage in a discussion. Additionally, the consultant computes predicted rating for the 25 technology profiles based on both, *a priori*, and the executed judgments. By computing these ratings, the consultant is able to eliminate the effect of inconsistencies in the ratings that were given to the profiles by the participants. Using these predicted ratings, the consultant computes correlations among all possible pairs of participants. This enables him to compute the average correlations *within* the managers', engineers', factory information specialists', and technicians' groups, as well *across* the groups as measures of consensus. The leader of the unit is impressed at the relative high degree of consensus within and across the different the groups in his unit. For instance, he sees that the engineers have a high degree of consensus among their *a priori* policies for the assessment of the value of technology transferred as reflected by a mean of all correlations among pairs of engineers at 0.76, with a standard deviation of 0.20. He also notices that this mean drops somewhat for the judgmental policies obtained from the engineers' ratings of the profiles. For these policies, the corresponding mean of all correlations among pairs of engineers is, nevertheless, still an impressive 0.63, with a lower standard deviation of 0.17. The unit leader is not surprised to see that the corresponding means of correlations obtained from Factory Information Specialists, for the *a priori* policies, is quite a bit lower at 0.49, with a standard deviation of 0.23, and for the judgmental policies obtained from the ratings of the profiles, is 0.43, with a standard deviation of 0.28. Not surprised, the unit leader reasons that these lower figures reflect the fact that the Factory Information Specialists perform advisory functions, and do not hold line responsibilities. Curious, he checks out the corresponding mean correlation for the Technicians' *a priori* policies. The figure is 0.25, with a standard deviation of 0.61. "Just what I expected," he thinks. But lo! The corresponding figure for the Technicians' judgmental policies is an impressive 0.62, with a standard deviation of 0.14. He tells himself to reexamine his assumptions regarding the insights the Technicians bring to the problem of technology assessment. This is partly because he has discovered that the measure of consensus between him and the deputy leader is only 0.40 for the policy obtained from their respective ratings of profiles, even though *a priori* the consensus was at 0.68.

The unit leader asks the consultant for measures of consensus across the managers and engineers. He is told that for the *a priori* policies and the judgmental policies, these are 0.73 with a standard deviation of 0.14, and 0.62 with a standard deviation of 0.23, respectively. Himself an engineer, he's pleased. The consultant goes on to report that the corresponding measures of consensus across managers and factory information specialists is 0.62 with a standard deviation of 0.13, and 0.47 with a standard deviation of 0.29, respectively. For consensus across managers and technicians the figures are 0.42 with a standard deviation of 0.53, and 0.37 with a standard deviation of 0.28, respectively. The unit leader also notes that the level of consensus over the entire group is measured by a mean correlation for *a priori* policies of 0.59 over *all* participants with a standard deviation of 0.39, and a mean correlation for judgmental policies of 0.58 over *all* participants with a standard deviation of 0.30.

In light of these figures, and having gained improved insight into the concept of the value of technology transferred as seen by himself and others, the unit leader decides to form the unit's policy for assessment of the value by taking the mean of all judgmental policies executed by the 2 managers and the 13 engineers, these 15 being members of his unit with line responsibilities. The consultant is asked to compute this policy by computing an average rating over these fifteen participants for each technology profile. The resulting policy, which is adopted by the unit, is shown in Figure 5.

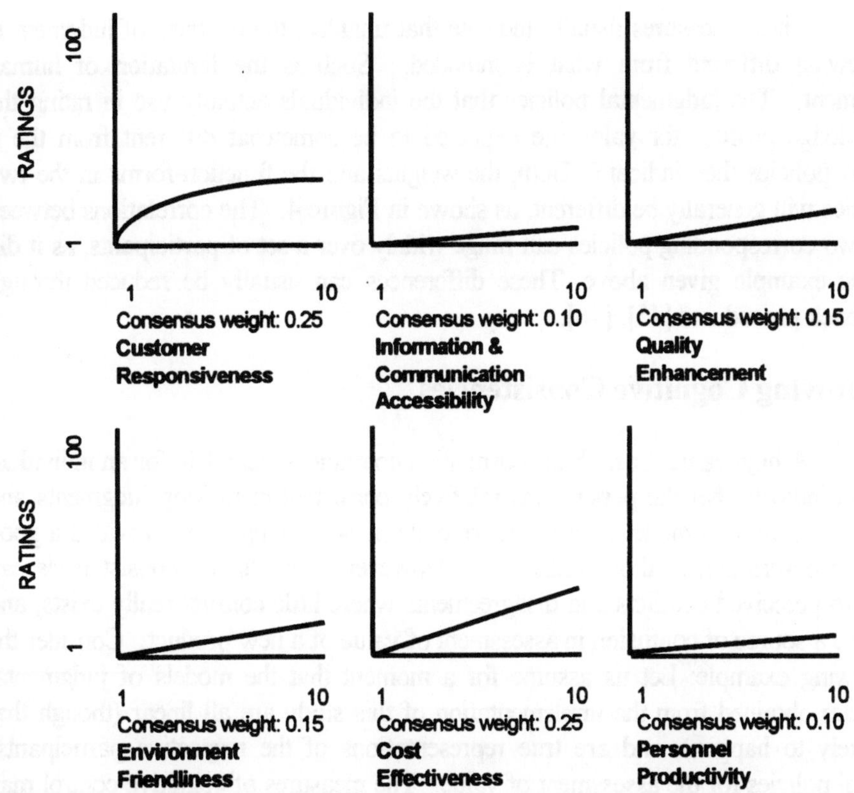

Figure 5. Final set of weights and function-forms adopted by the unit

Measuring 'Self-Knowledge'

Comparisons can be made of the *a priori* policies with the policies obtained from the judgments to determine the degree to which participants have an understanding of their own covert judgment process. We refer to correlations obtained from the corresponding pairs of policies as measures of the participant's 'self-knowledge.' In the case of the engineering unit discussed here, the consultant has computed these figures for the managers, engineers, factory information specialists, and technicians, and has found the means of these correlations to be 0.91, 0.77, 0.71 and 0.43 respectively. The overall range of these measures is from -0.69 to 0.97.

These measures usually indicate that unaided, the exercise of judgment is somewhat different from what is intended. Such is the limitation of human judgment. The judgmental policies that the individuals actually use in rating the knowledge profiles for value are expected to be somewhat different from the *a priori* policies they indicate. Both, the weights and the function-forms in the two policies will generally be different, as shown in Figure 4. The correlations between the two corresponding policies can range widely over a set of participants, as it did in the example given above. These differences can usually be reduced through feedback procedures [45], [46].

Improving Cognitive Consistencies

A high value for multiple correlation coefficient, near 1.0, for an individual would indicate that the person was relatively consistent in making judgments and that the regression model used to describe the person's judgments provided a good 'fit' or description of those judgments. However, even slight inconsistencies can lead to perceived conflicts and disagreements where little conflict really exists, and can be a source of confusion in assessment of value of a new product. Consider the following example: Let us assume for a moment that the models of judgmental policies obtained from the implementation of this study are all linear (though that unlikely to happen), and are true representations of the respective participants' actual policies for the assessment of value. The measures of cognitive control may then be used as measures of consistency, as per earlier discussion. Suppose that a pair of participants achieve measures of cognitive control at 0.80 and 0.90, respectively. In this situation, even with identical policies, the two participants may perceive limited mutual consensus with the correlation between the two being less than 0.80x0.90, or 0.72 (corresponding to at most about 50% of the variation in the judgments of one being explained by the judgments of the other). For the mathematical basis of this example, see Equation (1) above.

To appreciate the uniqueness of the approach presented in this chapter, a comparison of the procedure based on social judgment theory described here with that of the DELPHI technique [35], [36] would be useful. The DELPHI technique was an outgrowth of a series of studies at the RAND Corporation. By 1970 it was being widely acclaimed as a means to generate a consensus of judgment in a group. The DELPHI technique is characterized by three distinct features: (a) a *guarantee of anonymity* to the participants in the group; (b) a primarily *statistical compilation* of the group's response, and (c) a *controlled, iterative feedback* of the group's response to each member of the group prior to another set of judgments.

As in the case of the DELPHI technique, the procedure described in this chapter also offers anonymity to the participants participating in this proposed study. The procedure described here also compiles statistics on the participants' judgmental responses. However, the data compiled would include information not only on the overall judgments (as in the DELPHI technique), but also on the components or parameters of the judgments (unlike the DELPHI technique). Finally, the procedure would include a controlled feedback of the participants' judgmental policies to each member of the participating group, prior to another set of judgments. In this way, not only would the overt judgmental differences made explicit (as in the DELPHI technique), but the covert policy differences, too, is made explicit (unlike the DELPHI technique). This would allow the identification of those specific parameters (i.e., factors, relative weights, and function-forms) of the individual judgmental policies that contribute to disagreements among participants. With the parameters made explicit, the participants are able to control the policy to be implemented by revising their judgmental policies (in terms of factors, relative weights and function-forms). The DELPHI technique, limited to revising overt responses, does not offer such opportunities. As in the DELPHI method, the procedure described in this chapter, or a modification thereof, may be repeated until the desired level of consensus is reached or the alternative policies under consideration are explored.

CONCLUSION

In conclusion, we recapitulate the approach described in this chapter: This chapter presents a mixed-mode approach to the assessment of value of knowledge developed and transferred within an organization by its knowledge experts in the course of its technology portfolio development. The approach first developed a soft model of managerial judgmental policy for the assessment of value of knowledge, and then interfaced it with the hard econometric model to compute the economic value through *relative contribution* or *use value factor*. This approach is particularly suitable for the assessment of value when the transfer of technology or knowledge is in the *strategic* phase of its application to product, process or service development. Hard approaches based on *firm-specific human capital theory* and *human resource accounting theory* do not lend themselves for application in the strategic phase of technology application. During this phase, the value of technology, and of knowledge, is subjective. Different individuals may assign perceive different value. In this phase, mixed-mode approaches integrating psychometric based on social and industrial psychology with econometric approaches offer greater promise. The human judgment process is *covert*, *inaccurately reported*, and *inconsistent*. It can be described in terms of *factors* influencing judgment regarding value, *relative emphasis* placed on each factor, *relationship* between overall judgment of value and each factor, and *consistency* of judgment. It is effectively analyzed by the application of social judgment theory framework, as described in this chapter. It facilitates the assessment of the value of knowledge transferred through determination of the valuation policy; application of this policy to the specific technology or knowledge of interest; and conversion of the value rating into an economic value. It also provides information on technology managers' policies regarding the value assigned to knowledge transferred; relative importance of different factors in value assessment; the degree of consensus among managers; degree of 'self-knowledge' among managers; and potential for improving cognitive consistencies of judgment. Not only does the managers gain improved insights into their policies, they also gain improvement insights into the domain of value as it is perceived by others.

REFERENCES

[1] Porter, M.E. (1985). *Competitive Advantage: Creating and Sustaining Superior Performance*. New York: The Free Press.

[2] Berle, A.A. (1965). *The American economic republic*. New York, NY: Harcourt, Brace and World.

[3] Kendrick, J.W. (1984). *Improving company productivity*. Baltimore, MD: Johns Hopkins University Press.

[4] Kopelman, R.E. (1986). *Managing productivity in organizations*. New York, NY: McGraw-Hill.

[5] Joll, C., McKenna, C., McNabb, R., and Shorey, J. (1983). *Developments in labor market analysis*. London, UK: Allen and Unwin.

[6] Thurow, L.C. (1970). *Investment in human capital*. Belmont, CA: Wadsworth.

[7] Akerlof, G.A. (1981). Jobs as dam sites. *Review of Economic Studies, 67*, 37-49.

[8] Flamholtz, E.G. (1985). *Human resource accounting*. San Francisco, CA: Jossey-Bass.

[9] Thurow, L.C. (1975). *Generating inequality: Mechanisms of distribution in the U.S. economy*. New York, NY: Basic Books.

[10] Viren, M. (1979). *Human capital and wage differentials in a dynamic theory of the firm*. Helsinki, Finland: Societas Scientiarum Fennica.

[11] Mahoney, T.A. (1983). Approaches to the definition of comparable worth. *Academy of Management Review, 8*, 14-22.

[12] Monti-Belkaouri, A., and Riahi-Belkaouri, J. (1995). *Human Resource Valuation: A Guide to Strategies and Techniques*. Westport, CT: Quorum Books.

[13] Steffy, B.D., and Maurer, S.D. (1988). Conceptualizing and measuring the economic effectiveness of human resources activities. *Academy of Management Review*, April, 271-286.

[14] Hashimoto, M. (1981). Firm-specific human capital as a shared investment. *American Economic Review, 71*, 475-482.

[15] Cascio, W.F., and Ramos, R.A. (1986). Development and application of a new method for assessing job performance in behavioral/economic terms. *Journal of Applied Psychology, 71*, 20-28.

[16] Arkes, H.R., and Hammond, K.R., (eds). (1986). *Judgment and Decision Making: An Interdisciplinary Reader*. Cambridge University Press, New York.

[17] Cooksey, R. W. (1996). *Judgment Analysis: Theory, Methods, and Applications*. San Diego, CA: Academic Press.

[18] Behling, O., and Eckel, H. (1991). Making sense out of intuition. *Academy of Management Executive, 5*:46-54.

[19] Kaplan, M.F., and Schwartz, S. (Eds). (1977). *Human Judgment and Decision Processes in Applied Settings*. Academic Press, New York.

[20] Doherty, M.E., and Brehmer, B. (1997). The paramorphic representation of clinical judgment: A thirty-year retrospective. In W.M. Goldstein and R.M. Hogarth (eds). *Research on Judgment and Decision Making: Currents, Connections, and Controversies*. New York, NY: Cambridge University Press, pp. 537-551.

[21] Keeney, R.L., and Raiffa, H. (1976). *Decisions with Multiple Objectives: Preferences and Value Tradeoffs*. Wiley, New York.

[22] Edwards, W., and Tversky, A. (1967). *Decision Making: Selected Readings*. Penguin Books, Middlesex, England.

[23] Kahneman, D., and Tversky, A. (1979). Prospect theory. *Econometrica, 47*:263-291.

[24] Anderson, N.H. (1974). Cognitive algebra. In L. Berkowitz (Ed.). *Advances in Experimental Social Psychology, 7*. Academic Press, New York.

[25] Jones, E.E., and McGillis, D. (1976). New directions in attribution theory research. In J.H. Harvey, W.J. Ickes, and R.F. Kidd (Eds). *New Directions in Attribution Research*. Hillsdale, NJ: Erlbaum.

[26] Stewart, T.R. (1975). Policy capture. In C. McMillan, *Mathematical Programming*, Second Edition, 635-646. Wiley, New York.

[27] Zeleny, M. (1982). *Multiple Criteria Decision Making*. McGraw-Hill, New York.

[28] Brehmer, B., and Joyce, C.R.B. (Eds). (1988). *Human Judgment: The SJT View*. Elsevier Science Publishers B.V. (North-Holland)., New York.

[29] Hammond, K.R., McClelland, G.H., and Mumpower, J. (1980). *Human Judgment and Decision Making*. Praeger, New York.

[30] Zadeh, L.A. (1973). Outline of a new approach to the analysis of complex systems and decision processes. *IEEE Transactions on System, Man, and Cybernetic, 3*: 28-44.

[31] Zadeh, L.A., Fu, K-S, Tanaka, K, and Shimura, M. (eds) (1975). *Fuzzy Sets and their Applications to Cognitive and Decision Processes*. New York, NY: Academic Press.

[32] Saaty TL (1990). *The Analytic Hierarchy Process: Planning, Priority Setting, and Resource Allocation*. RWS Publications: Pittsburgh, PA.

[33] Saaty TL (1994). How to make a decision: The analytic hierarchy process. *Interfaces* **24**: 19-43.

[34] Brunswik, E. (1956). *Perception and the Representative Design of Psychological Experiments*, Second Edition. Berkeley, CA: University of California Press.

[35] Linstone, H.A., and Turoff, M. (1975). *The DELPHI Method: Techniques and Applications*. Addison-Wesley, Reading, Massachusetts.

[36] Rohrbaugh, J.W. (1976). Conflict management in decision-making groups: A comparison of social judgment analysis and the DELPHI technique. Unpublished doctoral dissertation, University of Colorado.

[37] Nisbett, R.E., and Wilson, T.D. (1977). Telling more than we can know: Verbal reports on mental processes. *Psychological Review, 84*:231-259.

[38] Ericsson, K.A., and Simon, H.A. (1980). Verbal reports as data. *Psychological Review, 87*, 215-251.

[39] Wiederman, M.W., and Dubois, S.L. (1998). Evolution and sex-differences in preferences for short-term mates: Results from a policy capturing study. *Evolution and Human Behavior, 19*, 153-170.

[40] Dhir, K.S. (1987). Formulating Management Policies for Value Engineering/Value Analysis." *IEEE Transactions on Engineering Management, EM-34* (3)., August 1987, 161-171.

[41] Dhir, K.S. (1991). Analysis of Human Judgment in Valuation of Resources. In R. Frantz, H. Singh and J. Gerber (Eds)., *Handbook of Behavioral Economics, 2B, Behavioral Decision Making*, 377-395. Greenwich, Connecticut: JAI Press.

[42] Dhir, K.S., and Savage, T. (2001). "Assessing the Value of Language: A Judgment-Analytic Approach." *Proceedings of the 2001 Western Decision Sciences Institute Conference*, Vancouver, British Columbia, Canada, April 3-7, 2001.

[43] Connolly, T., Arkes, H.R., and Hammond, K.R., (Eds). (2000). *Judgment and Decision Making: An Interdisciplinary Reader*, Second Edition. New York, NY: Cambridge University Press.

[44] Draper, N. and Smith, H. (1998). *Applied Regression Analysis*, Third Edition. Wiley, New York.

[45] Harmon, J., and Rohrbaugh, J. (1990). *Organizational Behavior and Human Processes, 46*, 34-54.

[46] Jaeger, R.M. (1995). Setting standards for complex performances: An iterative, judgmental policy-capturing strategy. *Educational Measurement: Issues and Practice, 14* (4), Winter, 16-20.

6

HARD DECISIONS, SOFT DATA: LOCALISED CONTEXT-RICH SOLUTIONS TO PROBLEMS OF NEW PRODUCT DEVELOPMENT

Michael Enright
School of Business
Swinburne University of Technology, Melbourne, Australia

ABSTRACT

This chapter draws upon conventional approaches to market orientation, planning and new product development and examines the extent to which they are applicable to smaller firms. It argues that for smaller firms, marketing decision making remains largely in the realm of human-centred methodologies, characterised by intuitive approaches. This applies when marketing strategy gives way to marketing implementation, as in new product development. The results of recent field work in two localised industries are considered for the alternative trajectory they provide for the study of marketing decision making, particularly the inherently risky process of new product development.

Keywords: marketing, new product development, market orientation.

INTRODUCTION

New product development is a matter of considerable risk. In marketing writing, it is generally held that new product failure rates are high [1-5]. However, this has not deterred marketing authors from reinforcing the

M.G. Nicholls et al. (eds.),
Mixed-Mode Modelling: Mixing Methodologies for Organisational Intervention, 171–207.

basic structure of the existing and conventional new product development process. New product development is at once constructed in an oft-repeated sequence whilst at the same time it is apparently either not working properly or is not being applied effectively enough to reduce the new product failure rates. Marketing thought generally settles on the proposition that the new product development process is a rational, discursive and sequenced model and that adherence to it enhances product success rates. What is this model, why is it adhered to and why, given the seemingly high failure rate for new products, does it not necessarily work? If it does work why is it not more widely adopted in quest of reduced failure rates? Before addressing these questions and proposing an alternative interpretative framework – a more context rich approach – it is appropriate to review the marketing construct in light of two of its key philosophical buttresses. These are the marketing concept itself and the concept of market orientation. From these spring a third, the conventional new product development process. The new product launch may be seen as one of the most significant and oft-repeated manifestations of marketing practice.

THE TENETS OF THE MARKETING CONSTRUCT

Since the mid-1940s, symbols of marketing thought have been aggregated into a corpus of beliefs about what marketing can achieve as an organisational decision making process. This is reinforced in general marketing texts with their consistent set of claims about what marketing has to offer the adherent. These are marketing's tenets. They are produced and reproduced in similar form, all using very similar sources. They are at the core of conventional marketing teaching and marketing thought. Variations of the official belief do arise, but often, that official belief remains an overriding framework in discussion. This is not to suggest that in the research literature, departures from these wisdoms do not occur. Yet until the emergence of postmodern marketing writing in the early 1990s they are nominal. In result, the wisdoms are regularly reinforced and buttressed in successive editions of generalist textual works: the very works that almost always constitute required reading in under-graduate and post-graduate marketing courses.

Foremost among the textual works are those of Kotler [1], Kotler *et al* [2], McCarthy *et al* [4], Stanton *et al* [5], Zikmund and d'Amico [6], McColl-Kennedy and Kiel [7] and Assael *et al* [8]. Whilst variations in interpretation occur they constitute, re-constitute and refine a key number of tenets.

1. that marketing is an ordered response to customer needs.
2. that through the function of marketing research, customer needs can be anticipated.
3. that the process of marketing planning facilitates the provision of products, be they goods or services, and that this can be undertaken in advance of the user or consumer of the product being cognizant of its final form.
4. that marketers can identify clusters of customers, known as target markets, with which they can communicate *via* the process of marketing communication.
5. that new product development processes can deliver new products to targeted customers in the most effective way.
6. that organisations staffed with marketing practitioners are more effective in these activities.
7. that the more one knows and understands of marketing theory and practice, the more commercially successful one will be.
8. that the marketing philosophy is a post-Second World War phenomenon of north American origin.
9. that the marketing philosophy is in its fourth stage of historical development and that this stage is one of social responsibility.

This is a bold set of claims. Almost all of the texts are in a citation chain, either each using the same sources or each other as a reference, repeating the argument almost verbatim. Nowhere is this more evident than in the first tenet, that marketing is an ordered response to customer needs. This is a statement of belief, with no epistemological basis. Not one of the nine tenets is proven fact by virtue of universal applicability. Organisations that claim a market orientation still have failures. The failures, be they at a product item, product market or organisational level, are presented as examples of some form of non-compliance with marketing's tenets. This is particularly the case with the specialist texts dealing with new product development. Almost all open with a discussion on the high rate of product failures. These serve as prolegomena for remarkably similar, sequentially driven new product development processes. As with their general text contemporaries, these works view marketing as a discipline operating more in structured, repeatable and therefore readily measurable environments.

MARKETING AND THE CONCEPT OF MARKET ORIENTATION

From these tenets emerges the concept of market orientation. Along with 'marketing' and 'marketing concept', the term 'market orientation' is prominent in discussion on how theorists and practitioners seek to understand the subject. For the past four decades, the terms, 'marketing' (or 'marketing discipline'), 'marketing concept', and 'market orientation' have tended to be used interchangeably and have enjoyed common and continued use in textual works, scholarly papers and in the language of business practitioners. More recently, there have been attempts at developing separate definitions for each term. In 1990, research by two separate groups, Kohli and Jaworski [9] and Narver and Slater [10], focussed attention on the matter of market orientation. They observed that whilst market orientation appeared to be a precondition to organisational performance and profitability, the relationship was not entirely clear. At best, it was conditional. Kohli and Jaworski [9] contended that "a market orientation may or may not be very desirable for a business" (p15). Narver and Slater [10] claimed, "for every business, at some point the incremental costs to increase its market orientation will exceed the incremental benefits"(p33). Both sets of researchers nevertheless concluded that market orientation is a central outcome of the marketing concept. Additionally, Kohli and Jaworski gave a hierarchy to the three definitions. To them, the marketing concept is a central component of the marketing discipline, a philosophical "cornerstone" [9] (p1). In turn, market orientation refers to that set of activities concerned with the implementation of the marketing concept. See Figure 1.

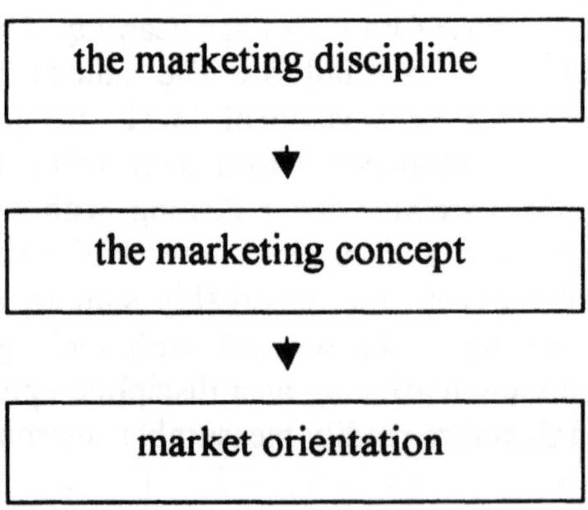

Figure 1. A Hierarchy of Marketing Process after Kohli and Jaworski, 1990

Kohli and Jaworski [9] provide a decidedly prescriptive definition of market orientation.

> "Market orientation is the organisation wide *generation* of market intelligence pertaining to current and future customer needs, *dissemination* of the intelligence across departments, and *organizationwide* responsiveness to it." [9] (p6).

Equally prescriptive is the Narver and Slater definition of market orientation.

> "Market orientation is the organization culture that most effectively and efficiently creates the necessary behaviors for the creation of superior value for buyers and, thus, continuous superior performance for the business." [10] (p21).

The terminology in both of these observations directly relates to new product development. In arriving at their particular definition, Narver and Slater acknowledged the work of Kohli and Jaworski and found common ground to the extent that they saw market orientation as a continuum. Narver and Slater were however more strident in their conclusions on the efficacy of market orientation and performance. To them, market orientation is a prerequisite for performance.

These two studies set the scene for subsequent research [11-18] that continues apace into this century [19-21]. The result has been a tendency to set aside the possibility that other systems of marketing – with concomitant but differing approaches to the market orientation question - might be out there. This was reflected in the concluding comments of the original 1990 research of Kohli and Jaworski.

> "Much work remains to be done in terms of developing a suitable measure of market orientation and empirically testing our propositions." [9] (pp16-17).

And of Narver and Slater,

> "Our...research must be replicated in diverse environments and over time to increase confidence in the nature and power of the theory." [10] (p34).

Such conclusions conferred value on market orientation, moving it from idealised concept to extant phenomenon. The implication, one carried further in the subsequent research, is that only the measurement of market orientation remained. In so doing, marketers have taken a most positivist stance on the efficacy of the concept. There is a desire to see marketing advance along a particular ideological path, to see it advance as a science. The research was empirical, the approach scientific and the expectations were and are that future research would buttress the market orientation phenomenon rather than call it into question. Prior to their research, the marketing concept and market orientation were widely used, if variably applied generalisations, particularly in textual works. Now, the discipline had seen the codification of the terms, their inclusion into an emerging marketing lexicon.

Other research sought to synthesise marketing and market orientation with attempts to expand its role in business and society. In 1991, Anderson and Hoyer [22] called for marketing to be seen as the means by which any organisation could achieve control over its environment. This was seen as the logical extension of marketing as a process and entirely consistent with the marketing concept. In many respects, the treatment of the marketing concept in Anderson and Hoyer's paper coalesced with the concept of market orientation. In 1992, Whittington and Whipp [23] questioned the effort being put into marketing's technical development and argued that, "In concentrating on the substance of marketing, the profession may be neglecting its trappings" (p52). They urged marketing to concentrate on its potential to develop as a professional ideology, stating that the relationship between market orientation and performance was tenuous. Whittington and Whipp concluded that "the true contribution of marketing to performance remains unconvincingly thin" (p61). Interestingly, Whittington and Whipp also used the term 'marketing' to describe what their sources referred to as 'market orientation', making for a disturbing tendency to coalesce – or confuse - the terminology. By now, these terms were not enjoying clearly separate definitions. The proposition for a rigidly defined marketing profession that systematically professes an ideology resonates with the earlier works of Buzzell [24] and Hunt [25, 26], both of whom portrayed marketing as a science in need of more rigour, more reason and more rationalism. The marketing-as-science proposition has gained in popularity over the years. These calls by the marketing community to take on the mantle of science most probably emanate, Brown [27] has observed, from the writings of Converse [28] in 1945.

There are two threads here: an apparent urge to define terms such as 'market orientation' and a desire to treat the domain of marketing as a science. They weave together into the broader quest of marketing as a profession. Adherents to the marketing cause are almost universal in their defence of the claim that marketing is a profession. Yet there remain a variety of interpretations of what constitutes market orientation within that called-for profession. Equally, there is a range of interpretations placed on what has already been written about it. From the works cited so far, a number of interpretations arise. 'Market orientation', may equate with 'marketing', it may be desirable but only in certain situations, not really proven to be linked with performance, an absolute precondition for performance, central to the marketing concept, or, marginal to the point where it should be set aside in favour of a more vigorous pursuit of marketing as a professional ideology. The question of what marketing and market orientation constitute has become difficult to decipher. To add to the double conundrums of 'what do we mean by market orientation' and 'is there really a difference between marketing and market orientation', Firat and Dholakia [29] argue that marketing is "the dominant mode of discourse in the contemporary global society"(px). This puts the question of definitions into a somewhat different perspective. Potentially, it makes definitions redundant.

In their research into market orientation in 1993, Jaworski and Kohli [13] re-affirmed their definition of the term and cited the 1990 work of their contemporaries, Narver and Slater [10], for the claim that market orientation and performance are causally linked. They reiterate that the marketing concept is "the philosophical foundation of a market orientation" [13] (p54). In their research, the market orientation argument assumes the proportions of a paradigm, one that is only mildly moderated by external market, competitive and technological forces. This is the setting for all marketing activities, including new product development.

Drawing on another earlier piece of research [30], Narver, Slater and Tietje [17] have more recently developed further the argument that formal organisational structures designed to engender market orientation may not be successful of themselves. They propose that market orientation is dependent upon two sets of influences that an organisation can recognise and harness: the abstract, that emanates from management, and the experiential, that emanates from customers. These they call respectively the "programmatic" and the "market-back" approaches. This is similar to the concepts developed by Schaffer and Thomson [31] of "activities-centered" and "results-driven" programmes, a point acknowledged by Narver and

Slater in their paper. Their proposition is illustrated in Figure 2. These researches are a far cry from the trappings-over-substance contentions of Whittington and Whipp [23] who pressed for an alternative approach to market orientation. They called for a market orientation of the very people who profess marketing before any further effort is put into the definition of the term. For those who question the robustness of the marketing discipline, theirs is a cogent argument. Marketing has, after all, had its detractors, even from within its own ranks.

Ponderings over the efficacy of the whole modern marketing construct continue to emerge. Soderland [32] argues for new approaches to

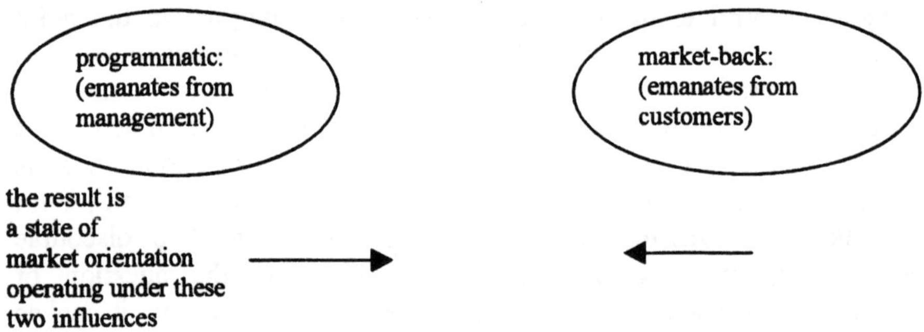

*Figure 2.*The Dual Generators of Market Orientation, after Narver, Slater and Tietje [19]

business intelligence for an era when "post-modern phenomena must be approached by post-modern methods" (p10). On a much wider philosophical front, but involving a direct attack on business management schools, Saul [33] deplores what he sees as the positivism of elites, especially for the way in which they have employed a claimed scientific rationalism at the expense of common sense. Saul's denouncements perhaps go too far in conferring monotheistic tendencies on business, and, presumably amongst them, marketing elites. However, they do highlight the dualities that exist when a group built on inherently soft decision making processes seeks professional status through the kind of value-free discourse that science is perceived to offer.

These issues had some impact on new product development but it was not enduring. As early as 1981, Bennett and Cooper [34] doubted the veracity of marketing's claims to a healthier business life. They acknowledged the existence of market forces but challenged the right and place of marketing to interpret and act on those forces. They observed that "Twenty years of adherence to the marketing concept may have taken its toll on American enterprise...The marketing concept has diverted our attention from the product and its manufacture...we are particularly scornful of the efforts of our own profession, namely marketing academics"(p52). They called instead for a reinstatement of a more product-oriented approach, a proposition they termed the "concept of product value" (p57ff). Arguing that market orientation was an over-applied aspect of the 1950s and 1960s they concluded that "We must go beyond the marketing concept"(p59). Bennett and Cooper wrote of products – both new and extant – as the core of business success, not market orientation. Twenty years on, this view has remained singularly unsupported.

Greenley's [16] 1996 research into market orientation in UK companies had sought to move the market orientation question from one of degree of orientation – which appears to have been proving remarkably difficult to assess – to that of form of market orientation. Three functions were identified as giving form to market orientation: market intelligence, planning and monitoring and control. Yet these were similar to elements identified in the earlier Kohli and Jaworski and Narver and Slater researches. Indeed, these elements are and have been some of the central tenets of marketing itself, well before the re-emergence of inquiry into market orientation. In light of current research, the market orientation question appears to continue to turn on its extent and measurement [14, 15, 17, 18]. But has a straw man been erected in the process? Many definitions of marketing itself are available. Whilst there are variations of interpretation, there is general consensus among marketing writers that the marketing concept is central to a claim to marketing orientation. Further, as Brownlie and Saren [35] have indicated, there is broad agreement as to what the marketing concept is, at least among academics. What is at issue - and this is something to which Brownlie and Saren [35] allude - is by whose criteria should such an orientation be established.

Management presumably does not seek elevated states of market orientation for its own sake but rather enacts processes by which their existence is better assured through the marketing of products at profitable volumes (be they limited or unlimited) to sufficient numbers of customers. Such activity may or may not align with the pronouncements of those who abide by the market orientation construct. Whether a profit-driven or not-for-profit results-based organization, it is axiomatic that some sort of product, some sort of customer base and some sort of exchange, monetary or other, takes place. The *raison d'être* of new product development lies in such structures.

The Conventional Planning and Implementation Schemas

Traditional approaches to marketing decision making are spread throughout the marketing literature. A review of the models in the general texts shows it to be based on specialist strategic planning texts [36-38]. The process centres on three rhetoricals: where are we now? where to we want to be? and, how will we get there? This disarmingly simple sounding set of propositions is then invariably treated in such a way as to embrace every other organisational function, from production through to human resources. Recent work [39, 40] suggests that if such complexing of the simple is possible, it becomes an extremely difficult proposition to unravel into actionable components.

Accompanying this tendency of marketing decision making to aggregate all other functions to it is another characteristic, that of broadly defining the answers to the three planning questions into two supposedly related but often quite separately treated processes; the strategic planning process and the new product development process. Perhaps not surprisingly, each seems designed to support the two key aspects of the marketing concept that formed the basis of the discussion in the first part of this chapter; the extent of market orientation and the robustness of an organisation's new product development protocols. This is outlined in Figure 3 below.

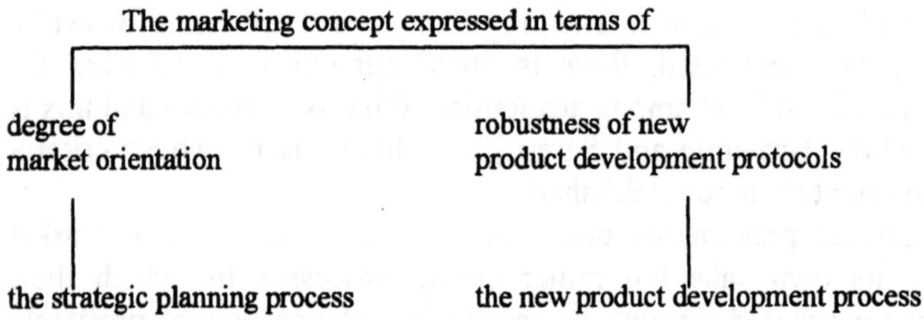

Figure 3. The Relationship Between the Marketing Concept and its Two Key Aspects

Taking the material from the texts and the learned journal literature, the strategic planning process can be outlined in synthesised form. This is shown in Figure 4.

1. mission statement
2. corporate objectives
3. situation analysis
4. strategy plan development
5. implementation
6. control and adjustment

Figure 4. The Strategic Planning Process

In similar vein can a synthesis of the new product planning process be constructed. This is shown in Figure 5.

1. strategic planning/marketing planning
2. opportunity identification
3. concept generation/idea generation
4. business analysis
5. concept/idea evaluation
6. concept/idea screening
7. product development
8. test marketing
9. financial evaluation
10. commercialisation/introduction/launch
11. post-launch follow-up/management

Figure 5. The New Product Development Process

The marketing theorists never seem to have got the models quite right. Despite their desire for sequenced stages that characteristically are invoked by a descending order of management functionaries, there is considerable overlap. These are attempts at hard models that do not gain greater strength from one another. Instead, they seemingly become more brittle when attempts at articulation are made between the two. The fifth stage of strategic planning, the implementation stage, is arguably where new product development commences, yet this strategic approach, by virtue of this fifth stage and also by virtue of a sixth stage of control and adjustment, apparently controls new product development. On the surface, this may seem consistent with a senior management sense of responsibility to monitor the new product development process. Yet it is a somewhat misplaced duty of care, for it calls for the strict sequencing of the new product development process in ways that distort and corrupt the new product process itself because it places demands for extreme precision in sales forecasts, costings, revenue projections and market share goals on the new product development process. The new product development process is inherently soft and hard models are at odds with this intrinsically risky process. There is no evidence that new product development can be subjected to such science-like precision and sequencing. Those products that are and become successful are outnumbered by those that fail (however that may be measured in the organisation). The inductive reasoning that argues that some scientifically launched products were successful, therefore all new products should be so-launched is an irrelevant transference of logic. Products fail because of lack of sales, not for lack of science. Nor do products necessarily succeed because they ignored structured, sequential and measurement-demanding processes. The successful ingredient appears to be appropriate scanning more than a presumption of accurate measurement.

Nor is the new product development process itself a self-contained sequence, for its first and second stages, strategic planning/marketing planning and opportunity identification, rest squarely in the aforementioned strategic planning process itself. The overlap is shown in Figure 6, which from an operational perspective brings together the whole sequential construct, from marketing concept to new product.

This is marketing's construction of market orientation leading to enhanced new product success. New product development is neither by origin nor in its present nature a purely marketing department-based activity and technically does not therefore reside solely within marketing's responsibility. Operations management writing, for example, clearly treats new product development as part of its domain [41, 42]. Yet marketers have tended to assume leadership if not sole control over the new product development process, borrowing heavily from operations management thinking in the process. Such an outlook springs from the marketing-driven argument that new product development stems from the marketing concept and the notion of market orientation. It makes new product development a fief of the strategic planning process for no apparent reason other than to secure control. Why has this occurred? It may have a much to do with the following observations.

First, as just noted, marketing is not the originator of market orientation or new product development. Rather, it is a manifestation of an emerging ideology – modernist, post-1940s marketing – that sees these vital functions as necessarily falling within its domain. Second, marketing is a function more than it is a profession founded on precision. Because it is not a process, such as production or cost accounting, its attempts at sequencing to cope with complex situations are problematic.

Third, marketing, or market-related activities were extant before the emergence of the modernist form of the domain toward the middle of the

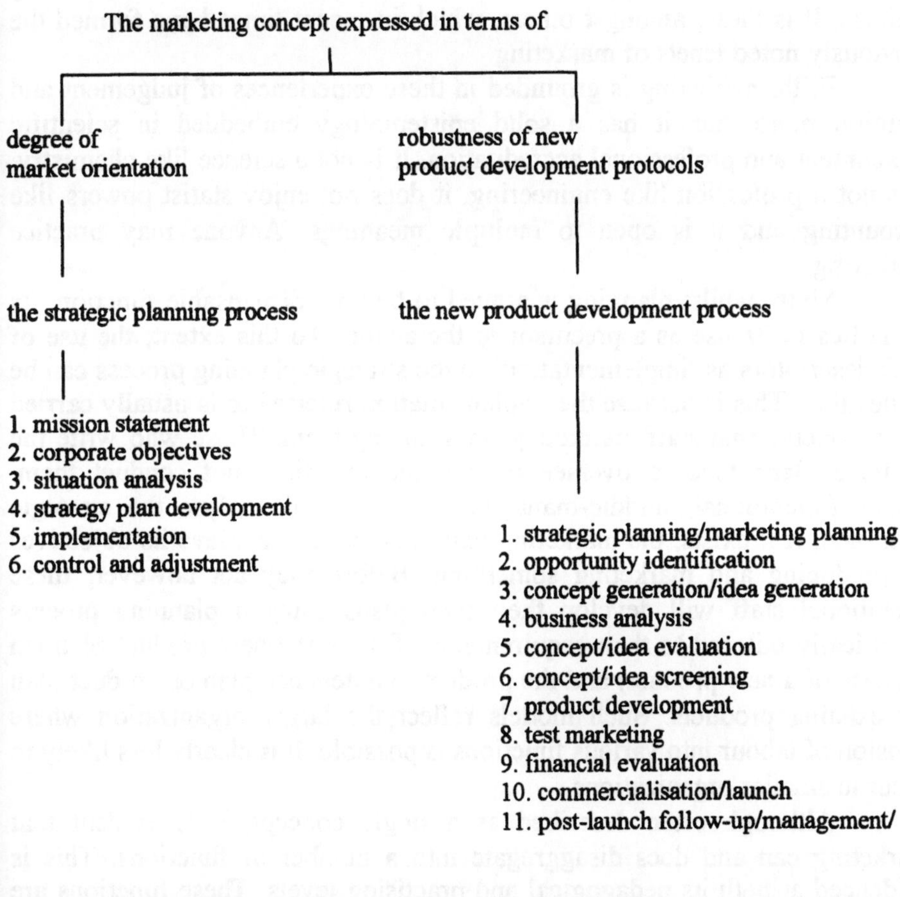

Figure 6. An Operational Perspective on The Marketing Construct

last century [43]. They were conducted by company owners and by their sales force. To market a product was a flourish, nurtured by complicated mixtures of opportunism, control of distribution channels, physical proximity to markets, astute advertising, competitive prices, the better product amongst the total available to customers, a streetwise familiarity with the market that only those in close proximity to it could attain, and foresight. Whether these factors are seen as shrewdness, exploitation, bourgeois sentiment or mercantilist ethic is less significant now than the claim by marketers that these are somehow their tools and theirs alone. From the list of factors immediately above may be discerned some basic constructs of modern marketing; the so-called marketing mix, adoption and diffusion rates, product typologies, market research and above all, planning regimes. It is these, amongst others, which in recent times have formed the previously noted tenets of marketing.

Fifth, marketing is grounded in these experiences of judgement and intuition more than it has a solid epistemology embedded in scientific detachment and professional accreditation. It is not a science like chemistry, it is not a profession like engineering, it does not enjoy statist powers like accounting and it is open to multiple meanings. Anyone may practice marketing.

Sixth, whilst planning is argued to be an indispensable function, its value lies in its use as a precursor to the action. To this extent, the use of such descriptors as 'implementation' in the strategic planning process can be misleading. This is because the implementation referred to is usually carried out by operational staff, marketing ones among them. Those who write the strategic plans tend to oversee their implementation, not conduct them. Others (operational, middle-management staff) will analyse the strategic plan (and, if it exists, the marketing plan) and seek to achieve its objectives by producing and marketing something. Before they act however, these operational staff will develop their own plans using a planning process specifically tailored to their requirements. This is the new product plan (in the case of a new product) and the product maintenance plan or product plan for existing products. Such models reflect the larger organization where division of labour into various functions is possible. It is clearly less likely to occur in smaller organizations.

Although often described as a single concept, it is evident that marketing can and does disaggregate into a number of functions. This is evidenced at both its pedagogical and practising levels. These functions are accompanied by a series of planning regimes that seek to simultaneously meet the strategic (long range), annual marketing (medium range) and short-term (new product development) planning desires of the marketing function. These planning desires of the marketing function can manifest themselves in a number of ways that are usually dependent on the nature of the organisation. There appear to be two key variables in the development of marketing's planning processes. One is the size of the organisation and the second is the extent to which it claims (and has embraced) what is commonly understood to constitute a market orientation.

ALTERNATIVE APPROACHES TO MARKET ORIENTATION: THE COUNTER-EXAMPLES OF TWO LOCAL INDUSTRIES

A means to explain why marketing's accepted wisdoms find variation in their applicability to different kinds of organisations emerges from field research into two consumer retail industries that claim a market orientation which lies well outside the paradigms and accepted discourse of mainstream research. The two field studies, conducted within a specific geographic region of Melbourne, made a qualitative examination of the extent of market orientation and the presence of formalised new product development procedures in two high growth sectors: the garden nursery and mountain bike industries [44, 45]. The results provide a rich picture of the way these business people made marketing decisions, particularly in the area of new product development.

When seeking to investigate the behaviour of individuals or groups, a large number of differing techniques are available to researchers. Craig and Hart [46] have concluded that there is no clear-cut best method of researching the area of new product development. The majority of general marketing research and, more specifically, new product-related research has been quantitative in nature, focussing on issues of technique such as processes, strategies and people-related factors [46]. Whilst such research permits an accounting of the new product development process in its conventional and hence supposedly measurable form, encased in pre-defined success criteria, it does not necessarily enable a ready interpretation of events on the ground in business practice. Such research also provides limited insight into why some businesses either do not use or have discarded what may be termed here as the traditional marketing practices such as the new product development process. Qualitative research, whilst having only been used sparingly in the past, is an especially helpful way to reveal managerial motives and reasoning. It was on this initial premise that research into such specific industries was formulated as a qualitative, in-depth exploration of managerial attitudes towards marketing in general and the new product development process in particular. It was not the goal of this research to provide statistical data hinting at success factors, but rather to uncover what was actually being done in relation to market orientation and new product development, and to gain an understanding of the reasoning behind these actions. Unique characteristics of the individuals and their businesses were considered in order to explain the degree of fit between accepted theory and current practice.

Some further explanation for the choice of these two industries should be given here. In the first instance, both the retail garden nursery and the mountain bike markets are experiencing rapid growth in Australia. On this point, the samples for both surveys were of accord. Second, the garden nursery and the mountain bike markets permitted a ready access to outlets that essentially occupied the same geographical area. Third, both the garden nursery and the mountain bike markets are relatively high-profile ones. In the case of the garden nursery industry, the creation of new outlets and the introduction of ever-increasing numbers of plant types and varieties attests to the strong and growing demand for garden plants, shrubs, trees and requisites. Gardening is very popular in Victoria, that part of Australia officially known as "The Garden State". In similar vein, mountain bike activities, whether at the leisure-lifestyle or the competition level, are experiencing strong growth, particularly since its inaugural acceptance as a sport in the 1996 Summer Olympics at Atlanta. Fourth, both have readily accessible retail sectors which evidence a capacity to jointly and severally engage goods and services product offerings into its total product offering and an ability on the part of individual retailers to be instrumental in the creation of product offerings to the consumer. This factor was clearly evidenced amongst the respondents in both surveys. Fifth, both the retail garden nursery and retail mountain bike industries display relative freedom from advanced corporate structures, extensive forward or backward integration or exposure to the marketing techniques that often accompany such structures. It was in these respects that both sectors were judged as appropriate places for the investigation of the extent of market orientation and new product development practices.

Despite the impact that marketing education has had on influencing business professionals, even casual observation of most industries will suggest that many of the basic principles of academy-style marketing are yet to be adopted by a large number of organizations. The field studies allowed an examination of these two local industries in order to determine the extent to which marketing practices have been formally or informally adopted. Each survey was confined to ten outlets. In the case of the garden nurseries, these ranged from very small enterprises employing as few as one equivalent full-time staff member to those employing as many as twenty. For mountain bike outlets the range was from three to ten. The outlets surveyed form a rough corridor, reaching out from the eastern edge of the Melbourne metropolitan centre into what can be described as middle- to upper-middle-class suburbs. The ten outlets for each survey were within sufficient proximity to each other to constitute a zone of direct competition, as established and recognised by both respondents and researcher. They represented, according to their estimates, around eighty per cent of the turnover of the area. Data was collected via a series of in-depth, face-to-face interviews based on a semi-structured questionnaire format. The respondent was a part owner or the owner or executive principal of the outlet. The interviews were held at the business premises during trading hours.

The goals of the research were threefold. To what extent did the respondents display a market orientation? To what extent were they making use of the conventional new product development process for bringing new products to the market? Did the findings suggest that marketing practitioners and theorists need recognise that some variations occur in marketing orientation and the new product development process in such localised businesses?

The Extent of Market Orientation

It transpired that for these two surveys, a substantial amount of the interviewing needed to be made using what can be described here as 'lay' rather than marketing descriptors and nomenclature. No respondent possessed formal undergraduate marketing qualifications, relying instead on seminars, dealer training or their own reading. All, however, had knowledge of business practice and most had established some protocols that either mimicked or were used instead of the conventional marketing approach. Because of this, interpretation of the responses and *in situ* observation of the respondents, their businesses and dealings with retail customers were very important considerations in the survey approach.

The qualities that were deemed by the respondents as essential pre-requisites to a market orientation were the innate ones; direct experience with their respective products at a personal level, expertise in running a business and a capacity to sell product. As one respondent observed,

> "there's no use in doing marketing courses when the business is going to have to run on common sense anyway."

and another,

> "if you don't ride mtb's, [mountain bikes] how can you sell them? Of course we're market oriented, or we wouldn't still be in business."

and another,

> "you can't train someone to be market oriented; they can either sell or they can't. We have staff who know what the customer wants and how to sell it to them."

This mixing of selling and marketing concepts was almost universal throughout the samples. Time and again, respondents freely used terminology from both fields with what some marketing purists might see as a breathtaking lack of understanding of either. This situation reinforced the need for the interviewer to move beyond traditional marketing nomenclature and make assessments based both on the researcher's own marketing knowledge and direct experiences both with the garden nursery and mountain bike markets.

The surveys sought to establish the extent to which respondents fitted the conventional notions of a market orientation. Looking closely at the actions of the business people in relation to the key components of marketing revealed that despite the lack of formal training, localised methods had arisen. These issues emerged as soon as the matter of market orientation had been broached. Whatever their use of marketing terminology, it quickly surfaced that nearly all respondents had a conviction that not only were they market oriented, they were also ready to claim full awareness of their respective business's organisational resources. How did these claims stand up against conventional wisdoms?

Only two respondents - both principals in the same business - had received formal marketing training and in both cases, this was confined to a minor number (no more than two) marketing subjects within a general business degree. The majority of each sample felt that marketing competence was a matter of innate and experientially acquired skills over time. Both samples were characterised by an almost universal absence of the conventional view of an all-embracing marketing concept as the foundation for the marshalling and employment of organisational resources.

When asked to describe the business they were in, respondents generally went well beyond the limitations of nominating a goods category. From an apparently extremely successful mountain bike outlet, one that specialised in premium-priced, high-end product came this observation,

> "We are not bikes and we are not even mountain bikes - we are in the business of making money out of specialisation for enthusiasts."

Respondents displayed an apparently sound knowledge of where their business was coming from in terms of sales by product categories. Respondents were asked first to nominate that part of their business that was generated by goods and by services. Few had trouble in separating these.

> "we know we have to have a certain amount of stock in each area - mtb's, changeover or upgrade front forks, tyres tubes, gear clusters, and so on - you get to know what the proportions are through experience."

and from a garden nursery respondent,

> "we like to position ourselves as a boutique nursery with a gift orientation...people come here for gift ideas."

In this way was the notion that they were primarily in a goods retail business tempered by an almost universal acknowledgment that service factors were critical to business success. It was widely acknowledged that no amount of product breadth and depth would offset customer concerns over any lack of readily available advice and perceived expertise. All respondents acknowledged the importance of service, one going so far as to say,

> "the garden business is ninety per cent services - advice, help - and we're a social venue too."

and another,

> "Goods are ninety-nine per cent of our dollar sales, but service and advice is probably about seventy per cent of our costs; by that I mean [the costs of] staff and the information counter."

On the matter of the "social venue", two-thirds of the respondents actively pursued business in the belief that customers patronised their business because "we are someone to talk to". Those nurseries and mountain bike outlets that claimed to compete on price were equally convinced that service - particularly in terms of a preparedness to have social interaction before the sale - was an integral component of their business.

When asked what made their business unique to the competition, there was a universal discard of the goods issues. What emerged was a very strong claim on the part of all respondents to a competitive superiority predicated on service factors. These ranged from 'approach' to customers through to claims of the best customer service. If the researcher were able to give one phrase under which all of these ambit claims could be aggregated, it would be a claim to a sales-based, problem-solving capability.

In summary, the respondents acknowledged ignorance of formal marketing training. Whilst they were unfamiliar with the bulk of theories and terminology, their actions indicated an awareness of competition, customers and environmental demands, balanced with organisational needs: the basis of a marketing orientation, as laid down in the foundation works of Narver and Slater and Kohli and Jaworski. Goals were vague for the most part with a general desire to grow being expressed, but very little in terms of premeditated mechanics for how these goals would be achieved. Yet the respondents claimed to have a good idea of what their role was, and through their actions indicated an ability to segment the market and position themselves amongst their competition. The picture that emerged was one of disdain for or disinterest in learning and using the formal approaches and *lingua franca* of marketing. All respondents nevertheless firmly believed they were market oriented. In terms of their service levels, understanding of total product offerings and preparedness to view customers as the focus of their business activities, they seemingly were. What was lacking were formal planning protocols and the familiarity with marketing terminology that encodes conventional views of market orientation and new product development.

The initial results of the two surveys have been dealt with in enough detail here. The purpose of this chapter after all, is to attempt to position these research findings in the context of conventional wisdom about the dimensions and nature of what constitutes a market orientation and what constitutes an appropriate new product development process. It is apparent that there exists a substantial variance between the conventional wisdom and these two industries' actualities. It is appropriate now to attempt to explain the variance. In so doing, an approach is taken that seeks less to prey upon the notion of difference or non-conformity and rather to look for the continuities. These two industries evidence - no matter how unconsciously or casually - a form of market orientation and new product development. To explain the variances and the parallels, the notion of plurality is offered as an explanation that marketing is, in its observance, subject to varying approaches. It is to the concept of pluralism within traditions that we will now turn.

MARKETING AS PLURALISTIC TRADITIONS

Earlier, reference was made to the work of Saul and the possibility that the marketing domain is a pluralistic one. In this marketing has parallels with studies in the social sciences, especially those in the field of anthropology. To look beyond the marketing construct as it is usually presented and to absorb some of the contribution of anthropological research may contribute to a broadening of our capacity to view the marketing domain not only for what it purports to be but also for what it represents; a cultural construct that resides within business and organisational life. A prominent anthropological contribution will now be looked at to provide some explanation for the dissonances discerned between the major conventional themes of marketing and the practices of the respondents in the garden nursery and mountain bike businesses. It argues that a tradition can be defined in terms of its small and great themes.

The concept of small and great traditions has its roots in anthropological studies. It belongs to a humanist who, despite his 'humanism', nevertheless made considerable impact on the emerging social sciences during the nineteen-fifties. Robert Redfield's enormous contribution to bridging the gap between 'scientific' and 'non-scientific' lines of thought, and between the presumed robustness of empirical approaches as opposed to the presumably flaccid conceptual approaches provides a rich and relevant field within which to consider the dynamics of the variations between what he termed small and great traditions [47-49]. For the purpose of this chapter, his most relevant work is *Peasant Society and Culture*, first published in 1956. This makes it contemporary with such foundation pieces of the marketing discipline as Converse's [28] marketing-as-science (1945), Levitt's [50] marketing myopia (1960) and Borden's [51] marketing mix (1965) contributions. Three propositions will be now put forward. They are predicated on the assumption that market orientation and new product development are central factors in conventional views of what constitutes a marketing culture. The propositions are by no means proven. Nor are they necessarily presumed to be universally applicable. Rather, they are an attempt to explain the existence of small traditions in these industries.

The first proposition is that in order to survive, the small marketing cultures of the garden nursery and mountain bike industries need to remain in philosophical and actionable communication with the broader marketing community outside them. This is how they not only maintain a perception of their own futures. It is also the means by which they feel they belong to the broader business community. It is also, in a business sense, how they survive.

The second proposition is that such industries are what Redfield so eruditely describes as "perpetually incomplete" [49] (p68). They have to know what goes on in the minds of their larger counterparts, be they competitors or co-operators, of direct or indirect nature. This is why they talk, no matter how simplistically, of marketing as a core function of their respective operations. They do arrive each morning at their place of business, and commence the Aegean Stable task of sorting business fact from prospect fiction, in a not dissimilar fashion to their great tradition counterparts in much larger corporate structures. Are they that different from the great tradition or that disturbingly similar?

The third proposition is that the small-tradition industries are not so much local phenomena of wayward or primitive marketing than they are examples of the purist replenishment of business from its primal source; its customers. Put another way, these small tradition industries are as in touch with the realities of their markets as their great tradition counterparts. They, perhaps even more than their great tradition counterparts, are in constant contact with the market's realities.

Recognition Of The Small Traditions

Although referring to peasant communities within the broader society or nation, this is exactly the point Redfield [49] (p70) made, and it bears quotation here.

> "The great tradition is cultivated in schools or temples; the little tradition works itself out and keeps itself going in the lives of the unlettered...The tradition of the philosopher, theologian, and literary man is a tradition consciously cultivated and handed down; that of

the little people is for the most part taken for granted and not submitted to much scrutiny."

Obviously there are more than two traditions and hopefully, it may be perceived that there is more than one marketing culture in which an organisation may operate. The garden nursery and mountain bike business people that were the subjects of the field surveys frequently aspire to marketing's great traditions as much as they are aware that their placement so deeply in the market demands that they intuitively scrutinise a situation rather than resort to marketing's meta - narratives, university courses and attendant conventional wisdoms.

For the fieldwork respondents, there is no single, 'correct' marketing philosophy or culture. The findings from these two industries would suggest that if there were, then they would be at such variance from it as to be deemed as not being market oriented. Yet if a concurrency notion is taken into account, they display what can be seen as a marketing orientation. They are not primitive or underdeveloped forms of marketing as measured in a linear sense against other, often larger industries. Rather, they are representative of marketing's small traditions.

A view that accommodates a plurality of marketing thought, a multiplicity of approaches, of a compounding of traditions, would still allow a clear recognition of the essential differences between say, a large corporation's strategic plans and a garden nursery proprietor's thoughts of tomorrow's trade. Separate strategic planning and new product development regimes are operating. At the same time, each nevertheless rubs transactional shoulders with the other, intellectually feeds off the other and relies upon or defies the other, perhaps by being its distribution channel, its price leader, its supplier, its competitor or its promoter. In this way are the two traditions not so much different stages in some presumed advancement, as they are concurrently operable and interdependent.

Against the market orientation construct of Narver, Slater and Tietje [17] shown in Figure 2, are these two industries too "market-back" and insufficiently "programmatic"? Are they errant market entrants, shortly to be overwhelmed by the forces of conventional market orientation that will be brought to bear on them by a vigorous new competitor? Given the weighty, empirically treated, statistically validated studies of the conventional market orientation school – especially the works of Kohli and Jaworski [9] and Narver and Slater [10], - is the evidence from the Melbourne field studies for other forms of market orientation too flimsy or does the existence of a multiplicity of interpretations calls the validity of a single, encyclopaedic-style-definition of market orientation into question?

FROM CONVENTIONAL TO CONTEXT RICH APPROACHES

Here, a description of a context-rich variation to the conventional strategic planning and new product development processes is presented and discussed. It commences with, yet quickly departs from the conventional approach. The more conventional approach is inherently sequential and relatively inflexible. The progressive refinement of a product idea from concept to launch is accompanied by a developing rigidity in the product's character. How did the respondents in the field surveys of the garden nursery and mountain bike industries react to the conventional marketing construct shown in Figure 6? This section outlines their interpretations.

The marketing concept was held to be a means to an end, a way to financial advantage. Invariably, it was expressed in terms of personal achievement that resulted in independence, personal wealth and general well being. Absent was a belief in the marketing concept for its own sake. Being market oriented and being able to develop new products were almost universally described in terms of "better sales", "selling up" and a regular, repeat purchasing customer base.

The strategic planning process was seen as beyond the realm of all but the few respondents controlling larger operations. None comprehended the importance of articulating the new product development process with the strategic planning process, but successful new products were deemed vital to success. All respondents claimed a capacity to think strategically and in their various descriptions of dealing with financial institutions, suppliers and industry associations, they evidenced mission statement and corporate objective-like approaches. All claimed their plans for their businesses or themselves – often held by them to be indivisible factors – ran well past five years. They were cognizant of their strengths and weaknesses and eloquent on their goal setting and planning capacities. They just did not have them necessarily typed, filed, formally approved or open for committee review. As one observer noted, he was the committee, the finance director, marketing manager and key sales representative, as well as new product manager, accountant and production controller.

When asked their views on the strategic planning process, most respondents were surprised that such precision would be of any use. How, they asked, could such precision be achievable even for larger organisations, when the short and long term vagaries of the market place made their own small to medium enterprises so difficult to predict?

The qualities that were deemed by the respondents as essential prerequisites to market orientation were innate: experience in the respective industry, personal skills, expertise in running a business and a capacity to sell product. Nearly all respondents displayed an apparently sound knowledge of where their business was coming from, both in terms of customers and in terms of sales by product categories. Most respondents had involvement in their respective industry for more than five years, half of them more than ten. Some had been sales representatives for the suppliers before moving into the retail sector. A number were adamant that they were probably still the best 'sales representatives' some of these supplier organisations still had. Respondents were very knowledgeable of the customers they served, they had lost and the type they most wanted. They could describe their targeted markets in terms of age, gender, income and occupational status.

Although usually gained informally rather than through formal data collection or market research, these marketers displayed intricate knowledge of their competition, both direct and indirect. Yet they claimed ignorance of marketing in the sense that it would be described in marketing literature. While they were unfamiliar with the bulk of theories and terminology, their actions, the apparent well being of their operations, and their views on the threats to and the growth prospects for their businesses indicated an awareness of competition, customers and environmental demands, balanced with organisational needs – the basis for a market orientation. What of the new product development process?

The Extent of Formal New Product Development Processes

It needs to be emphasised that whilst being planners and retailers, these people are also decidedly performing the new product development function. They are relatively unique in retailing in that they not only conduct the final distributive function of assorting goods as stock on display, they also have an active part in creating – making or growing - the stock. For the nurseries this extended from being involved in the production of their own branded accessories through to the management, through a kind of backward integration, of how the stock would be priced, promoted, when it would arrive and how it would be presented. In the case of mountain bikes, these were literally made on premise. Standard lines were developed, as were specialised items. For example, any bike could be almost completely dismantled, re-equipped and transformed into a quite separate product. Several respondents also spoke of their capacity to "dress" or "surround" a prospect in product as soon as they walked onto the premises. It was considered a challenge to see how much could be added to the initial purchase inquiry. This is marketing at it deepest, perhaps most primitive, certainly its most intuitive and decidedly at its most fundamental. And at the end of each selling day, stocks had to be assessed, likely sales considered and a balancing act between liquidity and stock orders managed. To assess the extent to which the traditional new product development process was employed, the synthesised form described earlier in this chapter was shown to respondents and the process explained.

The process was rejected out of hand. It was seen as irrelevant, inapplicable to organisations of their size and type. Yet it was evident that all firms had engaged in some product management activities and had done so as an essential part of doing business. Lines had been added and dropped, ranges extended and brand names developed. All had engaged in new product development activities. Nor was there evidence that the new product development process might even have been a shared one between these outlets and their respective suppliers.

The efficacy of the new product development process was not so much questioned as its applicability to their types of business. There was little empathy with the proliferation of steps in the process. Yet there was universal claim that some or even all of the steps in the process were being undertaken in some way or other. This they claimed they did in some abbreviated form, intuitively rather than in a conscious and discursive way, or simultaneously rather than sequentially. Figure 7 portrays the process. It is a synthesis, formed from those in the field, of their approaches to the strategic planning and new product development processes typically applied in such organisations. It constitutes a radical departure from the theoretical models in the literature.

The product management function, especially new product development is inextricably intertwined with the more strategic aspects of the organization. It becomes lateral more than hierarchical, and tends to work "back" into time as much as "forward" in that a balancing act between supplies, supplier response, customer demand manifestations and customer patience all have to be worked simultaneously. To this extent, the new product development process in particular becomes more a matter of simultaneous occurrences than of sequential events. Nor are these events "managed" or in any way gateway-controlled by the manager. Rather, they are dealt with as circumstances demand. No better metaphor for this kind of intense temporal compression of the new product development function may be found than in the mind of the garden nursery operator who is able to locate, in his mental map of the site, every tree or shrub in stock that will fit a particular shape and height requirement specified by a customer who walks onto the premises. Customers, it is well understood, will not wish to wait if they wish to spend money. Similar mental mappings were described in the mountain bike industry. Products and sub-products, be it fertiliser for plants or oil for gears, will be mentally aggregated to meet those wishes. Familiarity with the customer is a key factor in such mental constructions.

The outlet becomes the new product development centre in such industries. When a product becomes popular over time, suppliers may try to standardise supply to correlate with the particular ingredients but will stop short of risky capitalisation of and investment into a standing product line. Why take such risks when markets are so fickle and retailers can sort the problem of the perfect product out with a particular customer, at a particular time, using a variety of stocks they must hold or quickly obtain? There was consensus among the outlet owners that they were the true product managers and that the suppliers, importers and agents in the industries welcomed the burdening of product management problems onto the shoulders of those at the rough end of the supply chain. Outlet operators are the ultimate product managers, juggling stock, orders, expected sales, an often elusive and increasingly price sensitive customer base, seasonal demand and competitive forces.

A PROPOSED CONTEXT-RICH APPROACH FOR NEW PRODUCT DEVELOPMENT

Before outlining a framework for a solution to the problems discussed, it is appropriate to make a number of observations. These have framed the approach taken and form the basis for the proposed context-rich

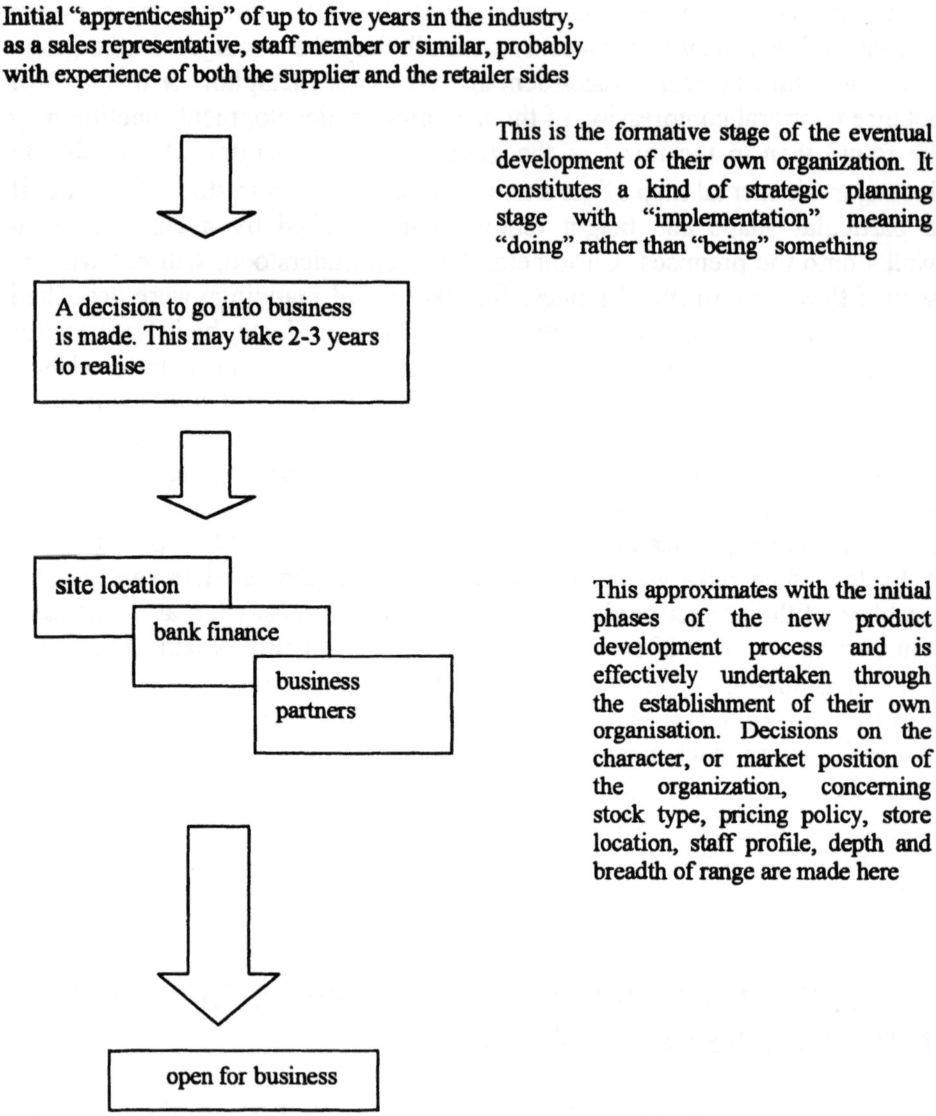

Figure 7. The Planning Process

The Organisation's Field of Controllable and Uncontrollable Variables
This approximates the product mix, marketing mix and environmental factors concepts of conventional marketing models and is the framework for their strategic-like desires. It is often described in this way, with up to fifty-five separate suppliers, none of whom control retail outlets and of which over thirty were traded with in the last six months.

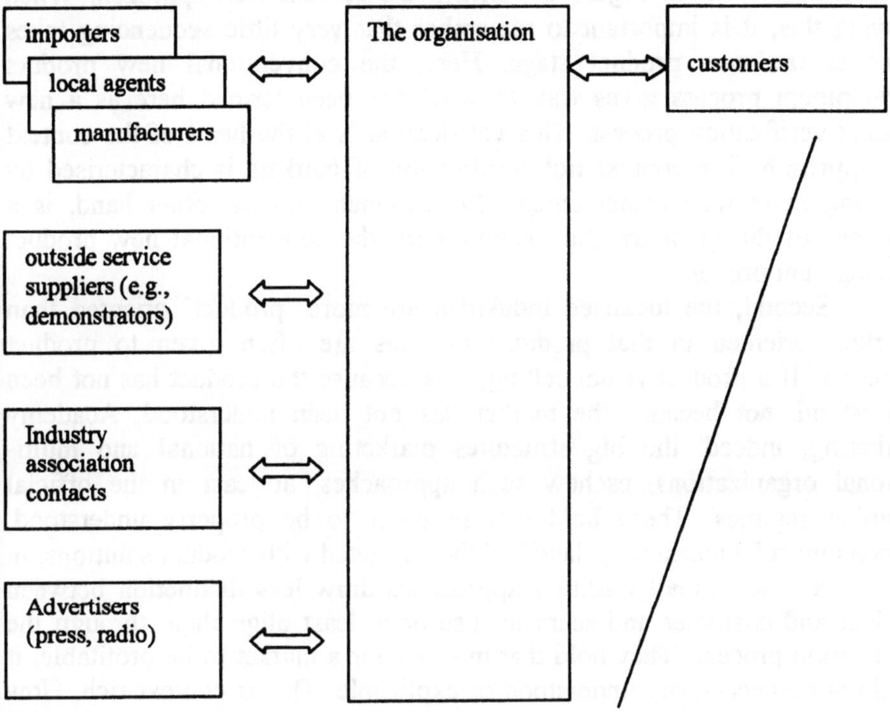

There are various classes of customers and their needs: this is the perception they hold of their
outward expression of their organisational goals. It approximates with the last stages of the planning process and the early stages of the new product development process outlined in Figure 6

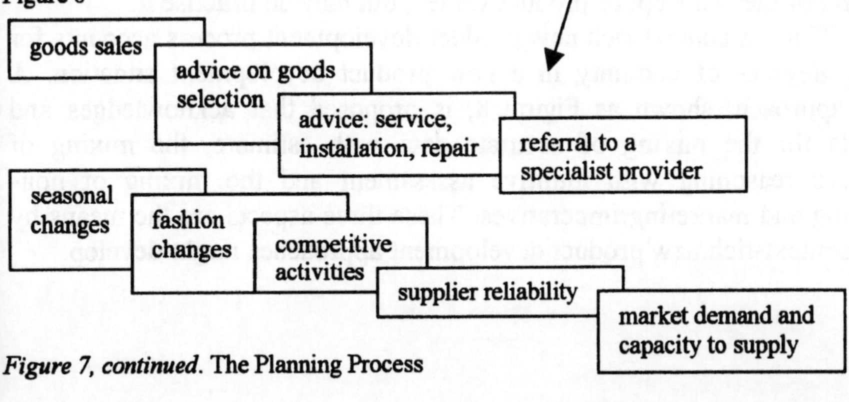

Figure 7, continued. The Planning Process

approach given here and shown as Figure 8. Firstly, the context rich approach is an interpretation of the methods uncovered in the fieldwork. These methods are intuitive, involving the simultaneous arrival of a number of issues that are resolved through product market decisions in an almost simultaneous fashion. Figure 8 portrays the context rich approach. When viewing this, it is important to remember that very little sequencing takes place at the new product stage. Here, the conventional new product development process gives way to what has been termed here as a new product verification process. This verification is at the heart of the context rich approach. The context rich verification of markets is characterised by scanning more than measurement. Measurement, on the other hand, is a hallmark of the great tradition counterpart, the conventional new product development process.

Second, the localised industries are more 'product' oriented than 'market' oriented in that product solutions are often given to product problems. If a product is not selling, it is because the product has not been understood, not because the market has not been understood. Academy marketing, indeed, the big structures marketing of national and multi-national organizations, eschew such approaches, at least in the official planning regimes. These hold that in order to be properly understood, markets must be measured, classified then targeted with product solutions, in that strict order. Small tradition approaches draw less distinction between product and customer and seem to fuse or at least align them through the verification process. They hold that in order for a market to be profitable, it need not be necessarily understood or explicable. This is context rich. How many product decisions in large organisations are written in market oriented reports that hide a product oriented decision process? The garden nursery and mountain bike respondents may never have heard of the work of Bennett and Cooper [34], let alone have read of their long-ignored call for a revisiting of the "concept of product value", but they do practise it.

Third, a context-rich new product development process accounts for varying degrees of certainty in a new product development situation. A model approach, shown as Figure 8, is proposed that acknowledges and accounts for the mixing of accurate data with estimate, the mixing of discursive reasoning with intuitive assessment and the mixing of non-marketing and marketing imperatives. These three aspects are the means by which context-rich new product development approaches might develop.

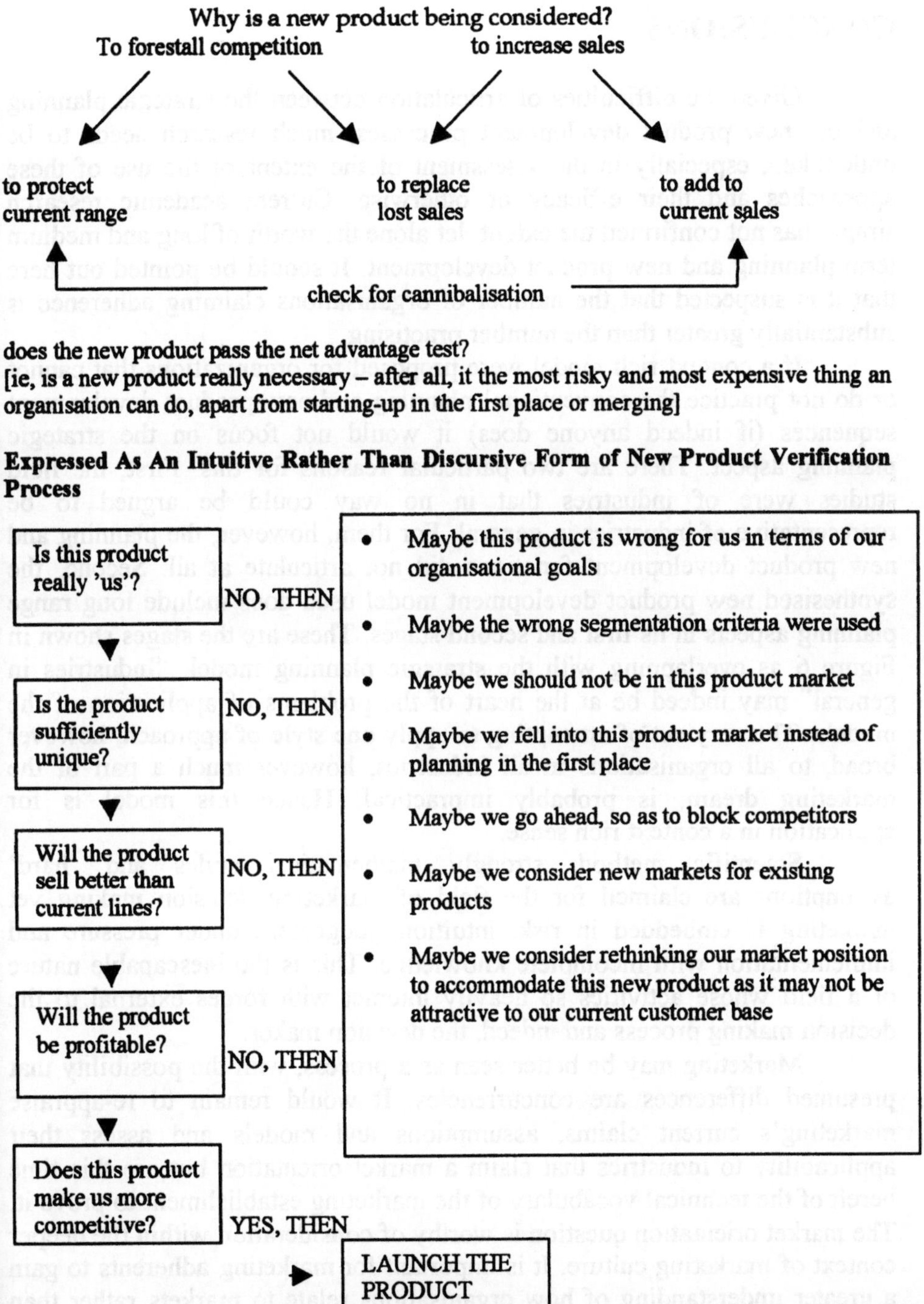

Figure 8. A Context Rich New Product Verification Process

CONCLUSIONS

Given the difficulties of articulation between the strategic planning and the new product development processes, much research needs to be undertaken, especially in the assessment of the extent of the use of these approaches and their efficacy or otherwise. Current academic research simply has not confirmed the extent, let alone the worth of long and medium term planning and new product development. It should be pointed out here that it is suspected that the number of organisations claiming adherence is substantially greater than the number practising.

If a context rich model were proposed for organizations that cannot or do not practice the conventional planning and new product development sequences (if indeed anyone does) it would not focus on the strategic planning aspect. There are two particular reasons for this. First, the field studies were of industries that in no way could be argued to be representative of industries in general. For them, however, the planning and new product development functions did not articulate at all. Second, the synthesised new product development model used does include long range planning aspects in its first and second stages. These are the stages shown in Figure 6 as overlapping with the strategic planning model. "Industries in general" may indeed be at the heart of the problems of application of the models. The very act of attempting to apply one style of approach, however broad, to all organisations in all industries, however much a part of the marketing dream, is probably impractical. Hence this model is for application in a context rich sense.

Scientific method, strongly mathematical styles and 'hard' assumptions are claimed for the field of marketing decision making yet marketing is embedded in risk, intuition, judgement under pressure and implementation with incomplete knowledge. This is the inescapable nature of a field whose activities so heavily interact with forces external to the decision making process and indeed, the decision maker.

Marketing may be better seen as a process, with the possibility that presumed differences are concurrencies. It would remain to re-appraise marketing's current claims, assumptions and models and assess their applicability to industries that claim a market orientation but are this time bereft of the technical vocabulary of the marketing establishment to prove it. The market orientation question is worthy of consideration within the deeper context of marketing culture. It is important for marketing adherents to gain a greater understanding of how organisations relate to markets rather than how firms 'be' something. This is a context-rich approach. The research to date has yet to satisfactorily tell us 'how', perhaps because it has not or cannot account for the organic aspects of an organisation's relationship with the marketplace. For small to medium enterprises at least, marketing-as-experience rather than marketing-as-science is arguably a safer place for marketing discourse than is a premature presumption that marketing has somehow already achieved unquestioned status as a science, a profession, or both.

Conventional new product development wisdom operates on the assumptions that objectives are fixed and constant, that a problem is somehow independent of time, that pay-offs are readily measurable and that a problem can be described as a closed system. In fact, not only does a new product development differ from product to product, it can also vary with experience and time. Conventional new product development locks in the measurable and the sequential, the internally controllable and the constant, just as it locks out and dispossesses the immeasurable and the simultaneously occurring, the externally uncontrollable and the variable. Those from the field studies favour stochastic approaches, experience and intuition over scientific management and discursive reasoning. The respondents in these industries were so involved in the full and complete marketing of their products as to consider such a model beyond their capacity to apply or adhere to. To this extent, they either considered their new product development processes as a jumble of events and actions or, at best, much more a concurrency of events and decisions than a neat sequence.

The strategic planning and new product development models are theoretical devices that go little way to explaining market realities for such industries. The models, possibly for similar reasons, appear to have little universal success elsewhere, even when applied to like organisations in the same industry. Perhaps too much is being expected of the planning and product planning processes, too much expected of models that cannot compensate for change. Market change overtakes the new product model. Really new, or discontinuous new products are more risky than the continuous or low level innovations. To adhere to the new product planning model, let alone presume it can be articulated with the strategic planning model is to uphold several tenets of canonical marketing practice. It is also an attempt to act out what may be termed "the marketing dream". This "marketing dream" is the stuff of models and is perhaps only applicable to mass markets serviced by large market entrants employing discontinuous, high innovation and hence, high risk, products. Further, modelling may only work when some as yet to be calculated ratio of internally controlled decisions to externally influenced ones exist. It is yet to be shown whether smaller markets, especially those occupied by small to medium enterprises, can be modelled. The challenge to market modellers is twofold. Can large-market new product development projects really be modelled so as to improve success rates? Can market modelling be applied, albeit with higher incidences of soft over hard decision areas, to small to medium enterprises?

REFERENCES

[1] Kotler, P. *Marketing Management: The Millennium Edition*, Prentice-Hall, New Jersey, 2000.

[2] McColl-Kennedy, J. and Kiel, G. *Marketing: A Strategic Approach*, Nelson Thomson, South Melbourne, 2000.

[3] Baker, M. and Hart, S. *Product Strategy and Management*, Prentice Hall Europe, London, 1998.

[4] Gruenwald, G. *How To Create Profitable New Products: From Mission To Market*, NTC Business, Chicago, 1997.

[5] Crawford, C. *New Products Management*, R.D. Irwin, Homewood, Illinois, 1996.

[6] Kotler, P., Armstrong, G., Brown, L. and Adam, S. *Marketing*, 4th ed., Prentice Hall Australia, Sydney, 1998

[7] McCarthy, E., Perrault, W. and Quester, P. *Basic Marketing: A Managerial Approach,* 2nd Australasian edition, Irwin, Sydney, 1998.

[8] Stanton, W.J., Miller, K.E. and Layton, R.A. *Fundamentals of Marketing, third Australian edition*, McGraw-Hill, Sydney, 1993.

[9] Zikmund, W. and d'Amico, M. *Marketing*, 5th ed., West, St. Paul, 1996.

[10] Assael, H., Reed, P. and Patton, M. *Marketing Principles and Strategy: Australian edition,* Harcourt Brace, Sydney, 1995

[11] Kohli, A. and Jaworski, B. "Market Orientation: The Construct, Research Propositions, and Managerial Implications", *Journal of Marketing*, vol. 54, pp. 1-18, 1990.

[12] Narver, J. and Slater, S. "The Effect of Market Orientation on Business Profitability", *Journal of Marketing*, vol. 54, pp. 20-35, 1990.

[13] Ruekert, R. "Developing a Market Orientation: An Organizational Strategy Perspective", *International Journal of Research in Marketing*, vol. 9, no. 3, pp. 225-245, 1992.

[14] Deshpande, R., Farley, J. and Webster, F. "Corporate Culture, Customer Orientation and Innovativeness in Japanese Firms: A Quadrad Analysis", *Journal of Marketing*, vol. 57, pp. 23-37, 1993.

[15] Jaworski, B. and Kohli, A. "Market Orientation: Antecedents and Consequences", *Journal of Marketing*, vol. 57, pp.53-70, 1993.

[16] Pelham, A. and Wilson, D. "A Longitudinal Study of the Impact of Market Structure, Firm Structure, Strategy, and Market Orientation Culture on Dimensions of Small-Firm Performance", *Journal of the Academy of Marketing Science*, vol. 24, no. 1, p. 27-43, 1996.

[17] Pulendran, S. and Speed, R. "Planning and Doing: The Relationship Between Marketing Planning Styles and Market Orientation", *Journal of Marketing Management*, vol. 12, pp. 53-68, 1996.

[18] Greenley, G. "Forms of Market Orientation in UK Companies", *Journal of Management Studies*, vol. 32, no. 1, pp. 47-66, 1996.

[19] Narver, J., Slater, S. and Tietje, B. "Creating a Market Orientation", *Journal of Market-Focused Management*, vol. 2, no. 3, pp. 241-255, 1998.

[20] Deshpande, R. and Farley, J. "Measuring Market Orientation: Generalisation and Synthesis", *Journal of Market-Focused Management*, vol. 2, no. 3, pp. 213-232, 1998.

[21] Avlonitis, G. and Gounaris, S. "Market Orientation and its Determinants: An Empirical Analysis", *European Journal of Marketing*, vol. 33, no. 11/12, pp. 1003-1037, 1999.

[22] Harris, L. "The Organisational Barriers To Developing Market Orientation", *European Journal of Marketing*, vol. 34, no. 5/6, pp. 598-624, 2000.

[23] Harris, L. and Ogbonna, E. "The Responses of Front-line Employees to Market-oriented Culture Change", *European Journal of marketing*, vol. 34, no. 3/4, pp. 318-340, 2000.

[24] Anderson, W. and Hoyer, W. "Marketing in the Age of Intelligence: The Case for Control", *European Journal of Marketing*, vol. 25, no. 8, pp. 32-54, 1991.

[25] Whittington, R. and Whipp, R. "Professional Ideology and Marketing Implementation", *European Journal of Marketing*, vol. 26, no. 1, pp. 52-63, 1992.

[26] Buzzell, R. "Is Marketing a Science?", *Harvard Business Review*, vol. 41, no. 1, pp. 32-40 and 166-170, 1963.

[27] Hunt, S. "The Nature and Scope of Marketing", *Journal of Marketing*, vol. 40, pp. 17-28, 1976.

[28] Hunt, S. "Should Marketing Adopt Relativism?", in Anderson, P. and Ryan, M. (eds.), *Scientific Method in Marketing*, American Marketing Association, Chicago, 1984.

[29] Brown, S. "Art or Science?: Fifty Years of Marketing Debate", *Journal of Marketing Management*, vol. 12, pp. 243-267, 1996.

[30] Converse, P. "The Development of the Science of Marketing – An Exploratory Survey", *Journal of Marketing*, vol. 10, pp. 14-23, 1945.

[31] Firat, F. and Dholakia, N. *Consuming People: From Political Economy to Theaters of Consumption*, Routledge, London, 1998.

[32] Narver, J. and Slater, S. "Becoming More Market Oriented: An Exploratory Study of the Programmatic and Market-back Approaches", *working paper*, University of Washington, 1991.

[33] Schaffer, R. and Thomson, H. "Successful Change Programs Begin with Results", *Harvard Business Review*, vol. 70, no. 1, pp. 80-89, 1992.

[34] Soderland, M. "Business Intelligence in the Post-modern Era", *Marketing Intelligence and Planning*, vol. 8, no. 1, pp. 7-10, 1990.

[35] Saul, J. *Voltaire's Bastards: The Dictatorship of Reason in the West*, Penguin, Toronto, 1992.

[36] Bennett, R. and Cooper, R. "The Misuse Of Marketing: An American Tragedy", *Business Horizons*, vol. 24, no. 6, pp. 51-61, 1981.

[37] Brownlie, D. and Saren, M. "The Four P's of the Marketing Concept: Prescriptive, Polemical, Permanent, Problematical" *European Journal of Marketing*, vol 26, no 4, pp. 34-47, 1992.

[38] Boyd, H., Walker, O. and Larréché, J-C. *Marketing Management: A Strategic Approach With A Global Orientation*, Irwin/McGraw-Hill, Boston, 1998.

[39] MacDonald, H. *Marketing Plans: How to Prepare Them, How To Use Them*, Butterworth-Heinemann, Oxford, 1997.

[40] Piercy, N. *Market-led Strategic Change: Transforming The Process Of Going To Market*, Butterworth-Heinemann, Oxford, 1997.

[41] Enright, M. and Dhir, K. "Clay Feet of Marketing Decision Sciences", *The Journal of Marketing Management*, vol. 9, no. 2, pp. 116-122, 1999.

[42] Nicholls, M. G. and Cargill, B. J. "The Development of a Change Management Tool to Assist in the Implementation of a Research Culture Change: An Australian Study", *Journal of Asia-Pacific Business*, 2000. (in press).

[43] Ulrich, K. and Eppinger, S. *Product Design and Development*, McGraw-Hill, New York, 1995.

[44] Chase, R., Aquilano, N. and Jacobs, F. *Production and Operations Management: Manufacturing and Services*, 8th ed., Irwin/McGraw-Hill, Boston, 1998.

[45] Enright, M. "Interpretations of The Origins of Marketing Decision Making", *Thirty-first Annual Meeting of the National Decision Sciences Institute*, Orlando, United States, 18-21 November, pp.314-316, 2000.

[46] Enright, M. "Marketing Orientation and New Product Development in the Melbourne Retail Mountain Bike Industry: a Qualitative Review of Local Practice in Comparison and Contrast with Conventional Wisdom", *Proceedings of the Australia and New Zealand Marketing Educators' Conference*, Melbourne, Australia, 1-3 December, 1997, vol. 2, pp. 835-848, 1997.

[47] Enright, M. and McDonald, H. "The Melbourne Garden Nursery Industry: A Qualitative Review of Marketing and New Product Development Orientation in a Retail Environment", *Journal of Product and Brand Management*, vol. 6, no. 3, pp. 175-190, 1997.

[48] Craig, A., and Hart, S. "Where to Now in New Product Development Research?" *European Journal of Marketing*, 26(11), 3-49, 1992.

[49] Redfield, M. (ed). *The Papers of Robert Redfield, vol. 1, Man, Nature and the Study of Society*, University of Chicago Press, Chicago, 1956.

[50] Redfield, M. (ed), *The Papers of Robert Redfield, vol. 2, The Social Uses of Social Science*, University of Chicago Press, Chicago, 1956.

[51] Redfield, R. *Peasant Society and Culture: An Anthropological Approach to Civilisation*, University of Chicago Press, Chicago, 1956.

[52] Levitt, T. "Marketing Myopia" *Harvard Business Review*, vol 38, no 4 , July - August 1960, pp. 45-56, 1960.

[53] Borden, N. "The Concept of The Marketing Mix", *Journal of Advertising research*, vol.5, pp. 2-7, 1964.

7

THE FUNDAMENTALS OF YIELD MANAGEMENT

Ian Yeoman and Anthony Ingold
Napier University Business School
Edinburgh, UK

ABSTRACT

Yield management or revenue management is the process of allocating the right capacity to the right customer at the right time at the right price in order to maximise revenue or yield. Within the context of operational research, it is the process of matching probabilistic demand to a set of finite resources in a manner that will optimise profit. The application of yield management has been described in a vast variety of service industries, including hotels, tourism and transport. These industries have similar characteristics i.e. constrained capacity and a perishable product. Operational research has made a significant contribution to the development of yield management systems by providing mathematical tools and modelling mechanism's. The purpose of this chapter, is to provide the reader with an introduction to the 'fundamentals of yield management'.

Key Words: yield management, revenue optimisation, service industries, price discrimination, intangibility, spontaneity, forecasting.

INTRODUCTION

According to the popular press and media a common discussion point amongst customers of service industries is why one person is charged

M.G. Nicholls et al. (eds.),
Mixed-Mode Modelling: Mixing Methodologies for Organisational Intervention, 209–227.

more than another for what is apparently the same service or product. Typical anecdotal questions include "Why is the passenger in the next seat on an aeroplane paying less than half of the fare that I have been charged?"or "Why is it costing me £70 to travel to London from Birmingham on the train when the passenger across the aisle has a ticket that cost only one quarter of this?". The answer to this perceived unfairness in costing is usually due to Yield Management (YM) sometimes also called revenue optimisation.

According to Schmenner [1], service industries differ in character to manufacturing industries in a number of significant ways:-

1. A service is often a duration or a moment in time, for example, a holiday, a journey.
2. Production and consumption in the service encounter are usually simultaneous and inseparable, for example, an encounter with a waitress in a restaurant.

   The service experience is intangible, for example, checking into an hotel.

Such services operate along a spectrum:-
From low to high perishability
From low to high simultaneousness
From low to high intangibility
From low to high customer intimacy

Given that service organisations operate in a wide range of markets which are composed of widely ranging elements that are expressed to differing degrees, then to define optimum pricing for any given service, in any set location and at a particular time provides a considerable challenge for members of the operational research community who may be involved. The problem has been expressed as one of matching a probabilistic demand to a set of finite resources in a manner that will optimise profit. [2] In the service sectors of hospitality, transportation and tourism, the tool, or set of tools, which has been used to solve this problem is YM.

Formulation of a definition

YM [3] had its origin in the deregulation of the US airline industry, although it is difficult to pinpoint an exact time for its inception. The major airlines, American, Delta, PanAM, United and Continental came under pressure in terms of capacity management from a new "start-up" airline - PeopleExpress. This new airline began operating a "no-frills" service out of the unfashionable Newark Airport (New York) at unbeatably low prices to a number of high volume destinations. American eventually countered this competition by use of a form of price discrimination. They offered some seats at a price which was lower than PeopleExpress could match economically, but maintained higher fares for those passengers who were willing and able to pay more. In this way, American were able to draw the low-spend passengers away from PeopleExpress, whilst maintaining the late booking, high spend business and first class passengers who gave a high yield. This eventually led to the demise of PeopleExpress and their eventual takeover by erstwhile competitor Continental. The full story of this dramatic period in aviation history is recounted by Cross [2].

The tools and techniques of YM are now widely recognised and used by an increasing number of service industries to maximise the utilisation of available capacity over time and to underpin financial viability. Service industries have a commonality: to sell a unit of inventory (time or space) and the service product is perishable. The application of YM has in a wide array of service industries, including hotels, package holidays, cruise, car rental, air and rail transportation and television advertising. These industries have similar characteristics of constrained capacity (expensive to add additional inventory units, e.g. airline seat or hotel room) and a perishable product (once a cruise liner has left port an unsold cabin is a lost opportunity). Such lost opportunity represents lost revenue which can never be recouped.

A commonly recognised broad definition of YM [3] "..the process of allocating the right capacity or inventory unit to the right customer at the right price so as to maximise revenue or yield." In the airline industry yield is normally represented as the revenue per passenger mile or kilometre (RPM/RPK) where yield is a function of both the price that the airline charges for its differentiated service options and the number of seats sold at each price [4]. In the hotel industry YM is concerned with the market sensitive pricing of fixed room capacity relative to an hotel's specified market segments. Here the goal of YM is the formulation and profitable alignment of price, product and consumer. Thus in the hotel sector YM has been defined as a "revenue maximisation technique which aims to increase net yield through the predicted allocation of available bedroom capacity to predetermined market segments at optimum price" [5].

Where service operations are constrained by capacity one of the main functions of management is to optimise utilisation of the available capacity to attain financial success. YM is thus used in industries which are capital intensive services with high fixed costs. Yield is therefore equated with maximisation of utilisation of capacity and pricing to optimise revenue. For example in the rail transportation industry the costs of selling an additional rail journey are almost inconsequential, but may add significantly to revenue.

Conditions, ingredients and boundaries

YM is applicable to service industries where capacity is fixed, demand is unstable and the market can be segmented. These industries also generally have low marginal costs and they often try to sell their perishable products to the consumer well in advance of the service delivery. Kimes [3] outlined a number of preconditions that are necessary for the successful implementation of YM. She also suggested a number of factors or "ingredients" which would be required for implementing YM as an operational system. These are expanded here to establish the operational boundaries of YM.

Preconditions

-Fixed capacity

Many service industries, like the examples given in this paper, tend to be capacity constrained and additionally have no opportunity to inventory their product or service. For example, hotels may increase capacity by adding a number of new bedrooms, or a new function suite. However, this involves a large capital investment and may cause temporary disruption to services. In addition if there is a downturn in the need for the services, the investment cannot be recouped.

-High fixed costs
As mentioned above, there is a high cost of adding incremental capacity. The cost of adding capacity for an airline normally involves purchase of additional aircraft. For a cruise company the cost of commissioning a new liner is a very serious consideration. In addition to the high cost of adding capacity, it is often the case that capacity cannot be rapidly adjusted.

-Low variable costs
The cost of allocating an additional consumer into unused capacity is relatively low, as already mentioned in the case of rail transportation. Another example may be drawn from the car hire industry where the cost of allocating a car to a new customer is simply to valet the car. One of the guidelines that capacity constrained organisations should follow is that they should eventually be prepared to sell their unused capacity, so long as it covers the variable costs with a small additional margin.

-Time varied demand
Capacity constrained organisations capacity is fixed, these organisations cannot easily adjust their capacity to meet peaks and troughs in demand. Kimes [3] explains that when demand varies, organisations can benefit from controlling capacity when demand is high and relaxing that control when demand is low. This management of time varied demand can be achieved through managing the uncertainty of arrivals and duration. Kimes and Chase [6] state capacity constrained firms must protect themselves from no shows or late arrivals. Therefore firms can use both internal (not involving customers) and external (involving customers) approaches to decrease uncertainty of demand. Decisions can also be made on reducing the duration uncertainty, which would enable management to better gauge capacity requirements and hence make better decisions as to which reservations to accept.

-Similarity of inventory units
YM is normally used in situations where it may be assumed that units of inventory are fairly similar. For example, airline YM systems are designed to deal only with seats, although there are different classes of seat. Similarly with the car rental business, cars are generally interchangeable, although different car types will be placed in different rate bands. These classes and bands may be opened and closed according to demand. As YM systems become more sophisticated, they may begin to be developed for more

complex tasks. Examples are YM for cargo in the airline industry [7] and YM for conference and exhibition management [8].

Ingredients

-Market segmentation

Service industries are usually able to determine their market segmentation policy by their customer's willingness to pay. This may lead to making restrictions on bookings, for example advance purchase requirements (APEX and Super APEX) or the imposition of cancellation penalties. The organisation will need to be able to model consumer buying behaviour according to their willingness to pay for the specific service. By distinguishing in this way between different segments of a market, the capacity constrained organisation is able to match a given customer type with an appropriate unit of inventory.

-Historical demand and booking patterns

In order that a capacity constrained service organisation may anticipate periods of high and low demand or indeed expected demand at any given time, a knowledge of the consumer buying behaviour is necessary. This information is usually held in the form of historical demand and booking patterns. This is one aspect of YM that has been transformed by computerisation, with the ability to hold the information on a database. Such a database can be compiled from the records held on a Central Reservation System (CRS). This information is essential to the process of forecasting, which underpins YM.

-Pricing knowledge

Economists describe YM as a form of price discrimination, although this is a simplification of the compilation of the tools and techniques of YM. In practice, hotels and airlines, for example, operate YM systems that depend on opening and closing price rate bands. In the case of the airlines, there may be as many as 20 or 30 different prices on any one aircraft. These bands are sometimes called hurdle rates. In order to stimulate demand in trough periods, capacity constrained service organisations may offer discount prices [9] although care must be taken that the price offered fully covers all costs. Conversely, at periods of expected high demand, low rate tariffs may be closed out. If the forecasting is faulty then an organisation may end up with too few customers, too many customers of the "wrong type" or potentially the worst scenario, too many customers and an overbooking situation.

-Overbooking
Despite what has just been stated, overbooking is usually seen as an important, if not essential component of YM application. However, overbooking levels are not left to chance but are carefully predicted on a probabilistic basis as part of the forecasting process. Predicted no-shows, cancellations and denials all form part of the calculation. In this way, the service provider may maximise uptake of the service, with a minimised risk of disappointing a customer who has booked in advance.

-Information systems
As the reader will realise by now, effective management of information is essential for implementation of YM, whether a relatively simple paper-based system is used, or whether it is one of the highly complex computerised airline systems. The use of information technology can help greatly in the sorting and data manipulation required. The use of artificial intelligence (AI) based systems have great potential for helping to cope with the complexity because AI can be used for problem solving, learning to perceive, reason, plan and analyse extensive data sets. Expert Systems (ES) are knowledge based software packages that can reflect the expertise in a given area of application [10]. One of the useful characteristics of ES is that they can manipulate non-numerical, qualitative data. Operational researchers are presently making considerable advances in their use.

Boundaries

There have been some concerns expressed over the global applicability of YM to all capacity constrained service industries [5, 11]. Although the airline, hotel, rail transportation industries for example, all share some common features, they are patently not the same. It could therefore be counter-productive for organisations in one industry sector to follow directly the YM practices implemented in a different sector. Each service industry sector must then analyse for itself what are its own unique characteristics, then identify which tools and techniques of YM may be used and how. These differences could be thought of as industry boundaries and some of these are set out below:

-Multiple units of inventory

In TV advertising, the rate will vary according to the number of time slots purchased, the schedule, the demand of that time slot and the time of day. With hotels, guests can arrive on a low rate and stay through a number of high rate days. This obviously leads to a problem with determining the right rate to charge the customer for the unit of inventory, when using multiple units. Many of these industries [6] (have a different unit of inventory based upon pricing and duration. Prices can be fixed (one price for the same service for all customers for all times) or variable different process for different times or different customer segments). Duration can be predictable or unpredictable.

-Multiplier effect

If an hotelier concentrates solely on the optimising the revenue to be generated from room sales then s/he may miss the revenue that could be generated from the other departments such as restaurants, conferences, leisure facilities etc. It is thus important that an integrated YM system is used. In the case of the tour operator there is similar complexity in that the package is a multiple packaged product. Concentrating only on maximising sale of air tickets and hotel rooms leaves out a number of important revenue generators such as car hire and sight-seeing visits.

-Rate structure

A YM approach will lead to the development of a range of prices for the products and services an organisation provides. Such a pricing structure may lead to consumer confusion and may also lead to frustration and alienation. In the case of the airline industry, this multiple pricing policy, whilst not understood, is generally accepted by the consumer. However, in the hotel industry, where YM has been practised for a shorter time period and is less globally used, the degree of acceptance is less. In the case of rail transportation, fare pricing is generally perceived by the public as muddled and perplexing [12]. It is probable that YM is seen by consumers as unfair, if not downright unethical. However, from the viewpoint of the users of YM there are some good arguments that could be posited for benefits deriving the consumer.

-Information distribution

The ability to make YM decisions is dependant upon accurate, reliable and timely information. Thus the management, gathering and distribution of this information is essential. Any yield manager must be fully aware and up to date with the available inventory s/he is selling and must be sure that the information provides a true reflection of status at any given time. The type of information and the use that is made of it will vary from industry sector to industry sector.

-Market segmentation
It has already been noted that one of the key characteristics of the use of YM is the need for a segmental market. The basis for this segmentation will vary between service industry sectors and will need customisation. Indeed in the hotel industry, for example, there will be variations in segmentation within the industry.

Modelling yield management systems.

One of the characteristic approaches of operational research is the building and use of models of systems. To this end Yeoman and Watson [13], have developed a systems model of yield management activity and this is presented in Figure 1 below. This model presents three activities of management: *Forecasting, People and Strategy.*

-Forecasting
The ability to forecast accurately is an essential prerequisite of YM [2, 14]. This means that users of YM must know the characteristics of their consumers in detail and in effect, producing a model of those consumers. Cross [2] states that YM is about the ability to make decisions based upon knowledge, not feelings. Forecasting is thus an essential element of YM that allows users to predict consumer behaviour, based on statistical principles. The better the ability to forecast accurately, the better business decisions are made and profit may be optimised. Such accurate and reliable forecasts will provide a rational view of any given market. Forecasting for YM requires account to be taken of all relevant factors for any given industry sector and occasion. To forecast in complex situations such as airline routes, normally requires use of information technology, as it is not humanly possible to compute the large volumes of multivariate data in the

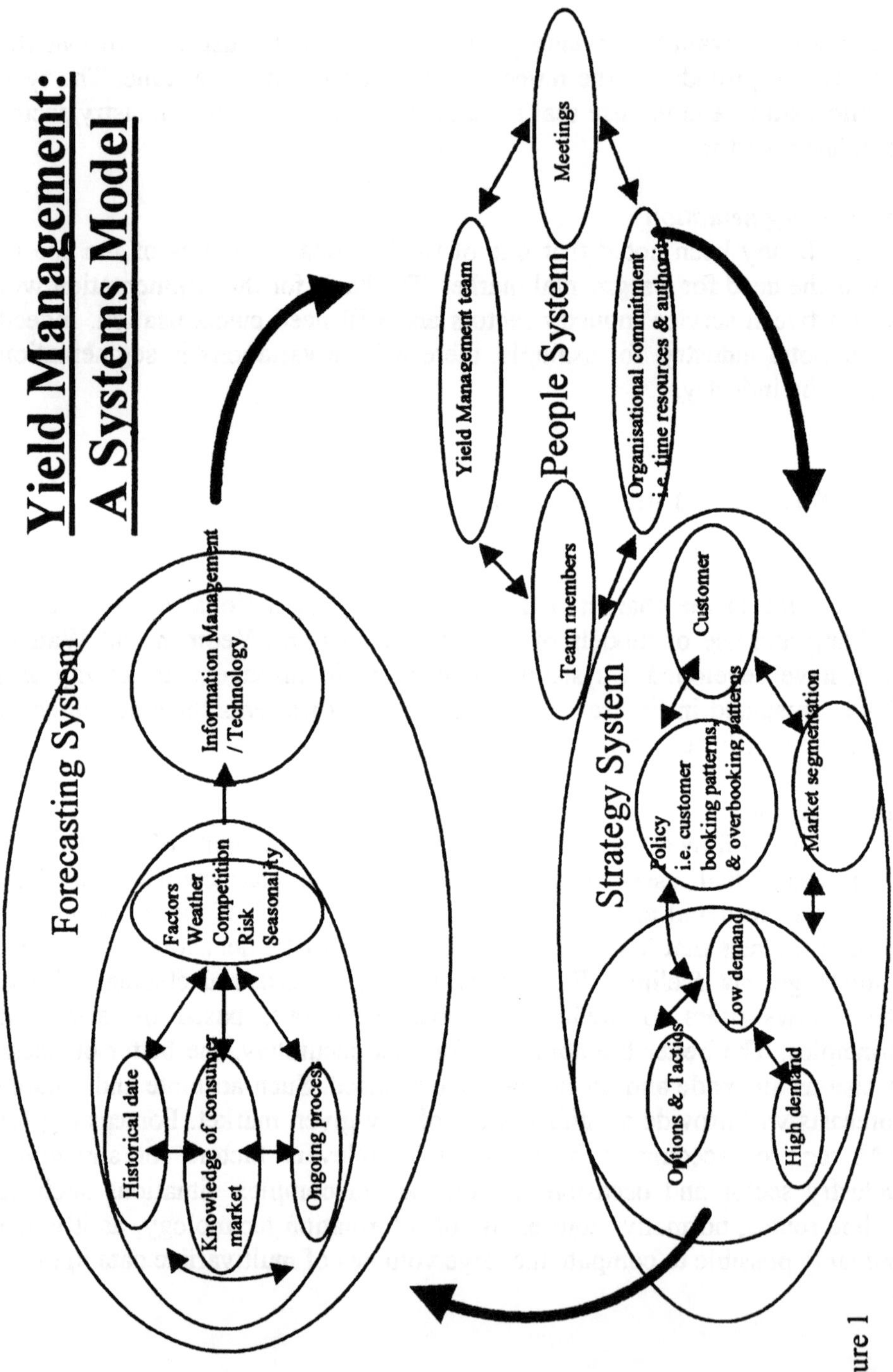

Yield Management:
A Systems Model
Forecasting System
Historical date
Knowledge of consumer market
Ongoing process
Factors
Weather
Competition
Risk
Seasonality
Information Management / Technology
People System
Yield Management team
Meetings
Team members
Organisational commitment i.e. time resources & authority
Strategy System
Customer
Policy i.e. customer booking patterns, & overbooking patterns
Market segmentation
Options & Tactics
Low demand
High demand

Figure 1

time-scale needed, for example processing one year of historical data overnight. However, YM is still a decision support system and data is presented that allows a yield manager to make probability based decisions.

The scientific basis of YM is drawn from an operational research base. This 'engine' underpinning YM thus allows the yield manager to concentrate on making the decisions rather than processing the data. The YM forecasting system is an iterative process, as Cross [2] states, YM is about "forecasting, reforecasting, reforecasting....".

-Strategy

Clear guidelines need to set out as to how a market is to be segmented. An evaluation of the customer purchasing behaviour is needed, in terms of the customers' needs and their willingness to pay [15]. The information that derives from the forecasting engine needs to be evaluated from the viewpoint of a range of possible options and tactics. These scenarios then need to be assessed for their potential effect on profit. An example of this might be to assess the effect of segmentation and pricing in high and low demand situations. These scenarios are usually modelled in computer simulation situations to quantify their effects prior to their application. An example of this is MERLIN, a modelling engine developed by Hood [16]. According to Cross [2], simulation in a YM context is about revenue, costs, displacement and profit. The process allows assessment of risk without actualising that risk, and many or perhaps all possibilities of a scenario may be taken into account. The modelling process can be said to be a keystone of good OR practice and it is the OR community that has developed the algorithms, systems and processes on which good yield decisions are based.

-People

At the bottom line the management of yield is a human activity. Whilst the YM engine and sub-systems produce the information and options from which to choose, it is the yield manager who ultimately makes the decisions and is accountable for the result. In a similar way to implementing a total quality improvement (TQI) strategy, implementing YM requires management commitment and a team approach. The functioning of the YM team must be understood and appreciated by other teams, e.g. sales and marketing, with whom they function in parallel. The YM team leader must have authority, must be respected and must believe in and understand YM. In the TQI scenario, such a person is often called a champion. The YM team then must be recognised to have responsibility, accountability and authority to manage yield, they are responsibility for the implementation of policy, decisions and tactics to manage and optimise yield, but the other teams must recognise their importance if the strategy is to work.

The systems model of YM [13] shown in Figure 1, presents YM in an holistic manner, where the sub-systems of forecasting, strategy and people present the interrelationships and dimensions of YM. Each sub-system has mutual interflows, and no one sub-system is more important than another. The model shows that all three are interdependent and in effect, synergistic. YM cannot function if any of the sub-systems are missing or weak and it is suggested that organisations should think of YM holistically.

The contribution of or to YM

Figure 1 shows, as has been discussed earlier, that OR has provided a fundamental foundation for YM. OR has made a significant contribution to the development of YM systems for capacity constrained service sector organisations by providing the mathematical tools and a modelling mechanism for development and testing. Cross [2] comments that "Operational research is the rocket science behind yield management".

The airline industry has been at the leading edge of the development and application of OR for YM. It is generally considered that YM was first developed by American Airlines, growing out of their CRS research and their SABRE development team. This was later spun off as Aeronomics Corporation. In the UK today British Airways has one of the largest and most active OR teams developing YM systems. Over the years a number of OR tools have been applied to yielding operations, from simple rule-based heuristics to sophisticated and multidimensional mathematical programming techniques. Most major airlines now use highly complex algorithms to aid with YM decisions. YM has been credited with improving profit margins on a very large scale, in some cases these could even be termed spectacular. For example Cross [2] records that YM contributed \$500 million annually to American Airline's profits, \$100 million to Marriott hotel group and in the case of National Car Rentals in the USA, YM is credited with turning the company around from imminent bankruptcy to a profitable and high growth organisation.

Raeside [14] categorised the quantitative approaches used for YM across a spectrum of service industry sectors:

-Mathematical programming
This approach is stated to be best for static situations and it is not well suited for dynamic situations where there is a continual inflow of information into the system, requiring constant updating. For example, linear programming may be used for the allocation of resources to different rate classes, such as aircraft seat classes or hotel room grades. However, Raeside [14] notes that studies into optimisation of airline booking systems have used dynamic programming and network models [17, 18, 19]. Williamson and Belobaba [20] have made use of greedy algorithms to allow virtual nesting of bookings in which the value of each fare depends upon the overall ticket revenue.

-Marginal revenue approach
This helps a yield manager to decide how many inventory units to sell at discounted rates and how many to keep for full-price customers. The method may also help to solve the problem of decision making in respect of overbooking levels. Pfeifer [21], Brumelle *et al* [22] and Bodily and Weatherford [23] advocate the use of simple decision rules to maximise profit in marginal revenue approaches.

-Threshold curves
The construction of threshold curves is based largely on historical data, experience and observation. The curve should show how units of inventory offered at discounted prices are shut out as the date of use gets nearer. This is a relatively simple method which is available to be used by even small organisations. The method can be paper based and has been used by airlines [24] and hotels [25]. The method is reliant upon accurate data, intelligent forecasting and continuous updating of the curve (on a daily basis), thus it may be very time-intensive. Applying this method an hotel will use its segmented demand forecasts to determine the optimal mix of guests for any given day.

Contribution of operational research: Practitioners viewpoints

Effective use of YM forecasting, optimisation and reservations control tools has commonly been associated with increases in total airline revenues of *two to five percent. Given that these revenue increases are realised with relatively low incremental costs, primarily those associated with yield management systems, development and operation. Most of the benefit of YM goes directly to airline operating profits. For a medium to large international airline, the annual revenue benefits attributed to even the most basic tools of overbooking and discount seat allocation can easily exceed US $100 million. The successful development and implementation of more accurate demand forecasting, network optimisation, and advanced origin-destination YM systems has the potential to provide further substantial increases in airline revenues.*

The importance of good yield management to airline profitability is clear. Since most airlines struggle to achieve operating profits much in excess of US $100 million even in the best of years, it could well be argued that, without YM, many airlines would not be able to turn a profit, and the profits of the strongest airlines could easily by reduced by half. Of course, this could also be said about many other aspects of airline management, including scheduling, route development, and capacity planning.

But that's the point - effective YM is critical to airline profitability, but it is not the sole answer to an unprofitable airline's problems. Even the best YM technology available cannot come close to overcoming the negative impacts of poor fleet planning and scheduling decisions, bloated cost structures, or simply bad airline management.

Professor Peter Belobaba
Principal Research Scientist,
Department of Aeronautics and Astronautics, USA
MIT University, USA
July 1997

In an industry without a track record of YM ,OR has a key role to play at every stage from feasibility and design to prototyping and implementation. There are several well researched factors required for YM to work successfully. In addition to the 'hard' conditions there are several 'softer' factors which affect the overall commercial success of the system. OR's expertise in data and forecasting has been crucial in identifying suitability of existing data and how to improve it. Finding a new use for old data is a good way of finding out what's wrong with it. Good YM depends on good forecasting which in turn depends on good data.

Introducing YM to an organisation inevitably means changing the way they do business. For YM to work there needs to be a physical and cultural change at the point of decision whether to accept or reject custom. OR has been involved here by project planning, process design and prototyping ideas and systems.

Finally OR's knowledge has been useful to evaluate results to (hopefully) ensure that the business gains maximum commercial benefit.

Matt Biglin
British Airways World Cargo
UK
March 1998

The importance of the Yield Management (YM) system to airlines cannot be overstated. In an industry with historically low margins, YM increases returns significantly. The YM system often makes the difference between a profitable flight and an unprofitable one.

YM systems control the sale of the seat inventory for the airline. Coincidence of consumer wants leads to heavy peaking and a need to efficiently allocate seats. The YM system allows filling of low demand flights with low fares while protecting seats for higher fare customers when demand is high providing flexibility in all demand situations. Peak load pricing can be approximated using YM through a market clearing mix of passenger types effectively "smoothing" realised demand for air transport.

Overbooking allows a more efficient use of seat inventory with fewer seats flying empty. Overbooking contributes greatly to airline profitability, especially when faced with double digit no show percentages by making full use of airline output.

Yield Management also mitigates the impacts of poor short, medium, and long term results from different functions within the airline. Poor market prices, fleet assignment, and fleet composition can be made less damaging through YM seat inventory controls. Furthermore, airlines realise greater returns with YM since the revenue from a "market clearing" price achievable through YM exceeds that in any single fare environment.

Theodore C. Botimer, Ph.D.
Continental Airlines, Inc. USA
January 1998

Yield Management is the science of micromanaging product supply to match the product demand at the same level to generate incremental revenues. Originally started in the airline industry, it is a practice which has found uses in industries ranging from car rentals, hotels, cruise, railroads, shipping to the entertainment industry.

> *"Yield Management has been so successful financially that it has become an article of faith in the airline industry, and is being copied by other marketers of perishable goods and services ranging from car rental concerns to utilities to broadcasters.*
> *...it is the single most important technological improvement in airline management in the last decade." - The New York Times, April 22, 1991.*

Since early 1994, a lot of companies in the aforementioned industries have started combining their pricing and yield management functions into Revenue Management (the terms Yield Management and Revenue Management are being used interchangeably since). As opposed to yield management being a reactive tactic to segment pricing, revenue management utilises demand forecasts to feed pricing as well as yield management strategies. Revenue Management is the art of selling the right product to the right customer at the right time for the right price. Or more technically stated: Revenue Management is the art and science of predicting real-time customer demand at micromarket-level and optimising the price and availability of the product. The Wall Street Journal recently described Revenue Management as a business strategy "poised to explode".

Revenue Management begins with forecasting demand for a product at a micro segment level. Users of Revenue Management segment their products based on the peculiarity of the customer demands. For example the airline industry segments travellers into business and leisure categories. Car-rentals and hotel chains segment into weekday/weekends or length-of-stay or standard versus deluxe products. Based on the demand forecast for each of these segments, a certain number of units of the product (for example seats on a flight) are made available to each of these segments that maximises overall revenue and product utilisation. The perishable nature of the goods involved precludes having clearance sales after the fact. In a lot of these industries the most valuable "business" customers tend to demand the product at the last minute and saving the right quantity of the product for them is one of the key concepts of revenue management. Another aspect of yield management is overbooking to account for expected wastage of the product.

Through offering numerous fare classes with varying travel restrictions for the same flight, the airline industry generates upward of $1B. in incremental revenue from revenue management strategies. Car rentals, hotel chains and opera houses offer different prices for different days of the week or different seasons or different times of the day and limit the availability within each price-segment to generate additional revenues estimated in the range of 1-10% using revenue management tactics.

A.Khandelwal
United Airlines, USA
17th December 1997

CONCLUSION

YM is a holistic approach to service organisations constrained by capacity. These constrained service organisations have a degree of commonality i.e. perishability, fixed capacity, high fixed costs and a unit of inventory that involves a period of time. To manage these characteristics, YM is a proven method that encompasses all of these details. YM is a process that involves making accurate decisions in a holistic manner, involving the sub-systems of people, forecasting and strategy. The modelling of elements from that sub-system, involves the contribution of Operational Research. Operational Research is a natural base in which YM can develop and improve through the foundation principles of OR. In particular hospitality, tourism and transport is benefiting from the rocket science approach to solving problems that OR makes.

REFERENCES

[1] Schmenner, R.W. *Service Operations Management*. Prentice Hall. Englewood Cliffs, New Jersey, 1995.

[2] Cross, R.G. *Revenue Management: Hard-Core Tactics for Market Domination*. Orion Business Books, London, 1997.

[3] Kimes, S. Yield management: An overview. In *Yield Management: Strategies for the Service Industries*. (I. Yeoman. and A. Ingold Eds.) Cassell. London, 1997.

[4] Ingold, A. & Huyton, J. Yield management and the airline industry. In *Yield Management: Strategies for the service industries*. (I. Yeoman. and A. Ingold Eds.) Cassell. London, 1997.

[5] Donaghy, K., McMahan-Beattie, U. & McDowell, D. Yield management practices. In *Yield Management: Strategies for the Service industries*. (I. Yeoman. and A. Ingold Eds.) Cassell. London, 1997.

[6] Kimes, S. E. & Chase, R. B. The strategic levers of yield management. *Journal of Service Research*. 1 156-166, 1998.

[7] Ingold, A. & Huyton, J. Yield management and the airline industry. Ingold, A. McMahon-Beattie, U & Yeoman, I. *Yield Management: Strategies for the Service Industries*. 2nd Edition. Cassell. London. (In press), 2000.

[8] Hartley ,J. & Rand, P. Conference sector capacity management. In *Yield Management: Strategies for the service industries*. (I. Yeoman. and A. Ingold Eds.) Cassell. London, 1997.

[9] Ingold, A. & Ho, R. Yield management in Hong Kong hotels. *Proceedings of the Third Annual International Conference on Yield Management*. University of Ulster, Northern Ireland, 1998.

[10] Russell, K. Expert systems. In *Yield Management: Strategies for the Service Industries*. (I. Yeoman. and A. Ingold Eds.) Cassell. London, 1997.

[11] Lee, D. & Johns, N. Yield management in hospitality SME's. *International Journal of Contemporary Hospitality*. 2/3. 66-69.

[12] Huyton J., Evans P. & Ingold, A. The ethics of yield management. *Proceedings of the First Annual International Conference on Yield Management.* Walton Hall, Birmingham, UK, 1997.

[13] Yeoman, I. & Watson, S. Yield management: A human activity system. *International Journal of Contemporary Hospitality Management* 2/3 80- 83, 1997.

[14] Raeside, R. Quantitative methods. In *Yield Management: Strategies for the service industries.* (I. Yeoman. and A. Ingold Eds.) Cassell. London, 1997.

[15] Huyton, J. & Peters, S. Application of yield management to the hotel industry. In *Yield Management: Strategies for the Service industries.* (I. Yeoman. and A. Ingold Eds.) Cassell. London, 1997.

[16] Hood, Merlin: Model to evaluate revenue management and loadings for Intercity. *Proceedings of the Second Annual International Conference on Yield Management. Held in Conjunction with the Operational Research Society 39th Annual Conference,* University of Bath, 1997.

[17] Rothestein, M. Hotel overbooking as a markovian sequential decision process. *Decision Sciences*, 5. 389-394, 1974.

[18] Boas ,J. S., Madsen, O. & Vidal, R. Booking policy for flights with two types of passengers. *European Journal of Operational Research*. 27, 278-288, 1986.

[19] Glover F., Glover, R., Lorenzo, J. & McMillan, C. The passenger-mix problem in the scheduled airlines, *Interfaces*. 58, 73-79, 1982.

[20] Williamson, E. L & Belobaba, P. P. Optimisation techniques for seat inventory control. *AGIFORS 28th Annual Symposium Proceedings*, 1988.

[21] Pfeifer, P. E. The airline discount fare allocation problem. *Decision Sciences,* 20. 149-157, 1989.

[22] Brummelle, S. L, Oum, J. I, Oum, T. H., Sawaki, K. & Tretheway, M. W. Allocation of airline seats between stochastically dependent demands. *Transportation science,* 24 183-192, 1990.

[23] Bodily, S. E. & Wetherford, L. R. 'Perishable-Asset revenue Management: generic and multiple-price yield management with Diversion. *Omega*. 23, 173-185, 1995.

[24] Huyton, J. & Ingold A. 'To yield or not to yield, that is the question.' *Proceedings of the Conference of the International Journal of Contemporary Hospitality Management*. University of Surrey, UK, 1990.

[25] Bradley, A. & Ingold, A. 'An investigation of yield management in Birmingham hotels'. *International Journal of Contemporary Hospitality Management.* 51, 13-16, 1993.

8

MANAGEMENT AND WELLBEING IN THE UK

Gillian Jack and Brian Lehaney
Centre for Knowledge Management,
University of Luton, UK

ABSTRACT

This chapter considers the increasing complexity of internal and external influences on organisational management and behaviour, with a specific focus on poor communications within the psychosocial working environment. It is argued that different management approaches impact in different ways on the wellbeing of the workforce and ultimately on levels of performance. As a consequence, some organisations may need to address their management styles and communications strategies, before they are able to embrace the concepts of knowledge sharing and knowledge management in practice.

An empirical investigation of a higher education institution suggests that the management of change is a significant contributory factor to wellbeing and performance. Further exploration identified the impact that people have on organisational competitiveness and performance. Recommendations were made that could contribute to the development of an appropriate Human Resource Strategy and a participative and interactive change management model was developed. In particular, a good communications strategy was seen as vital, and such a strategy should, in today's environment, be geared towards knowledge sharing.

Keywords: management, strategy, human assets, occupational health, communications, mixed-mode modelling, systems.

M.G. Nicholls et al. (eds.),
Mixed-Mode Modelling: Mixing Methodologies for Organisational Intervention, 229–257.

INTRODUCTION

Organisations are becoming aware of the wider social and health issues that impact on profitability, quality, and attitudes of staff. Such awareness has been influenced by various factors, which include changes in society and culture, new management trends, and development in Government policies, [1]. The welfare and interests of the workforce have come to be regarded as strategically important, not through sentimentality or generosity, but simply because the quality and disposition of the workforce reflects directly on the performance of the organisation [2] and [3]. In addition, there has been a wider recognition that the nature of western economies has shifted permanently from manufacturing to services, where knowledge, rather than physical assets, is at a premium [4].

Recent Government policy, now focuses greater attention on human factors than in the past [5, 6, 7]. Such an emphasis reflects the view that "In the end, the location of the new economy is not in the technology ... It is in the human mind", Webber [8] (p27). In practice, however, such views and initiatives may have limited impacts. For example, many organisations such as universities, are operating in fast changing environments, striving for greater competitiveness, increased profitability, effectiveness, high performance etc, amidst an era of downsizing, efficiency gains, and smarter working.

Organisational pressures are sometimes contradictory, and it is difficult to motivate a workforce to embrace, or even to accept, new strategies, if they have fears about their job prospects. Such fears are major psychosocial factors, and these are defined by Fraser [9] as elements that affect attitude and productivity, and include managerial and workplace interrelations and communications. The Government and the Health and Safety Executive (Dobson and Jowell [5]) now consider psychosocial factors to be connected directly to motivation and performance, and such factors should be regarded as high priority issues to be dealt with by employers concerned to improve wellbeing.

The foregoing discussion is especially important in a post-industrial society and for service organisations within that society. The relevance of knowledge within such organisations has been recognised for many years, with, for example, Bell [10] arguing that: "Post-industrial society is organised around knowledge." It is taken as axiomatic here that a university is a knowledge-based organisation, and within western culture such organisations will be in post-industrial societies. Hence, both for internal and external purposes, knowledge sharing and knowledge management within a university is important to its success and competitive edge. If knowledge sharing is to occur, and if it is to be managed, it is self evident that for the former, communication is vital, and for the latter, policies, procedures, and strategies will play a key role if anything other than ad hoc communications is to be achieved.

This research incorporates a case study of a higher education institution, and draws on other empirical work within the area. The potential improvements in performance and effectiveness that may be achieved by appropriate management practices are considered. A review of the literature considers influences on organisations in relation to health and wellbeing, and discussions of policies and practices in the context of psychosocial factors and influences on communications within organisations are developed. A university was used as the case study to explore management approaches with a view to improving organisational wellbeing and strategic performance, and to suggest possible approaches for other similar organisations.

Research Design

The study was qualitatively based and as such, emergent problems arose, for example, influencing variables, including feelings and opinions, and access to factual data, to provide a clear and accurate picture. Gummesson, [11] (p120) describes a fact as "definite and permanent, independent of subjective interpretation and independent of paradigm", however, he states that in qualitative or quantitative research, business planning and forecasting, it is unlikely that true factual data can be achieved. In essence, there is no direct access to 'factual data', but only to individuals' and groups' interpretations of data, which they themselves have received as others' interpretations of data or personal perceptions of situations.

Triangulation provides a recognised and useful approach to reduce such ambiguity and increase credibility, for example by a mixed-mode modelling approach, as was the case in this investigation.

This investigation was undertaken using four different forms of triangulation:

- data triangulation, which involves the use of information, derived from a range of sources;
- method triangulation which is the use of multiple methods to solve a single problem;

- investigator triangulation, which requires several different researchers to interpret the same data thus avoiding personal bias, or alternatively, the use of an external auditor to review information and confirm its validity;
- theoretical triangulation, which is a multi-perspective such as anthropology, psychology, sociology etc to interpret the same data.

The foregoing is relevant generally and specifically when considering case studies and similar research in organisations. Bulmer [12] (p151) highlights that "organisations have a number of special features (with) the need for the researcher to establish a workable and convincing role in which to gather data by interview, observation, surveys etc." Equally relevant is the comment of Crompton and Jones [13] (p72) on 'Researching White Collar Organisations': "In organisational research, it is not a mutually exclusive decision between quantitative and qualitative methodology. In reality, it is very difficult to study organisations without using both sorts of methods".

This investigation meets the requirements of triangulation, incorporating data and method triangulation and to some extent the concept of investigator triangulation. Method triangulation involved semi-structured interviews, unstructured interviews, and meetings with internal staff and external experts. Secondary research contributed to the design of a health-related questionnaire and fieldwork conducted in the University of Luton. Additionally, opportunistic interviews with a variety of staff and people external to the university contributed to the richness of information.

Investigator triangulation includes secondary research such as the University of Luton Market and Opinion Research International Survey (MORI), Health and Safety Executive research, and Health Education Authority research. Use of expertise such as a Health and Safety Executive representative, the University Health and Safety Manager and an Occupational Health Professional, contributed during discussion of concepts and offered guidance in terms of accuracy and realism. Data triangulation included fieldwork based on the University of Luton as case study and includes the authors' own survey.

A diverse combination of literature, contributed to the study. The discussion about Health and Wellbeing drew on authors such as Kingdom [14], Doyal and Gough [15], and Abercrombie and Warde [16], which contribute a social and political focus, demonstrating how policy development in health provision has reached such an influential position in the business world.

Information regarding occupational health and wellbeing is derived from authors such as Stranks [3] and Ridley [17] in addition to secondary research relating to different occupational health models in other organisations. Government policy is drawn from Dobson and Jowell [5] and the Health and Safety Executive [13, 6, 7] which highlight immediate and future issues for organisations.

There are many and varied texts available to explore management, change and organisational behaviour, for example Mullins [1], Handy [19] and Carnall [20] discuss different aspects of behaviour, management and organisations. Buchanan and Huczynski [21] focus on organisational behaviour. Pugh's "Organisation Theory, Selected Readings" [22] is extensively used to review the development of management, and consider theories in relation to psychosocial factors, applying key theoretical approaches to modern day situations. Texts such as Johnson and Scholes [23], Pearce and Robson [24], Ansoff [25] and Bowman [26] are used to review strategic management, and Buchanan and Boddy [27] for change management.

Commentary literature has been derived from journals, newspapers and Internet sources. 'Occupational Health Today' and the Health and Safety Executive's newsletters emphasise current thinking about health in the workplace. Journals such as 'Management Today', 'Institute of Personnel Management' and 'Administrator', in addition to other similar commentary literature, although in some cases fairly anecdotal, still contribute to the learning process and provide balance between the theoretical perspective and practical application and to some extent reflect the 'worldview' on related issues. All literature is considered in the context of management and psychosocial factors, with consideration given to occupational health provision.

The literature and initial data collection combine to provide clarification of the wider issues, influencing the development of an appropriate investigative model, which serves to meet the aim and objectives and reflects a participative approach that embraces the varied issues that may arise in organisational research.

The model shown in Figure 1 highlights six key stages of investigation within which clusters of activity are undertaken:

A is the identification of a problem or idea and the initial intentions about how to progress, including the formulation of 'loose objectives';

B is the first stage of constructive research, which is undertaken through literature using a combination of sources. This, in conjunction with the author's background knowledge and experience, and qualitative research, is intended to increase understanding and knowledge;

C represents the stage when issues can be clarified and objectives 'tightened' or established, particularly in relation to empirical research;

D focuses on the methodology and design of empirical research, on the basis of new knowledge and is intended as part of the mixed-mode modelling approach;

E represents the collection, analysis and interpretation of primary data collection, which further clarifies the organisational problem, as well as contributing new views to the conceptual understanding; this is achieved by cross-referencing and comparing with previous data gathered; it is at this stage that the mixed-mode approach consolidates and the process of triangulation strengthens, as more information is actualised;

F concentrates on feasible and desirable change that can now be considered with more confidence, and a plan of action to improve the situation formulated.

The entire process is iterative, both overall and within each stage. In addition, cross-referencing from one stage to another is a natural expectation. Hypothetically, the model can be divided between the conceptual and empirical approaches to the investigation, identified by the 'division' through the centre. In keeping with SSM, this model maintains a traditional qualitative approach with an action-oriented outcome.

This investigation was qualitative and utilised action research, within which data, method, and investigator triangulation approaches were used to help develop confidence in the results. These are shown in Figure 1. In addition to primary data, information was obtained from a university Market and Opinion Research International Survey (MORI), a Ceridian work/life study, the Health and Safety Executive, and the Health Education Authority. Expert comments were given by a Health and Safety Executive representative, the university Health and Safety Manager, and an Occupational Health Professional, and this expertise contributed to accuracy and realism, and provided practical inputs to some theoretical concepts. Data triangulation included fieldwork based on the university as case study and involved semi-structured and unstructured interviews, and the authors' own survey. The overall design may be seen as a mixed-mode modelling approach Lehaney [28] and Lehaney, Clarke [29].

Health and Wellbeing

The health and welfare of the nation has remained on the political agenda for, in excess of 100 years, when according to Thane [30] (p3) and Ridley [17] (pp337-500), humanitarians were seeking a better working environment to improve health, wellbeing and social conditions. Developments throughout this time included the establishment of the National Health Service as a centrally controlled, interventionist initiative, on the premise that "health care was a right for all people and an obligation of the state", Abercrombie and Warde [16] (p369).

Certain principles were established, including the financing of health care from general taxes, and the Government was to own the organisation and to employ its staff (see Lehaney [31]). However, with regard to the Government's employment of staff, Thane [30] (p230 and p424) points out that discussion and development of the NHS involved "leading members of the medical profession ... doctors and nurses were directly employed and paid by the Government often at higher rates than they had experienced before". Kingdom [14] (p452) explains that one of the major results of the medical profession's involvement with policy makers to this extent was the definition of the health service as "a means of curing and healing, and largely excludes preventative functions of healthcare, which aim to eradicate environmental conditions damaging to health".

George and Wilding [32] (p183) support this argument further, stating that from a Green perspective, "medical professionals relied on providing medicine to address an isolated condition based on the illness rather than considering the individual's lifestyle, environment and social factors that might be causing the illness in the first place". George and Wilding [32] (p182) make the direct connection with work, proposing that to improve health, among other social issues, "accidents at work (should be) reduced and the emotional pressures of the work ethos taken care of".

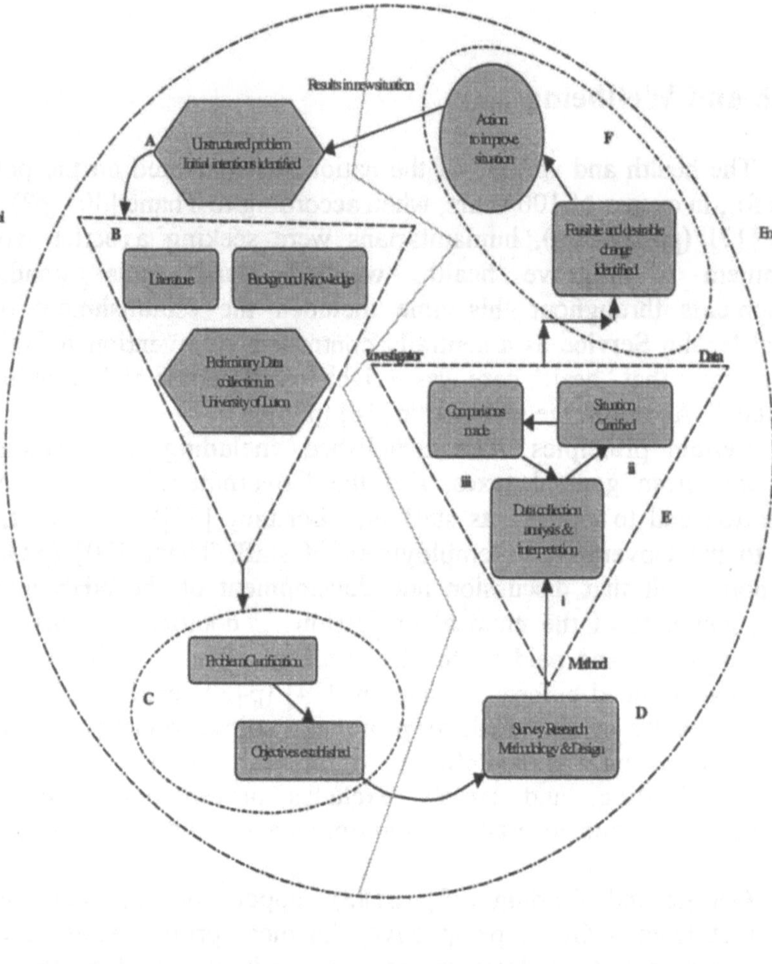

Figure 1. Framework for Investigation

From the 1960s to the early 1980s, a number of reports were commissioned regarding the running of the National Health Service. Sir Douglas Black (1980 in Kingdom [14]) conducted an investigation into the inequalities in health, revealing that many of the short comings related directly not to provision of medical care, but to unequal income, education, nutrition, housing and working conditions, as well as cultural differences, thus applying a sociological perspective. Ten years later this argument was still apparent as Doyal and Gough [15] (p202) stated when discussing human need: "There are direct hazards associated with the medicalisation of health problems – the use of the biomedical model to obscure the economic and political causes of ill health".

Doyal and Gough [15] explore issues relating to health and the work environment identifying three serious risks in the workplace:

a) excessive hours of work, which can physically and mentally exhaust people;
b) a hazardous work environment which can cause injury and disease, for example, exposure to chemicals, dust, noise etc;
c) forms of work that diminishes an individual's self-satisfaction and positive attitude. For example, "change management and consequent feeling of lack of control over job content can result in depression, anxiety and low self-esteem. In addition over work or underwork can undermine wellbeing" (Warr 1987, pp5-7 in Doyal and Gough [15] (p203)).

Considering this perspective and the current high cost of the National Health Service, i.e. approximately £23.3 billion of Government expenditure [31], it could be argued that today's Labour Government intends to address the sociological issues and concerns raised over the past 20 years by implementing preventive measures more forcefully, and devolving an element of responsibility to organisations via collaboration with the Health and Safety Executive. The Labour Government's green paper, "Our Healthier Nation" proposes such action in partnership with local organisations to improve the country's living conditions and health. This includes the health of the work force from an individual, social and economic perspective, with the expectation that "businesses can bring new skills to bear ... as well as improving the health and safety of their own employees", Dobson and Jowell [5] (p2).

With regard to individual cases, it is the Government's intention to ensure that people contribute full to working life. From a social perspective, the case is for equality in living standards, and from an economic perspective, Dobson and Jowell [5] (p6) state "to succeed in the modern world economy, the country's workforce must be healthy as well as highly skilled. The Confederation of British Industry has estimated that 187 million working days are lost each year because of sickness, a £12 billion social tax on businesses".

The responsibility on employers has increased incrementally and this trend is likely to continue. Government policy appears to gradually impact further on organisations, both directly from a health perspective and through employment legislation such as minimum wages and shorter working hours with more emphasis on quality of lifestyle. The Disability Discrimination Act (DDA 1996) places greater responsibility on employers to provide for those with disabilities or long-term sickness. Furthermore, through the new culture of partnerships in business between management and employees, it is the Government's intention to address problems of stress and insecurity in work [5] (p22). At an implementation level, the UK Health and Safety Executive (1997) report on research undertaken into workplace health, which reveal that the key risks to emerge requiring prioritisation are "psychosocial" [9] (p9).

Although health and safety management has been in operation for many years, the shift in emphasis is apparent as demonstrated in the foregoing. However, the increase in the amount of incidences where employees are taking employers to industrial tribunals, particularly with issues such as stress, leads one to assume that employers are not fully aware or co-operating. Alternatively, it could be that individuals are encouraged to take assertive action in what is increasingly becoming a litigious society. Wilson [34] (p1049) states " there are very few stress at work cases that go all the way to trial, many are settled, often subject to confidentiality clauses".

Occupational Health

In addition to litigation, commercial organisations appear to have become more vociferous in the marketing of 'Employee Assistance Programmes' or similar occupational health type services. For example, the 'Lancaster Stress and Counselling Services' advertise their ability to reduce problems that organisations may be experiencing in relation to workforce stress and associated sickness absence. (The Lancaster Group 1997). Current debate in the profession of occupational health, however, questions the benefit of such a service in reducing sickness absence and improving performance and effectiveness to both the satisfactions of the employer and the employees. This is explored further when focussing specifically on occupational health.

Occupational health in the workplace predates 1848 when the Public Health Act was introduced. Thane [30] (p40) and Waldron [35] (pp6-16) regard this as being the first act of Government social intervention and as Waldron states "marked the establishment of the Welfare State". During and following the Second World War, developments in health and safety accelerated, which can be demonstrated by examples of the various legislation and events that occurred [3, 17, 35]. In 1948, two years after the establishment of the National Health Service, the first doctors were appointed specifically to monitor and advise on work related health. Ridley [17] (p323) states that eventually, by 1972, it was recognised that this system was too limited to deal with other emerging factors regarding health and safety in the workplace. It was replaced, therefore, by the Employment Medical Advisory Service, followed by the Health and Safety at Work Act in 1974. The Employment Medical Advisory Service was formed to give advice to "employers, employees, trade unions and others on medical matters related to work".

Waldron [35] (p8) raises a similar argument in relation to occupational health, stating that "medical intelligence ... from the testimony of individual physicians, had an early influence on the development of health and safety measures", indicating a rather reactive treatment service, as opposed to a holistic preventative service. Although organisational wellbeing received attention to varying degrees, the use of terminology and emphasis is clearly placed on physical aspects and hazards. Ridley [17] (p325), for example, states "the main hazards are of three kinds, physical, chemical and biological, although occupational psychological factors may also cause illness". This statement demonstrates the lesser emphasis that psychosocial factors attracted at the time of writing, whereas these factors are increasingly becoming more dominant.

The provision of occupational health requires a different approach depending on the nature of the organisation and the people within the organisation. Waldron [35] (p16) supports this by describing the organisation's "personality, behavioural problems and state of health". For example, manufacturing industries appear to have special requirements according to the production process, the emphasis being placed on chemicals used, machinery etc. Acting on this principle, therefore, it suggests that service organisations, with a particular focus on human interaction will have special requirements according to the process employed to deliver the service.

The most significant differences between service-oriented organisations and manufacturers relate to use of occupational health and emphasis placed on a particular aspect, for example, psychological factors feature heavily in service organisations with greater use of counselling services and stress management. A common perspective derived during primary research is that these services should operate in a pro-active and more strategic way to be beneficial, otherwise it will become a reactive treatment service, which, although positive and supportive of individuals does not address the broader cross-organisational and human resource issues.

Gardner and Taylor [36] (p20) state that the overall principle of occupational health is the "maintenance and care of healthy people in the working environment rather than the care of people when they are ill. The objectives and responsibilities of an occupational health department can only be as good or limited as the company policy allows". This could be viewed as a simplistic and narrow statement; as although a company may wish to invest in a comprehensive proactive and preventative service, similar to many activities beyond the core business of organisations, cost is usually an obstacle. Chrissie Owens [37] (p1), an occupational health professional, highlights the fact that "the absence of a tangible business case for occupational health and the perception that it is nice to have" is a major obstruction to development. She continues by describing "the growth of risk management and litigation, which provide evidence to change this situation".

Consolidating these ideas, and in the current 'climate', following recent Government policy [41] as well as increasing media exposure, one could infer that wellbeing will become a major issue in organisations, perhaps rising up the management agenda to a strategic level, if not already the case. Sinead Stewart [38] (p2-3) a practitioner with Leicestershire Occupational Health Service, reports that media hype has led to employers identifying occupational health as being the answer to performance and effectiveness in organisations. Stewart argues, however, that occupational health is not the solution to "costly sickness absence problems". She explains that the role of occupational health in the reduction of absenteeism is "ill defined ... literature dating as far back as Taylor, identifies that a multidisciplinary approach is essential to effective management", therefore an effective organisation.

In contrast to this view, the Director of the British Occupational Health Foundation, Michael Landenburg, advocates that occupational health can help reduce absenteeism and maintain the health of the workforce in a proactive way. Landenburg [39] (p2) states "the success of any commercial enterprise clearly depends on the health and consequently the productivity, of its employees. This in turn depends upon ... avoiding or at least minimising work related ill health". Landenburg continues by describing the UK's integration in the European continental market and competition in the world economy. He suggests that it is necessary for businesses to maximise on productivity and economies consistent with good quality, a key aspect of which is the reduction of huge costs due to work related ill health.

Recent surveys highlight that over two million people are suffering from illness they thought was caused by work [10] (p11). There is no information, however, that identifies specific types of work or sectors of employment. It is also difficult to establish an undeniable correlation between ill health and work, as lifestyle outside the workplace will obviously be a contributory factor. More current research, however, conducted by the Health and Safety Executive, Occupational Health Strategy Group [41] provides an indication of future trends and expectations on organisations and managers in terms of new policy, which is targeted for implementation in Spring 2000.

The following points are highlighted for consideration in the context of this investigation:

a) when referring to the meaning of occupational health, concerns have been raised about the need to emphasise mental as well as physical health, to treat all elements equally, and to emphasise that ill health is best tackled by multi-disciplinary teams;
b) the future vision for occupational health should: embrace the positive contribution that work can have for health; address the effect of health on work, as well as the effect of work on health; provide for health in the workplace not just the prevention of ill health; include the effects of work on society;
c) the future trend of health related issues include casualisation of the workforce, increase in homeworking, litigation, stress and back pain due to changing nature of work;
d) with regard to systems and procedures, there is an emerging desire for greater enforcement on health issues as much as safety systems and support for larger financial penalties and longer prison sentences. It is recommended that managers

should have statutory responsibility and accountability and better partnership working with employees, therefore more training for managers on health issues including monitoring and evaluation of health. Additional proposals include systems such as self-reporting of accidents, sickness absence and work related ill health to trigger investigations and take action. Areas mentioned most frequently and of greatest concern that need improvements include stress and mental health;

e) better systems need to be established to get information into small to medium sized companies e.g. by using locally based contacts including universities;

f) GPs were seen as increasingly crucial, as the first point of contact with workers who are ill from work, but concerns have been expressed about their lack of awareness and training to recognise the links of ill health with work.

It remains questionable as to whether or not the provision of occupational health in the future can or can not either reduce sickness absence or improve performance. There appears, however, to be little doubt from the Government [42], and leading management theorists e.g. Peters and Waterman [2] that the active care of employees, delivered through appropriate management approaches, will improve performance and productivity, as well as minimise the financial risks of litigation and subsequent compensation payments. Management is discussed in more detail next, with an introduction to the theory of management, setting in context theory and practice as well as highlighting the associated impact on wellbeing.

Models of Management

Government policy, in conjunction with the Health and Safety Executive [42], appears to be devolving responsibility, to introduce a preventative model of care, based on individual, social, and economic perspectives, of which businesses are regarded as key players. The Health and Safety Executive Occupational Health Strategy Group [41] indicated that organisations may be placed under greater pressure to make provision for wellbeing. However, in some 'modern' organisations the ethos of a classical management approach is still apparent and potentially affects wellbeing and performance [43, 44, 45].

The Classical or Scientific approach to management is characterised by:

a) rational and coherent systems;
b) vertical work structures with specific objectives designed to improve productivity and performance;
c) scientific selection and systematic training of the workforce on the premise that people are motivated purely by money;
d) scientific organisation of work, differentiating between management and the workforce introducing a formal hierarchical structure;

(Taylor 1947 in Pugh [22] (p 205)).

The intention of the classical school of thought was to introduce greater control through systems, structures and training, and was based on the power of knowledge to implement an authoritative management approach. For example, Burns [46] (p13) referring to classical management states that "once the knowledge is ... possessed by managers, it becomes possible not only to establish what workers actually do with their time, but also ... how they carry out a given task".

The above is despite progressive management theory, shifts in society, changing working patterns and greater demands of the workforce requiring a new social approach to management, which proposes that people are assets that should be nurtured. For example, the emergence of the Human Relations approach to management and in particular the Hawthorne experiments, moved thinking forward in relation to psychosocial factors. This approach considers people and social factors at work, as much as tasks, and demonstrated the need for employees to be able to discuss issues indirectly associated with work, as well as issues directly relevant to work (Mayo 1949, in Pugh, [22] (pp350-351)).

Important progression was made as a result of the Hawthorne experiments including "new ideas concerning the importance of work groups and leadership, communications, output restrictions, motivation and job design" Mullins [1] (p52). Modern features of organisations, however, include "secondments", "vertical team working", "core" and "peripheral" staffing, "homeworking", all of which erode membership of a specific group and to some extent communication and motivation, and can result in knowledge migration.

Managers need to remain aware of the complexity of activities that reflect modern organisations, and to some extent the Systems and Contingency approach to management helps enable such awareness. This theoretical perspective recognises diversity and influences on organisations.

Buchanan and Huczynski [21] (p453) define the Systems and Contingency approach as being an attempt to "... understand the multi-variate relationships between components of organisations and to designing structures piece by piece as best fits the components (with) each situation analysed separately. Systems and Contingency implies that within the same organisation there may be units of bureaucracy, units operating in a matrix structure and units which are divisionalised". The Systems and Contingency approach is especially relevant to knowledge management, since it recognises and addresses explicitly the understanding and appreciation of internal and external influences, structural diversity, organisational, dominant and sub-cultures. In doing this, it highlights the complexity of issues surrounding the management of tacit and explicit knowledge.

The evolution of management theory tends to reflect social and environmental changes, including Government policy and business competitiveness and, more recently, social issues in organisations have become more dominant. Part of the most recent shift relates to social responsibility. Clarke and Clegg [47] (p33) expand on this when discussing changing paradigms in management, and they suggest that changes come in waves with various theorists introducing their own perspectives: "... the growth of new social interests in the environment becomes reflected in new relationships with the environment, with groups representing it ... customers, suppliers and other stakeholders". These social interests and environmental relationships imply that tacit and explicit knowledge is a major factor in new wave management. The management of such knowledge is therefore also of importance, but whilst knowledge management is implicit in the above, it has now emerged as a discipline in its own right, and extends far beyond the concept of social interests and relationships with the environment.

Clarke and Clegg [47] consider the shifts in society that influence organisations, with one significant factor being increased levels of education of the workforce. This reflects the previously discussed view that people are assets that should be nurtured. However, a recent Ceridian work/life study [48] highlighted the stress senior managers experience that can affect their ability to nurture, to motivate, to increase performance and to maintain wellbeing of colleagues and the workforce. This could adversely affect managers' abilities to cultivate the appropriate environment for knowledge creativity and sharing.

The strategic importance of human assets is emphasised by Bowman [26], who surmises that to manage strategically requires the management of "... formal and informal power relationships between people, their attitudes to change, their values and beliefs, the culture of the organisation, the status of relationships and the morale of staff". This was demonstrated further using Porter's [49] "Value Chain Analysis" to exemplify the influence of the workforce on strategy. In higher educational institutions, the value of people and expertise coming into the organisation, the value that students place on the quality of delivery and the value that employers place on the student they might recruit as the final 'product', represent overall competitive performance. It follows therefore, that the motivation and wellbeing of human assets, who deliver the entire process, cannot be considered simply at an operational level, but must be considered at a strategic level, and strategic wellbeing is key to organisational success, knowledge creation and sharing at each link of the value chain.

The Case Background

The case organisation has undergone radical change throughout the past nine years, with greater pressures being placed on the workforce. For example, academic staff were pressed to increase quality and quantity of research, consultancy and publications, whilst facing new approaches to the assessment of course provision. The university had the dual pressures of trying to enhance corporate performance and attract income during a time when costs had to be considered very carefully.

The start of the new era can be traced to the 1988 Education Reform Act, with a number of major changes to the sector occurring subsequently. A key factor was the transformation of what was previously a public sector organisation, into a market led business that would be required to consider customer demand, commercial financial management and high quality provision. Such transformation meant radical change and for many represented the erosion of traditional views of education as a public service.

As the organisation developed, and became a university in 1993, senior management considered that further change was required, and a flatter and highly delegated management structure was devised. Although the institution expanded and diversified rapidly, it was necessary to maintain standards of quality, and staff faced increasing pressures to improve performance. Furthermore, the speed at which change was necessary required clear lines of communication, accountability, responsibility and responsiveness. All of this was in the context of a large increase in student numbers, and a new modular, semester-based, teaching scheme.

A Quality Network introduced in 1991 stressed the importance of honesty, trust, respect, empowerment, consultation, teamwork and equal opportunities. However, not all staff had the opportunity to engage in these formal initiatives and peer/social support and informal communication was difficult to achieve in practice. Training and personnel development opportunities were limited because low staffing levels meant that opportunities of release to attend training sessions were at a premium.

Formal communication and participation in decision making was inadequate as was demonstrated in the MORI survey (1999). The results of the MORI survey provided an overview of staff attitudes in the university, revealing that the main issues of concern related largely to poor organisational communication. Management styles were considered classical in this respect, which, as indicated previously, involves managers actively choosing to retain knowledge because knowledge is power, whereas, human centred approaches actively advocate participation and involvement. If this is taken one step further, the knowledge management approach is that sharing knowledge results in corporate power.

Communication and therefore knowledge sharing repeatedly emerged as the common denominator in many different forms and was regarded as highest priority for staff if improvements were to be made. The concept of communication has many facets ranging between the formal and explicit to informal social interaction, and the provision of tools and facilities to enable effective communication to take place. Good communications are key to knowledge management and knowledge creation, and Nonaka and Takeuchi [50] (p3) describe organisational knowledge creation as "the capability of a company as a whole to create new knowledge, disseminate it throughout the organisation and embody it in products, services and systems".

Faced with the MORI results, the university recognised that it is unlikely to achieve effective knowledge creation and knowledge sharing whilst it is perceived by staff to use classical management methods, or at best a formal systematic approach. To improve this situation, there has been a new focus on management training, to create the right environment for human centred tacit and explicit knowledge management. It is anticipated that this could improve the resolution of issues that result from poor communications, and that it would look explicitly at improving communications so that such issues should be rare. In general, it is hoped to contribute to improving the psychosocial environment and wellbeing.

This could also be relevant when considering stress and job strain, for example, Karasek (1979), in Shaubroeck and Fink [51] (p140), discusses a "job demands – control model" asserting that "Job strain increases as job demand increases". If an employee's abilities match the demands of the job and they are empowered to deal with and solve associated problems, then a positive outcome will result. If, however, demands are high and control is low, high strain is maintained.

Johnson and Hall (1988), in Shaubroeck and Fink [51] (p171) introduce a newer model: "Demands – Control – Support" suggesting that "Social Support (buffers) the effects of demands in conditions of low control" therefore high demanding jobs, with both low control and low social support or interaction may result in high strain. To consider individual levels of stress, however, may not be feasible. Perhaps a culture that embraces knowledge sharing and reciprocal peer support could be more effective in reducing stress, particularly if the change that an organisation experiences is fast and radical.

Results

The return rate on the survey was 19%. "Time constraints" were given as the main reasons for non-response. In addition, many unopened envelopes were returned because the targeted member of staff had either left the university or had been relocated. It is interesting to note that post was returned rather than forwarded on, as this is an additional, unexpected, issue concerning communications.

Table 1 shows the breakdown of respondents by position in the organisation. Academics showed a particularly low level of response.

Table 1: Response Rate by Staff Category

Position	Number of Responses	Response Rate by Staff Category
Senior Management	3	3.2%
Middle Managers Supervisors	18	12.6%
Academic staff	18	18.9%
Administrators	46	48.2%
Manual Staff	2	2.1%
No stated position	8	8.4%
Total	95	100%

Table 2A shows responses to the statement "This organisation really cares about the health and wellbeing of staff", whilst Table 2B provides a breakdown of respondents by staff category.

Table 2A: This organisation really cares about the health and wellbeing of staff

Score	Statement	Responses
1	Strongly agree	-
2	Agree	18
3	Neither agree nor disagree	38
4	Disagree	23
5	Strongly disagree	13
Not Stated	Not stated	3
	Mean	4.3
	Median	4

Table 2B: Responses by staff category

Categories of Staff	Average Scores
Senior Management	2
Middle Management Supervisor	3.06
Academic	3.53
Administrator	3.32
Manual	4
Unknown	4

The single largest group (38) neither agreed nor disagreed with this statement. However, the mean score was 4.3, which suggests overall that there is a negative rather than positive view. The greatest deviation from the mean was, unsurprisingly, from Senior Management, who believe that the organisation cares about the health and wellbeing of staff. It could be assumed, therefore, that this was not communicated enough to staff, or senior management attitudes did not demonstrate their beliefs in practice. Considering the fast and radical change that the university has experienced this infers that management attitudes are perceived to engender the characteristics of the Classical approach. Supporting this inference further were the results of the MORI survey that confirmed the workforces' perception that the organisation is bureaucratic, demanding, and authoritarian.

Table 3A shows responses to the statement "My department manager talks to me and/or takes an interest in my general wellbeing", whilst Table 3B shows responses by staff category. The spread of responses to this statement was fairly evenly distributed with 40 in agreement, 34 in disagreement and 21 neither agreeing nor disagreeing. The mean score was 3.6.

Table 3A: My department manager talks to me and/or takes an interest in my general wellbeing

Score	Statement	Responses
1	Strongly agree	7
2	Agree	33
3	Neither agree nor disagree	21
4	Disagree	20
5	Strongly disagree	14
Not Stated	Not stated	-
	Mean	3.6
	Median	4

Table 3B: Responses by staff category

Categories of Staff	Average Scores
Senior Management	3
Middle Management Supervisor	2.39
Academic	2.83
Administrator	3.11
Manual	3
Unknown	4.25

Feedback received from one middle manager suggested that "The departmental manager does not have time to talk, or take an interest in general wellbeing, but he does care" (Administrator). This situation may indicate that levels of work for managers prevent them from taking time for staff, which can result in poor communications, demotivation, lack of leadership and poor performance.

Alternatively, there may be a case in relation to time management and making time for staff, but "in your face" pressures are difficult to remove from their position of precedence. On the issue of leadership, Peters and Waterman [2] (p83) state that the leaders who throw themselves into a relationship with followers can make the followers feel elevated, who then become more active themselves, thereby improving performance. Perhaps the most interesting result is that the largest disparity in scores occurs between senior managers and the management group immediately below them, with middle managers showing greater confidence than their superiors.

Table 4A shows responses to the statement "Management is not aware of rising stress or de-motivation in the workforce", whilst Table 4B

Table 4A: Management is not aware of rising stress or de-motivation in the workforce

Score	Statement	Responses
1	Strongly agree	27
2	Agree	32
3	Neither agree nor disagree	17
4	Disagree	10
5	Strongly disagree	7
Not Stated	Not stated	2
	Mean	2.1
	Median	2

Table 4B: Responses by staff category

Categories of Staff	Average Scores
Senior Management	4.33
Middle Management Supervisor	2.28
Academic	2.53
Administrator	2.09
Manual	2
Unknown	2.75

shows responses by staff category. This statement appeared to have made a significant impact with relatively few respondents remaining neutral and 59 respondents agreeing that management is not aware of rising stress or de-motivation, of which 27 strongly agreed. The mean score was 2.3. Significantly it is senior management that disagree most strongly, but the reasons for such disagreement are unclear.

Additional comments indicated that "Senior managers are aware of the problems but they are not high on the agenda so little attention is paid to health and wellbeing. Further, the pressures to perform and deliver means good health practices etc are put on the back burner" (Senior Manager). A Middle Manager stated that "The fault lies not with immediate managers, but with the system itself and therefore the decision-makers at the top. Staff no longer feel motivated". A glimpse at the responses by staff category in Table 4B suggests that there is a void between senior management perception and the perceptions of the workforce in general.

Table 5A shows responses to the statement "Senior management takes occupational health and wellbeing seriously", whilst Table 5B shows responses by staff category. The dominant division of responses to this statement was between those that remained neutral (37), and the 20 respondents who disagreed. Thirteen agreed. The mean score was 3.7, indicating that the workforce may not have agreed that senior management takes occupational health and wellbeing seriously. The largest split was between senior management who agreed that they do take health and wellbeing seriously, and manual workers, who disagreed. This could reflect poor communications, as, for example, additional feedback from the survey indicated that several respondents found this statement difficult to make a judgement against, because it is "specific to senior management views and there is little communication to suggest what that view might be" (Academic).

In general, many of the foregoing issues can be traced to problems of communications. Without understating possible issues of substance, it is important that these are dealt with, to ensure that there is some common understanding of procedures, policies, and university vision.

The university senior management has subsequently addressed many issues associated with stress and communications by establishing a human resource team, with new posts and appointments. The team's responsibilities include corporate team briefings, management development and training, and the redevelopment of a unified administration and structure. As part of this team, a new appointment was made, with the explicit responsibility to focus on cross-organisational working, knowledgesharing, and student and staff satisfaction. In addition, action is being taken to improve facilities to support informal communications and socialisation, introducing opportunities for informal peer support which will enhance the concept of corporate ownership and teamwork, whilst contributing to the wellbeing of staff.

Table 5A: Senior management takes occupational health and wellbeing seriously

Score	Statement	Responses
1	Strongly agree	-
2	Agree	13
3	Neither agree nor disagree	37
4	Disagree	20
5	Strongly disagree	15
Not Stated	Not stated	10
	Mean	3.7
	Median	4

Table 5B: Responses by staff category

Categories of Staff	Average Scores
Senior Management	2.67
Middle Management Supervisor	2.89
Academic	3.4
Administrator	3.46
Manual	4
Unknown	3.88

CONCLUSIONS

This investigation set out to explore management approaches based on a case study of a higher education institution. It focussed on wellbeing in the workplace and the potential improvements in performance that could be achieved through appropriate management practice. The process by which this was undertaken involved a review of external health oriented influences on organisations, analysis of theories of management compared to practice and an overview of strategic management. A university was used as a case study, which enabled the application of theoretical concepts to be applied to a real situation, from which knew knowledge and understanding emerged. The key points to emerge were as follows:

Managers may be placed under greater pressure to make provision for wellbeing in organisations which include all aspects of 'psychosocial factors', including efficient communication and interrelations.

Management practice appears to be developing at a slower rate than management theory. A Classical management approach is still apparent and potentially affecting wellbeing and performance both at an operational and strategic level. The Ceridian work/life study highlighted the stress senior managers are experiencing which can impact on the motivation, performance and wellbeing of colleagues and the workforce.

The background to the case study highlighted the radical change experienced over the past 10 years and the impact on staff. Change management was explored which revealed deficiencies and from this, in addition to the MORI survey and empirical research, the author elicited the following key issues relating to management and wellbeing:

- Appropriate training in relation to change management to include awareness and consideration for psychosocial issues that directly affect work, particularly for staff who work to unusual patterns.
- An appropriate strategic management process that recognises people as a community with a common objective, rather than an organisation may be effective.
- A strategy to improve knowledge sharing and communication will provide continuity and support to staff and shift power bases from individual and departmental level to corporate level. This may then cultivate a participative and interactive process, a sharing of and respect for both explicit and tacit knowledge.
- A suitable infrastructure that impacts on the culture and philosophy of the organisation, may have long term benefits in moving the organisation to a motivating, organised, caring and high performance environment that the workforce would prefer.

- Practical aspects such as resource allocation and methods for monitoring and evaluating are also of considerable importance both for credibility and continuous improvement.
- Monitoring of staff and student perceptions through student and staff satisfaction surveys, as well as qualitative feed back from personal observations, team briefings, review forms and informal social interaction.
- Consideration should be given to individual and group perceptions, which could be progressed using a human-centred model of change, however, the appropriate management skills to facilitate this process will be critical to its success.

The university senior management has addressed many of the above issues, and is considering ways to address the remaining ones. A new human resource team, with new posts and appointments, has been created, with particular responsibilities for corporate team briefings, management development and training, and the redevelopment of a unified administration and structure. Within this team, a new appointment has been made, with the explicit responsibility to focus on cross-organisational working, knowledge sharing, and student and staff satisfaction. In addition, action is being taken to improve facilities to support informal communications and socialisation, introducing opportunities for informal peer support which will enhance the concept of corporate ownership and teamwork, whilst contributing to the wellbeing of staff.

Most importantly, senior management have recognised the need for bottom up as well as top down communications. Formal and informal communications are recognised as being of importance, and surveys such as those discussed in this paper will continue.

REFERENCES

[1] Mullins, L. *Management and Organisational Behaviour*. London: Pitman, 1996.

[2] Peters, T & Waterman, R. *In Search of Excellent Companies.* London: Harper & Row, 1988.

[3] Stranks, J. *Management Systems for Safety*. London: Pitman, 1994.

[4] Stewart, T. Intellectual Capital. *The New Wealth of Organisations*. London: Nicholas Brealey, 1997.

[5] Dobson, F & Jowell, T. *Our Healthier Nation*. London: HMSO, 1998.

[6] Health & Safety Executive. *Developing an Occupational Health Strategy for Great Britain, Discussion Document*. London: HMSO, 1998a.

[7] Health and Safety Executive Behavioural and Social Sciences Research Group. *Mainstream Research News January, 3*,4-6, 1998b.

[8] Webber, A. What's So New About the New Economy? *Harvard Business Review*, Jan-Feb, pp24-32, 42-42, 1993.

[9] Fraser, T. M. *Human Stress, Work and Job Satisfaction*. International Labour Organisation, 1984.

[10] Bell, D. *The Coming of Post-Industrial Society*. London: Heinemann, 1973.

[11] Gummesson, E. *Qualitative Methods in Management Research*. London: Sage, 1991.

[12] Bulmer, M. *Doing Research in Organisations*, edited by Bryman A. London: Routledge, 1988.

[13] Crompton, R & Jones, G. *Researching White Collar Organisations*, 1988.

[14] Kingdom, J. *Government and Politics in Britain* London: Polity Press, 1991.

[15] Doyal, L. & Gough, I. *A Theory of Human Need* London: Macmillan, 1991.

[16] Abercrombie, N. & Warde, A. *Contemporary British Society* Cambridge: Polity Press, 1988.

[17] Ridley, J. *Occupational Health and Hygiene*, Safety at Work, 1994.

[18] Health & Safety Executive *Economic Impact of Health and Safety, Discussion Document*. London: HMSO, 1997.

[19] Handy, C. *Understanding Organisations* London: Penguin, 1993.

[20] Carnall, C. *Managing Change in an Organisation*. London: Prentice Hall, 1995.

[21] Buchanan, D. & Huczynski, A. *Organisational Behaviour*. London: Prentice Hall, 1991.

[22] Pugh, D.S. *Organisation Theory Selected Readings*. London: Penguin, 1990.

[23] Johnson, G. & Scholes, K. *Exploring Corporate Strategy*, London: Prentice Hall, 1993.

[24] Pearce & Robinson. *Strategic Management Formulation, Implementation and Control.* Boston: Irwin, 1991.

[25] Ansoff, H. *Corporate Strategy.* London: Penguin, 1996.

[26] Bowman, C. *The Essence of Strategic Management.* London: Prentice Hall, 1990.

[27] Buchanan, D. & Boddy, D. *The Expertise of the Change Agent.* London: Prentice Hall, 1992.

[28] Lehaney, B. Mixed-Mode Modelling. In *Operational Research Keynote Papers,* 1996. (D Johnson and F O'Brien, eds). Keynote paper in the Mixed-Mode Modelling Stream of OR38, the Annual Conference of the Operational Research Society, Warwick. pp 150-157, 1996.

[29] Lehaney, B. Soft Systems Methodology (and Simulation) for Mixed Mode Modelling? 1997. In *Operational Research Keynote Papers,* 1997. (F O'Brien and A Orman, eds). Keynote paper in the Mixed-Mode Modelling Stream of OR39, the Annual Conference of the Operational Research Society, Bath. pp 16-33 (with Steve Clarke).

[30] Thane, P. *Foundations of the Welfare State.* London: Longman, 1982.

[31] Lehaney, B. Simulation Modelling in Administration by Consensus Organisations. *Unpublished PhD Thesis. Brunel University,* 1999.

[32] George, V. & Wilding, P. *Welfare and Ideology.* London: Harvester Wheatsheaf, 1994.

[33] UK Health & Safety Executive. *Economic Impact of Health and Safety, Discussion Document.* London: HMSO, 1997.

[34] Wilson, P.J. Stress at Work *New Law Journal 9th July 1999*, pp1036-1048, 1999.

[35] Waldron, H.A. *Occupational Health Practice.* London: Butterworth Heinemann, 1989.

[36] Gardner and Taylor. *Health at Work.* London: Associated Business Programmes, 1975.

[37] Owens, C. *Occupational Health Today.* 4,1,1, 1996.

[38] Stewart, S. *Occupational Health Today,* 4,1.2,3, 1996.

[39] Landenburg, M. Introducing the New Director of the Foundation. *Health at Work, Autumn, 11,* 2-3, 1998.

[40] Bilbao. Questionnaire – Economic Impact of Occupational Health and Safety. *The European Agency for Safety and Health at Work. June,* 11, 1997.

[41] Health and Safety Executive, Occupational Health Strategy Group. *Developing an Occupational Health Strategy for Great Britain, Discussion Document,* London: HMSO, 1999.

[42] UK Health & Safety Executive. *Developing an Occupational Health Strategy for Great Britain, Discussion Document,* London: HMSO, 1998.

[43] Heller, R. A Nation of Half Time Workers. *Management Today,* August, 21, 1998.

[44] Mann, S. Give a Little Gain a Lot. *Professional Manager, 8,2,32,* 1999.

[45] Thomas, A. The World is your Office. *Management Today,* July, 79, 1999.

[46] Burns, B. *Managing Change* London: Pitman, 1992.

[47] Clarke, T. & Clegg, S. *Changing Paradigms, the Transformation of Management Knowledge for the 21st Century.* London: Harper Collins, 1998.

[48] Davis, E. Does Your Life Work. *Management Today, August 1999,*48, 1999.

[49] Porter, M. 1985. In Johnson G & Scholes K. *Exploring Corporate Strategy.* London: Prentice Hall, 1993.

[50] Nonaka, I. and Takeuchi, I. *The Knowledge Creating Company. How Japanese Companies Create the Dynamics of Innovation,* New York: OUP, 1995.

[51] Shaubroeck, J. & Fink, L. Facilitating and Inhibiting Effects of Job Control and Social Support on Stress Outcomes and Role Behaviour: a Contingency Model. *Journal of Organisational Behaviour, 19,* 167-195, 1998.

9

THE USE OF MIXED-MODE MODELLING IN DETERMINING BEST PRACTICE FOR A BUSINESS

Miles G. Nicholls and Barbara J. Cargill
School of Business
Swinburne University of Technology, Melbourne, Australia

ABSTRACT

In this chapter a soft model of the human resources management function is developed. This model is then interfaced with a conventional hard production planning model with the resulting overall model then used to develop 'best practice' using a soft heuristic solution algorithm explicitly incorporating Management *per se*. This approach constitutes *mixed-mode modelling* which aims at producing more holistic and thus realistic representations of, in this paper's context, business processes. Additionally, this modelling concept aims to expand the usual limited thinking associated with the development of, in this instance, a production plan using the traditional hard operations research type models. The human resources management function has been used to illustrate the approach, however, in reality other functions would be incorporated as well. An illustration of the ultimate determination of best practice is given.

This research is based on ideas foreshadowed in papers presented at the 30th Annual Meeting of the Decision Sciences Institute, New Orleans, USA, November 21st - 23rd, 1999 and the 30th Annual Meeting of the Western Decision Sciences Institute, April 3rd - 7th, Vancouver Canada, 2001.

M.G. Nicholls et al. (eds.),
Mixed-Mode Modelling: Mixing Methodologies for Organisational Intervention, 259–292.

Keywords: mixed-mode modelling, production scheduling, human resources management.

INTRODUCTION

The approach to modelling adopted in this chapter rests on the idea of *mixed-mode modelling*. Mixed-mode modelling attempts to formally represent problems in an interdisciplinary and holistic way. For applications such as discussed in this chapter, mixed-mode modelling is perhaps more suited to arriving at best practice with the explicit incorporation of Management *per se* than say the Theory of Constraints espoused by Goldratt [1] which does not facilitate soft model integration to the same extent. The application discussed in this chapter is a mixture of soft and hard paradigms, with the hard model being that of the production planning process and the soft model being that of the human resources management (HRM) function with Management explicitly included throughout the models as well as in the solution heuristic. The interested reader is referred to [2, 3, 4] for more details on the philosophy of mixed-mode modelling. For prior applications of mixed-mode modelling with respect to the marketing function, production planning and Management *per se* see [5]. The reader is referred to [6, 7, 8] where the concept of incorporating the HRM function has been foreshadowed.

This chapter selects a challenging and critical area to include in the mixed-mode modelling approach to business solutions, namely HRM. The difficulty lies in the development of a suitable paradigm to represent HRM and then to develop a methodology of explicitly incorporating it into the overall solution process. This modelling of production scheduling, HRM and Management *per se* as an example of the mixed-mode modelling process is followed by the development of a solution heuristic that provides the best practice (rather than the global optimal solution). Other critical business functions such as finance, marketing etc could also have been included, however, the areas chosen here serve well enough to illustrate the modelling approach and solution methodology using mixed-mode modelling.

The need for the development of an integrated or holistic model incorporating the HRM function of a manufacturing business stems initially from the need to counter the effects of two commonly encountered mind-sets.

Firstly, the attitude towards HRM in a production planning context is more often than not to ignore it as being an imposition and a peripheral activity that does not warrant serious consideration. Secondly, the HRM function is not generally seen as having a great deal of impact on the operation of the production planning operations, other than the provision of the required labour force. Witness to this is the fact that the HRM function is consistently absent from production planning and scheduling applications (a sin committed even by one author of this chapter [9]), together with the apparent absence of any systemic representation of the human resources function with the objective of at least, establishing the amount of labour available. The development of models, hard or soft, in the HRM area tends to be oriented towards staff planning and assignment [10, 11], recruitment [12] and career development [13]. The actual explicit recognition of labour *per se* as being important and needing management is rare (an example of an exception being Burns and Carter [14]). The actual integration of HRM and production scheduling with Management in the determination of best practice appears (at best) to be rare indeed.

The production plan is traditionally determined using an optimisation approach (using for example linear or mixed integer linear programming) with the HRM function left to supply labour and keep clear of the 'main game'. However, the HRM function is far more important than the above scenario would suggest [6] and potentially affects the profitability of the business significantly. Indeed, the HRM function may be a pivotal aspect of a sweeping change management strategy within an organisation, leading to an overhaul of management style, a cultural transformation and/or a significantly different approach to all usual organisational goals, including profitability amongst the indicators of corporate success [15] (p10). Figure 1 below illustrates the way in which HRM, production planning, Management and marketing (for example) interact and play a role in determining the 'best practice' for the business. The delivery of 'optimal' solutions is not sought by business since they seek best practice, recognising that in reality optimality is simply a concept and illusory (and often costly if sought). The reader is referred to [5] for more specific details of the interaction between production planning, Management and marketing holistic models.

However, unlike the marketing function, HRM is substantially qualitative in nature and more difficult to encapsulate in a soft model or

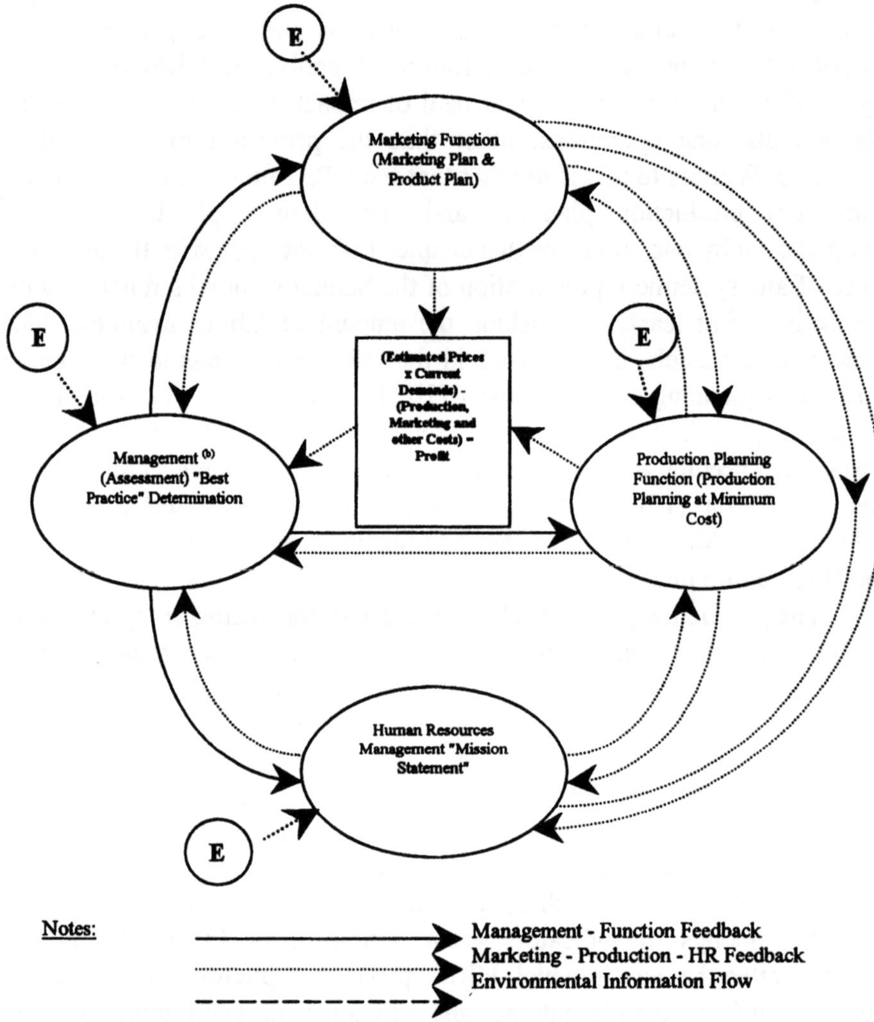

(a) Environment e.g. Economy, External Costs, Fixed Costs etc.
(b) Note that Management and Marketing are functional differentiations here and that the same people may be in both areas

Figure 1. Interaction of the Marketing, Production Planning and Management Areas

paradigm. HRM functions invariably have three overarching objectives namely, attracting, retaining and motivating capable employees to and within an enterprise. (see Schuler *et al* [16] (pp18-19)). Beyond this, the HRM labour reduction. The solution (obtained using Heuristic A) is then checked for feasibility and if it is not feasible, it is modified (using a HRM modifying procedure, Heuristic B). Note that feasibility here is also taken to include attaining the primary mission, a percentage reduction in labour. The feasible solution (if one exists) is then passed on as an input into the production planning model (i.e., the labour availabilities). If no feasible solution exists for the HRM model then management is consulted and the process restarted.

Step 1:

Management establish the mission statement for the HRM model and determine the availability of labour for the first period in the selected planning horizon, and ensure all information is placed in the HRM model (a simple spreadsheet). The HRM model is then run taking into account only natural attrition as a means of labour reduction. The solution (obtained using Heuristic A) is then checked for feasibility and if it is not feasible, is modified (using a HRM modifying procedure, Heuristic B). Note that feasibility here is also taken to include attaining the primary mission, a percentage reduction in labour. The feasible solution (if one exists) is then passed on as an input into the production planning model (i.e., the labour availabilities). If feasible solution exists for the HRM model then management is consulted and the process restarted.

Step 2:

The production planning model is then solved using the input from the HRM model employing linear programming. The solution, if not feasible due to labour shortages, will require the HRM modification procedure again. If the solution is feasible and thus in LP nomenclature 'optimal', then the feasible pair of solutions to the HRM and production planning models are stored, and the alternative HRM solution generated using Heuristic B. This process is continued until no further feasible solutions are available, or the necessary number of potential best practice solutions have been generated.

Step 3:

> The solution pairs generated are then evaluated using Heuristic C, which facilitates Management arriving at either their preferred choice, or requesting some additional solutions to be investigated. It might even be that because there is no feasible solution to the problem, that they might need to reassess their mission statement.

Note that in reality, the pursuit of optimality often costs more than accepting 'best practice' (i.e., a local optimal solution) with the rewards available from the best practice often little different from the optimal. An example of this [9] occurred in the master production scheduling of the manufacture of tobacco products, where a local optimal mixed integer solution arrived at with simplifying assumptions was almost indistinguishable from the global optimal which took considerably greater time and effort to arrive at. Additionally, the incorporation of subjective assessment (i.e., the explicit involvement of Management in the determination of best practice) in the solution process outlined in this paper, makes the objective of obtaining 'optimal solutions' of the overall problem meaningless.

In the sections following, the HRM (soft) model is developed followed by the specification of a simple production planning model. Finally, the solution heuristic is developed and discussed with an illustration provided of the process of determining best practice. Included also, is a discussion of the advantages associated with this approach and the future research required to see it eventually applied in a real world environment.

The Human Resources Management Model

Introduction to Human Resources Management Function

The HRM function of a business is composed of many constituent sub functions and operations. The full cycle of activities is segmented in Schuler *et al* [16] into five main functions, namely:

- Planning for HR needs
- Satisfy the organisation's personnel needs
- Approving and remunerating employee behaviour

- Improving employees and the work environment
- Establishing and maintaining effective working relationships.

Other approaches do not differ markedly. Notably the fundamental purpose of legal compliance (previously mentioned) is threaded throughout these five functional areas, and forms such a crucial aspect of the organisational context, that any HRM model needs to clearly acknowledge the broader economic, legal, cultural, political and societal elements which have an impact on employment and work in general (see Tyson [15] (p56)). The Australian scene is no exception and has in fact, a colourful history of vexed labour relations [17] and legislative framework which have made organisational success problematic in many instances. The model discussed below is based on the Australian industrial framework but is readily adaptable to any country and its general conceptual validity is not impaired. The legal compliance dimension is given prominence simply because it constrains many other HRM functions in a production oriented environment whichever aspect of a more elaborated HR model is in focus.

Here, the HRM model is composed of two main subgroups, the prime drivers and the secondary drivers. The prime drivers include the industrial laws and regulations, the occupational health and safety regulations and the enterprise agreement that has been arrived at by Management, the workforce in conjunction with the other two prime drivers. The secondary drivers include Management, and the available human resource skills/knowledge and attributes together with the external environment, all comprising the determinants of the HRM function in this instance. The primary drivers together with management essentially establish the mission statement (and associated objectives) for the HRM function. The mission statement, as suggested before, could be for example the reduction of the manufacturers' labour force by say 10% by the end of the current planning period assuming labour is in excess. Figure 2 below illustrates the interactions of the sub models within the HRM function.

The enterprise agreement basically defines the terms and conditions of employment and work practices that are agreed to after formal negotiations between Management and labour for a specific business. This agreement must be within the guidelines and in agreement with the industrial laws and health and safety regulations currently in force. The enterprise agreement in conjunction with the industrial laws and regulations, the occupational health and safety regulations and the available human resources skill/knowledge and attributes, essentially determines what the initial labour availability will be by job and supervisory category for each month within the planning period. The cost of labour is also substantially determined by this process.

The mission statement *per se* together with the manner in which it is actually attained (i.e., the scheme as well as the *way* in which the scheme is implemented) will substantially determine the final availability of labour.

There will always be natural attrition within the categories of labour and this will also need to be taken into account. Additionally, in a background sense, the HRM practices adopted by the business will impact on the available labour. For example, management of the human resources by non-consensus methods with a deliberate lack of communication could result in a disgruntled work force with a consequent reduction in productivity, i.e., a reduction in the effective availability of labour, and the obverse of Schuler *et al* [16] 'motivating' of employees. Equally, poor consultation and communication by management may not generate the improved work practices which would enable the same or slightly reduced production to be maintained whilst simultaneously reducing actual labour force hours.

The drivers mentioned above which determine the initial availability of labour will also have a considerable input in determining the cost of the labour by skill and level of supervisory capacity. Productivity (as determined by some of the factors already mentioned) will also have an impact on the cost (e.g., an unhappy work force may result in less care taken in the production process and thus greater wastage and consequently, greater end cost of production). All this simply points to the organic and holistic workings of HR 'success' and the softness of the model needed to interface with production planning.

The determination of the scheme (i.e., the plan developed to affect the mission statement) is determined by a heuristic solution algorithm developed later in this paper. The solution heuristic encompasses

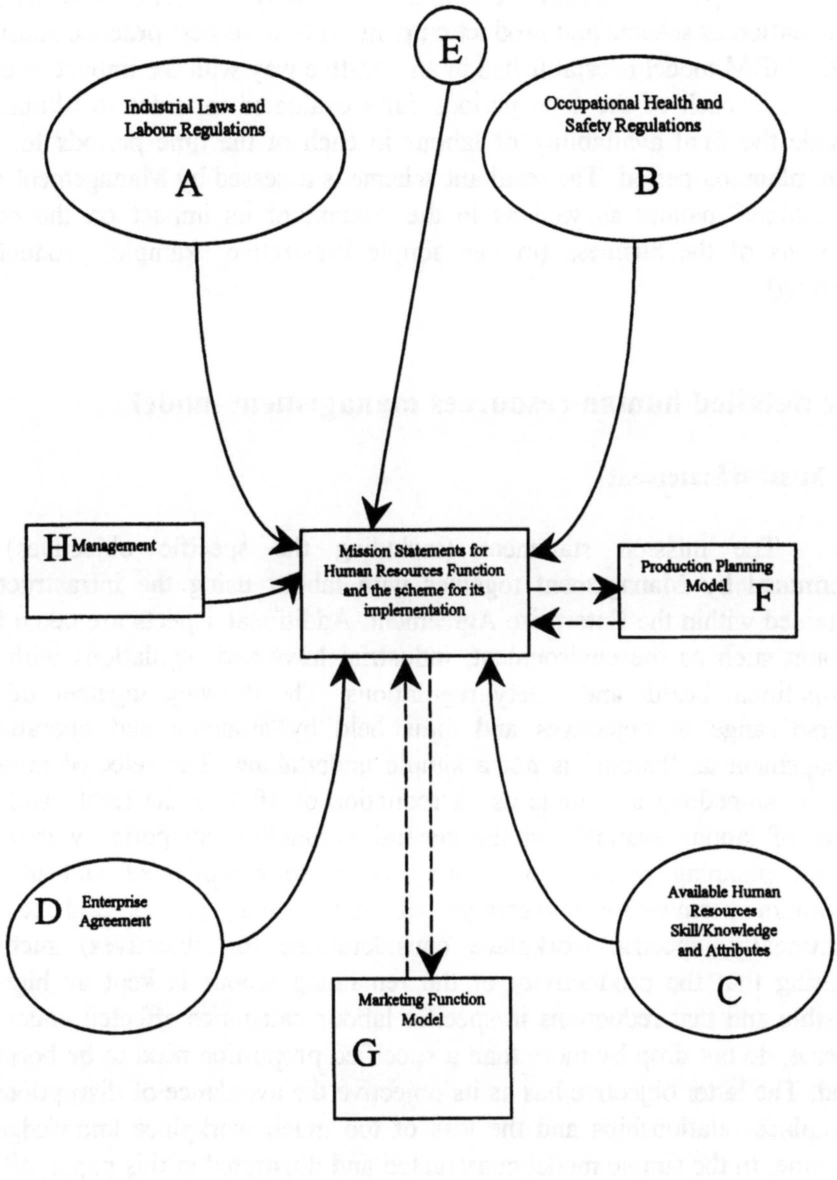

Figure 2. The Human Resources Model

determination of the set of best practice schemes for the HRM model together with the best practice production plan and ultimately the best practice overall combination of scheme and production plan. The set of best practice schemes for the HRM model is established in an iterative way with the impact of each decision in each of the time periods fully evaluated in order to ultimately provide the final availability of labour in each of the time periods for the entire planning period. The resultant scheme is assessed by Management in a stand alone manner as well as in the context of its impact on the other functions of the business (in this simple illustrative example, production planning).

The detailed human resources management model

The Mission Statement

The mission statement (including the specific objectives) is determined by Management together with labour using the infrastructure contained within the Enterprise Agreement. Additional aspects are taken into account such as the environment, industrial laws and regulations with the occupational health and safety regulations. The drawing together of the diverse range of objectives and aims held by strategic and operational management as 'labour' is not a simple undertaking. The selected mission may be something as simple as "a reduction of 10% in the final available hours of labour available in the general production categories within the current planning period", or it may be more complicated and include maximum permissible percentages of idle labour, profits and so on. Additionally, specific workplace considerations (or objectives) such as ensuring that the productivity of the remaining labour is kept as high as possible and that reductions in specific labour categories effected under the scheme, do not drop by more than a specified proportion need to be borne in mind. The latter objective has as its objective the avoidance of disruptions to workplace relationships and the loss of too much workplace knowledge at one time. In the simple model constructed and illustrated in this paper, all the above considerations will be incorporated into the model. Additionally, natural attrition will be accounted for also.

The Scheme for attaining the mission statement

The mission statement (in this example, the reduction of the finally available labour hours of specified categories of the workforce by a given percentage within the current planning period, the maintenance of the maximum possible productivity of remaining labour and finally ensuring that labour reductions from one period to another will not exceed a given magnitude) can be (fully or in part) attained by the adoption of each (or a combination of) the following actions (A) in addition to the naturally occurring attrition (n):

(i) voluntary departure of labour (with packages);
(ii) involuntary departure of labour (with packages);
(iii) outright redundancy of labour;
(iv) retraining of labour;
(v) alteration of the terms of employment i.e., reductions in the working week etc.;
(vi) switching labour (or a portion thereof) to part time or casual status;
(vii) natural attrition with selective recruitment to maintain skill stocks (attrition is greater than selective recruitment)

The eventual combination (or single selection) of the actions (i=1,. . ,I) listed above, and applied in various degrees (i.e., the proportion of the reduction chosen) over each of the months in the planning period will then constitute the scheme or plan of action which is required to be undertaken in order to meet the mission statement.

The scheme must be evaluated in terms of whether it meets the mission statement as well as what its effect are on the production planning model and other sections of the business. These evaluations and eventual determination of best practice are discussed later in the solution heuristic. Additionally, there may be cost minimisation requirements associated with the HRM function (or at least cost guidelines) that must be met. The actions taken here will help determine the final amount of labour available for each of the months in the planning period by category of targeted labour.

Productivity effects on the labour availability due to the manner of implementation of the scheme - final labour availability

As mentioned, the combination of the above activities together with the extent to which each is implemented in each month of the planning period forms the scheme to be used to attain the HRM mission statement (and each of the objectives within it).

The implementation of each of the possible actions in the scheme results in a reduction in the quantity of labour remaining after natural attrition has been accounted for in each period. In this HRM model, attrition is assumed to occur at the beginning of each month. For each category of labour targeted in the scheme (i.e., labourer-no specific skills, skilled artisan or supervisory) different final quantities will be available depending on the manner (M) in which the scheme was implemented, i.e., the final quantity of labour available is determined taking into account the action selected in the scheme to obtain the amount (e.g., 600 hours of unskilled labour removed through involuntary departure packages) and then the manner in which the scheme was implemented to obtain the final amount (e.g., little or no negotiation with the labour concerned and finally done in an acrimonious way leaving the work force generally angry). This latter effect is incorporated into the model through the use of likely productivities (m) derived taking into account the actions (A) and the manner (M) in which they were implemented. Note also that even for non-targeted labour categories, i.e., those categories where no planned reduction is required in a period, there will possibly be follow-on effects from the manner of implementation for the targeted categories. In this model however, the follow-on effects are assumed to be negligible. Theoretically, the effect could be positive where management have worked very collaboratively with labour to produce a climate of co-operation and joint challenge to raise productivity.

The productivities are arrived at *a priori* in a subjective way (perhaps representing possibilities or fuzzy values) by those involved in the HRM function and management *per se*. The reductions in productivities are arrived at using past experience and 'guestimates' of how the reductions are likely to be carried out given the circumstances, i.e., the people involved and the climate.

Some of the factors (M_j) (j=1, . . , J) that will have an impact on the productivity of the base labour after the implementation of the scheme are as follows:

(a) the mode of implementation of the scheme (e.g., consultative or non-consultative);
(b) the degree of industrial harmony maintained within the plant;
(c) the 'cheer factor' on the shop floor;
(d) the working conditions generally;
(e) the paradigm which Management have adopted to run the business;
(f) other factors (e.g., new equipment, specialised training programmes, work practice reform which all might even increase the level of productivity above that level it was before the reduction).

Note that most of these factors actually interact with each other to have composite (simple additive) and or compounding (multiplicative) effects possibly extending over more than one time period (see [15], [17]). However, the HRM model developed in this chapter will for simplicity ignore the compounding effects.

A simple formal representation of the HRM Function

Definitions

In order to allow a paradigm to be more formally expressed some definitions and symbols need to be introduced as follows:

Definition of coefficients:

$\mathbf{n}_{\iota,t}$ = the proportion of hours in labour category ι in period t that will be lost due to normal attrition at the beginning of period t.

$\mathbf{m}_{i,\iota,t}$ = the productivity level of the labour remaining after natural attrition and reductions as a result of actions taken in targeted category ι in period t. This net impact is a result of the manner of implementation (M_j) of all of the actions. For simplicity, this is assumed to be subjectively assigned by Management *a priori*. Note here, the possibility of (f) occurring, i.e., new equipment for example, increasing productivity ($m_{i,\iota,t} > 1$) is not considered. It nonetheless is a possibility in the real world.

Here:

$$m_{i,\iota,t} = f(M_j, a_{i,\iota,t}, E) \qquad (1)$$
$$(i \in I^+(t))$$
$$(\iota \in L^+(t))$$
$$(t=1, . . ,T)$$

Also: $$0 \leq m_{i,\iota,t} \leq 1 \qquad (2)$$
$$(i \in I^+(t))$$
$$(\iota \in L^+(t))$$
$$(t=1, . . ,T)$$

and

$$m_{i,\iota,t} = 1 \qquad (3)$$
$$(i \notin I^+(t)) \text{ and/or } (\iota \notin L^+(t))$$
$$(t=1, . . ,T)$$

where $I^+(t)$ is that subset of actions ($A_{i,t}$) in period t that have been selected to reduce category ι labour and $L^+(t)$ is that subset of labour categories that have been targeted for reductions using actions in period t. The set L contains all the labour categories and thus $L^+(t) \in L$. The set I contains all the possible actions, thus $I^+(t) \in I$.

$r_{\iota,t}$ = the maximum proportional reduction permitted in labour category ι from period t-1 to t due to operational considerations.

$Z1_T$ = the proportion that the total labour availability must have reduced by during the planning period. This is the first objective specified in the mission statement. This is specified by management.

Definition of variables (decision components)

$a_{i,\iota,t}$ = the proportional reduction of labour availability in category ι in period t (established with due recognition of the natural attrition that will occur) that HRM Management choose to achieve through action A_i. Note that $a_{i,\iota,t} = 0$ for non-targeted labour categories for all actions in t, i.e., $(\iota \notin L^+(t))\ \forall i$ and that for targeted labour categories;

$$0 < a_{i,\iota,t} \leq 1 \qquad (4)$$
$$(\iota \in L^+(t))$$
$$(i \in I^+(t))$$
$$(t=1,..,T)$$

where I^+ is that subset of actions selected for reducing the targeted labour category ι in t, and

$$a_{i,\iota,t} = 0 \qquad (5)$$
$$(\iota \in L^+(t))$$
$$(i \notin I^+(t))$$
$$(t=1,..,T)$$

Essentially $a_{i,\iota,t}$ and $m_{i,\iota,t}$ are linked in this simple model.

Definition of dependant variable (consequential components)

$FL_{\iota,0}$ = the initial or nominal availability of labour (in hours) for labour category ι for period t. This is arrived at through the physical raw availability from the previous period modified by the enterprise agreement (EA), industrial laws and labour regulations (IL) and health and safety regulations (HS) together with the general environment (E), i.e.,

$$FL_{\iota,0} = f(EA, IL, HS, E) \qquad (6)$$

The determination in (6) above is valid for targeted $(\iota \in L^+(t))$ (where $L^+(t)$ is that subset of labour categories selected in period t for reduction other than by natural attrition) and non-targeted labour categories $(\iota \notin L^+(t))$.

$FL_{\iota,t}$ = the final amount available of each labour category ι in time t after its reduction due to actions undertaken (if the labour category is targeted), natural attrition and the productivity effects. This is essentially a dependent variable.

Definition of availabilities

G_ι = the initial or nominal availability of labour (in hours) for labour category ι for period 0. This has been discussed above and may be considered as a right hand side for the convenience of the solution heuristic.

The Mission Statement and Other Associated Objectives

The mission statement and its associated objectives have in this chapter centred on the reduction of labour as an illustration only. This illustration assumes that there is an understanding by Management that labour is generally in excess. There will be more situations in practice where the mission will be to increase the level of productivity (i.e., $m_{i,\iota,t}>1$) through new technology etc., while simultaneously reducing the workforce.

The mission statement and its objectives for this illustration have already been generally outlined, however, more formally, they might be specified as follows:

The mission statement is:

$$\text{Achieve: } Z1_T = \sum_{\iota \in L} ((FL_{\iota,T} - FL_{\iota,0})/FL_{\iota,0}) \qquad (7)$$

Specifically, the mission statement in this illustration is to reduce the total availability of labour (in specific labour categories) by a given proportion by the end of the planning period (T) in such a way that 'harmony and the well being of the remaining labour force is to be maximised'. This mission statement has within it an implied objective i.e., to reduce the size of the labour force in selected labour categories. Note here that L is the set containing all labour categories. This objective statement can be restated and achieved by its inclusion in the constraints of the model, via:

$$\sum_{\iota \in L} (FL_{\iota,T} - FL_{\iota,0} + Z1_T\, FL_{\iota,0}) = 0 \qquad (8)$$

The overall mission will require the application of skilled management to ensure that the other HRM aspects of labour harmony and well being are achieved.

Some additional objectives that might well be required to be achieved are as follows:

(i) Maximise the productivity of all remaining labour over targeted categories over all periods:

$$\text{Max } Z2_t = \sum_{i \in I^+(t)} \sum_{\iota \in L^+(t)} m_{i,\iota,t} \qquad (9)$$

This can be incorporated into the solution heuristic quite easily and will be discussed in later sections.

(ii) Ensure that the maximum reduction in any labour hours availability in any category from one time period to the next is no more than $r_{\iota,t}$. (objective $Z_{3,t}$). This is easily achieved by the insertion of the following requirement into the HRM model representation.

$$FL_{\iota,t-1} - FL_{\iota,t} - r_{\iota,t}\, FL_{\iota,t-1} \leq 0 \qquad (10)$$

$$(\iota \in L)$$
$$(t=1, . . ,T)$$

An additional objective for consideration

One additional consideration Management might well wish to consider along with the attainment of the mission statement and objectives outlined above for the HRM function, is the minimisation of specific costs associated with the scheme.

The base hourly labour cost for a given period ($C_{\iota,t}$) is established in the main by the enterprise agreement together with the industrial laws and regulations. However, the cost for the remaining labour after the implementation of the scheme and the actual cost of 'paying out' for the labour reduction actions ($PC_{l,i,t}$) e.g., departure packages and legal costs, needs to taken into account.

The cost function that could be considered as a second objective is as follows:

$$\text{Min } C = \sum_{t=1}^{T} \sum_{l \in L} ((C_{l,t} / m_{l,t})\, FL_{l,t} + \sum_{i \in I} PC_{l,i,t}) \qquad (11)$$

The Formal Representation Model of the HRM Function

The model representing the HRM function can then be expressed as follows:

$$\text{Max } Z2_t = \sum_{i \in I^+(t)} \sum_{l \in L^+(t)} m_{i,l,t} \qquad (9)$$

such that;

$$FL_{l,t-1}(1 - n_{l,t}) - FL_{l,t} = 0 \qquad (12)$$

$$(l \notin L^+(t))$$

$$(t=1, . . ,T)$$

$$FL_{l,0} = G_l \qquad (13)$$

$$(l \in L)$$

$$FL_{l,t-1}(1 - n_{l,t}) - \sum_{i \in I^+(t)} a_{i,l,t}\, FL_{l,t-1}(1 - n_{l,t})\, m_{i,l,t} - FL_{l,t} = 0$$

$$(l \in L^+(t))(14)$$

$$(t=1, . . ,T)$$

$$\sum_{i \in I^+(t)} a_{i,l,t} \leq 1 \qquad (15)$$

$$(l \in L^+(t))$$

$$(t=1, . . ,T)$$

$$FL_{l,t-1} - FL_{l,t} - r_{l,t}\, FL_{l,t-1} \leq 0 \qquad (10)$$

$(l \in L)$

$(t=1, . . ,T)$

$$\sum_{l \in L} (FL_{l,T} - FL_{l,0} + Z1_T\, FL_{l,0}) = 0 \qquad (8)$$

$(t=1, . . ,T)$

all variables ≥ 0

In (9) above, the first objective (expressly incorporated in the mission statement) must be achieved over the planning period. This section of the mission statement is a management specified one of maximising the productivity of the remaining labour after natural attrition and where appropriate, reductions as a part of the scheme to achieve the first objective (the required reduction in labour). The scheme developed in order to attain the mission statement is essentially the actions undertaken and the consequential reductions in labour, i.e., the list of all $a_{i,l,t}$.

In the HRM model above, the objective is to maximise Z_2 for *each* t rather than to maximise Z_2 *overall* t. The latter objective would require a more complicated solution heuristic based on a 'first solution' arrived at say using LP. Management could then perhaps introduce their knowledge and subjective assessments into this first solution, with the implications being tracked and evaluated using a simple spreadsheet model. This injection of 'real world' knowledge is critical in arriving at a best practice solution. The latter objective function would differ from (9) only by the addition of a summation over all t.

The simple objective adopted in (9) allows the HRM model to be solved by Management, using their judgement and knowledge alone, with the aid of a simple spreadsheet. The use of LP is an option but not a necessity due to the simplicity of the problem. Research on the efficacy of using LP in the solution of the HRM model with (9) as the objective function is currently under way. While the term constraint is used below, in this soft model, the term labor flow or labor flow requirement would be more appropriate.

Constraint (12) establishes the final amount of available labour in the non-targeted categories in period t. The constraint takes into account the natural attrition.

Constraint (13) defines the starting quantity of all labour categories at the beginning of the first period in the planning horizon. This is defined as in (6) with a value G_l.

Constraint (14) performs the same task as does (12) but for the targeted labour categories. The difference here is that the labour available is reduced by the natural attrition as well as actions deliberately taken to reduce it further together with reductions (effectively through productivity losses in the remaining labour) as a result of the way in which the actions were carried out.

Constraint (15) simply ensures that the reductions that are carried out through the actions are not more than that amount of labour available (after natural attrition has been accounted for).

Constraint (10) as already discussed above, ensures that the reduction in labour from one period to the next is no more than the maximum allowed proportion.

Constraint (8) as already discussed, ensures that the proportional reduction in the available labour over the planning horizon as specified by management will be achieved.

Before the solution heuristic is developed for the overall problem and a numerical illustration given, it is necessary to specify a very simple production planning model. The next section develops this.

The Production Planning Model

The production planning model outlined in this section is a simple one for illustration only. Its objective is to maximise projects ($\pi_{j,t}$) meeting minimum demands ($D_{j,t}$) for final products ($x_{j,t}$) while ensuring the limited raw materials ($RM_{h,t}$) and available labour ($FL_{l,t}$ determined by the HRM model) are not exceeded in any time period t over the total planning horizon T (the same as for the HRM model). If the marketing function were explicitly incorporated as well, then the objective may have been to minimize costs.

The mathematical model is typically:

$$\text{Max } ZP_T = \sum_{t=1}^{T} \sum_{j=1}^{J} x_{j,t}\, \pi_{j,t} \qquad (16)$$

subject to

$$\sum_{j=1}^{J} x_{j,t}\, c_{j,h,t} \leq RM_{h,t} \quad (17)$$

(h=1, . ,H)
(t=1, . ,T)

$$CS_{j,0} = G_j \quad (18)$$

(j=1, . ,J)

$$CS_{j,t-1} + x_{j,t} - CS_{j,t} = D_{j,t} \quad (19)$$

(j=1, . ,J)
(t=1, . ,T)

$$\sum_{j=1}^{J} x_{j,t}\, d_{j,\iota,t} \leq FL_{\iota,t} \quad (20)$$

($\iota \in L$)
(t=1, . ,T)

$$x_{j,t},\ CS_{j,t} \geq 0$$

From constraints (19) it is clear that the production of final product can be made in one period and stored for another to assist in the meeting of demand. To this end a closing stock variable has been employed ($CS_{j,t}$).

This formulation means that the solution of the full planning period model is required as is the case for the HRM model, in order to provide a set of feasible solutions for Heuristic C. Thus for each set of $FL_{\iota,t}$ provided by the HRM model for the planning period (i.e., $\forall t$) the production planning model requires solution using a LP approach. The details of the solution procedure are discussed below.

The Heuristic Solution Algorithm for the Determination of Best Practice Together with a Numerical Illustration

The General Heuristic Solution Algorithm

The solution heuristic employed for the determination of best practice in this problem is a combination of soft and hard models and solution techniques. The overall solution is ultimately arrived at by Management using a guidance procedure. The heuristic solution algorithm is described below with the three main heuristic procedures involved in the algorithm discussed further on.

Step 1:

performed only once to determine the available labour ($FL_{\iota,t}$) *assuming that only natural attrition is permitted.*
Using: $FL_{\iota,0}$ and $n_{\iota,t}$ ($\iota \in L$), ($t=1,..,T$).
Set: k=1 (iteration counter), **Q_1 Q_2 = 0** (flags used later).
Set: $a_{i,\iota,t}{}^{k} = 0$, ($i \in I$), ($\iota \in L$), ($t=1,..,T$).
Perform: Heuristic A
[In this simple example a spreadsheet is applied to the HRM model represented by constraints (12), (13), (14), (15), (10) and (8) This provides the ability to assess the actions required (if any) to meet the $Z1_T$ objective.]

Calculate: $\Delta_k = Z1_T - \sum_{\iota \in L} ((FL_{\iota,T}{}^{k} - FL_{\iota,0})/FL_{\iota,0}))$
[This indicates whether the required reduction ($Z1_T$) has been met and if not, what the violation is.]
If: $\Delta_k = 0$ Then Set $Q_1 = 1$ and Go To Step 2.
Else: If $\Delta_k > 0$ Then Go To Heuristic B.
Else: Let K=k and Go to End [No Feasible Solution to HRM problem suggests that Management will need to review $Z1_T$ or $r_{\iota,t}$. If $\Delta_k < 0$ the labour reduction due to natural attrition exceeds the required amount set by management.]

Step 2:

Using $FL_{\iota,t}{}^{k}$, solve the LP Model defined by Equations (16), (17), (18), (19) and (20) for the optimal solution $x^*_{j,t}{}^{k}$. [The solution $x^*_{j,t}{}^{k}$ is then examined for feasibility]
If $x_{j,t}{}^{k}$ is infeasible Check [to see if labour constraints violated]
If using $FL_{\iota,t}{}^{k}$, constraint (20) is NOT violated, Set K=k=0 and Go To END [Labour Slack variables ≥ 0 and therefore no solution to LP due to another non-labour related constraint infeasibility]
Else Go To Heuristic B [determine more HRM solutions.]

Else If for $x^*{}_{j,t}^{k}$; Q1≠1 and/or Q2≠0 Go To RECORD subroutine
Else If Management don't want additional solution options: Set K=k and Go To END: [a Global 'Optimal' Solution obtained i.e., HRM model required no actions and met target reductions, while the production model is feasible and maximises profit. However, there may be alternative optimal solutions to the production planning problem involving different $FL_{\iota,t}^{k}$ values, therefore check for slack variables associated with constraint (20) = 0 with marginal values (shadow prices) = 0.]
Else go to RECORD subroutine
END

RECORD (subroutine) details of the solutions [for HRM and Production modelling problems]
Set k=k+1
If k≠K^T Go To Heuristic B
Else Go To Heuristic C [predetermined number of solutions obtained and now need best practice determined]

Heuristic B [Attains feasibility by adjusting actions in such a way that the $Z1_T$ is being aimed at while meeting the other objective,

$$\text{Max } Z2_t^k = \sum_{i\in I^+(t)} \sum_{\iota\in L^+(t)} m_{i,\iota,t}^{k} \;]$$

Select;($\iota\in L^+(t)$), ($i\in I^+(t)$)
Set: $a_{i,\iota,t}^{k} > 0$, for ($\iota\in L^+(t)$), ($i\in I^+(t)$), (t=1, . ,T) such that:

$$\text{Max } Z2_t^k = \sum_{i\in I^+(t)} \sum_{\iota\in L^+(t)} m_{i,\iota,t}^{k}$$

[Management's subjective decisions]
Determine: $FL_{\iota,T}^{k}$, Δ_k [Using the same spreadsheet in Step 1]
Set $Q_2 = 1$
If: $\Delta_k = 0$ Go To Step 2 [Solution Feasible]
Else Go To Beginning of Heuristic B [Solution not feasible and need to generate another set of actions and re-solve.]

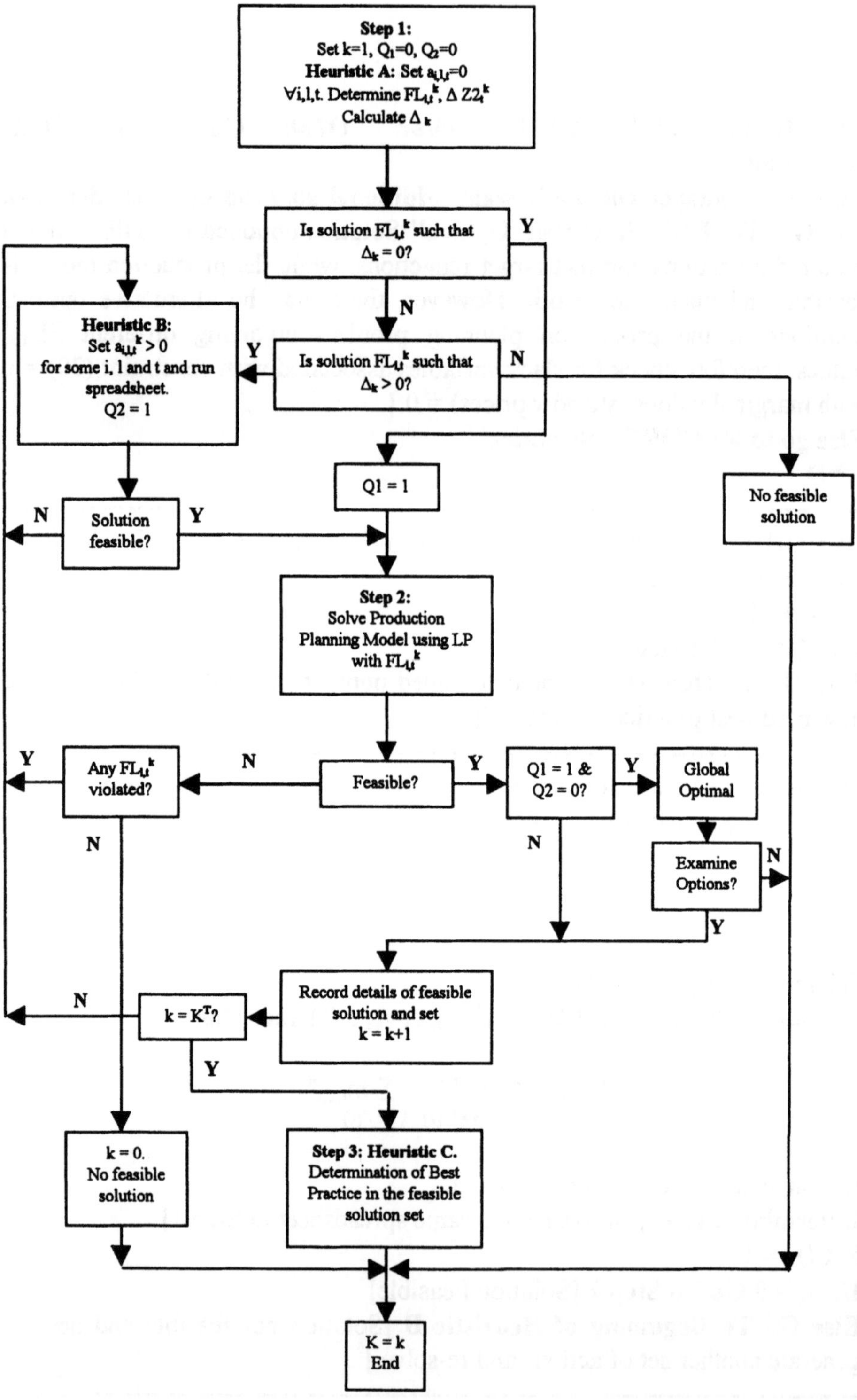

Figure 3. The Heuristic Solution Algorithm

Step 3:

Heuristic C *Determination of best practice*

This heuristic requires the direct involvement of Management in determining the best practice solution from the list generated in the heuristic solution algorithm above. Upon the determination of the best practice solution, the solution heuristic is at an end. The heuristic solution algorithm is illustrated in **Figure 3**. The specific details relating to the Heuristics are discussed below.

The heuristic has already been described in the algorithm details above. Essentially, it is a small spreadsheet that evaluates each of the equations (constraints) making up the HRM model, with the initial labour values and attrition rates input.

Details of the Heuristic Procedures Used in the Solution Algorithm

Heuristic Procedure A - Initial Evaluation

It allows for no actions to be undertaken whatever, thus its simplistic nature. The labour reduction obtained as a result of natural attrition alone is measured (as a proportion) and compared with the required level specified by management.

Heuristic B - Generation of Actions to Meet HRM Mission Statement

This heuristic uses the same spreadsheet approach used for Heuristic A, however, there are some additions that take into account the second objective associated with the mission statement, namely:

$$\text{Max } Z2_t^k = \sum_{i \in I^+(t)} \sum_{l \in L^+(t)} m_{i,l,t}^{\ k}$$

i.e., ensure that the labour productivity is as high as possible. This is achieved by adopting actions that have the smallest impact on productivity (assessed *a priori*). Thus when looking at the determination of:

$a_{i,\iota,t}^{k} > 0$, for $(\iota \in L^{+}(t))$, $(i \in I^{+}(t))$, $(t=1,..,T)$

the actions should be selected such that $m_{i,\iota,t}$, where possible, is the maximum. Then overall, the total across all labour categories for each time period (at least) should be a maximum. This requires Management to select accordingly. At each selection of an action, the spreadsheet is run and the effects evaluated in terms of meeting the first objective $Z1_T$ through measuring Δ_k. If after an action has been selected, the run of the spreadsheet indicates $\Delta_k = 0$, then the model is feasible and the process moves on. However, if $\Delta_k < 0$, then too much labour has been removed and the action taken needs to be reduced in severity. Similarly, if $\Delta_k > 0$, then too little labour has been removed and the action needs to be strengthened or new actions added. The collective wisdom of management is used in this process, with their experience coming to the fore to select a set of actions that give the desired result for all the mission statement's contents. A campaign of constructive work practice or process improvements or equipment upgrade as a part of a total change process may of course deliver enhanced productivity (as indicated previously) off a smaller labour base in parallel. In this illustration, excess labour has been assumed and thus major productivity increases are less the issue than labour reduction.

Should this heuristic be entered after either an infeasible LP solution to the production planning problem has been obtained, or Management want additional solutions generated after having obtained a global optimal solution, then additional knowledge and information comes with these solutions. This knowledge is in the form of what time period(s) and what labour category(ies) in which there are either shortages or full use made of available labour. This then allows Management to focus on those periods and categories to reassess their choice of actions and/or their selection of magnitude of reduction. The simple framework for this heuristic is available, but more development work is required to provide suitable guidelines for Management to operate this process.

Heuristic C - Determination of Best Practice

Best practice is essentially a managerial 'balancing act' of some complexity and ultimately judgement. Notwithstanding the preceding heuristics that are largely quantifiable there will inevitably be a large number of other variables and other considerations into any final management consideration.

A considerable amount of enterprise specific historic data and knowledge is required, for example, what has occurred before in the plant? What did or did not succeed? What will the local union leaders tolerate, accept or never accept? What local and particular socio-economic variables might alter the scenario? What particular cultural or even ethnic cultural characteristics of the labour force might come into play to suggest that some possible solutions, although logically preferred, may not actually deliver best result in practice? Inevitably this integrative judgement is qualitative.

Best practice is not only a function of considering all known variables. It is additionally an outcome of excellent implementation. Working positively with the dynamics of a change process to keep morale high, disruption low, co-operation strong is necessary. All consultation mechanisms must be maintained sufficiently to have a labour force willing to deliver in the short and longer terms, rather than one pressed by circumstances into short term compliance but resentful or debilitated in the longer term. Best practice also requires strong and clear leadership since an unclear vision or definition of mission will diminish any 'effective' solution.

In this case it can be seen that the recording of the solution details for each of the k 'iterations' of the heuristic solution algorithm provides a list of solution details for the HRM and the production planning models as follows:

$$(k,\ a_{i,l,t}^{k},\ FL_{l,t}^{k},\ Z2_{t}^{k},\ x*_{j,t}^{k},\ ZP_{T}^{k},\ SFL_{l,t}^{k}) \qquad (21)$$

Note that in (21) that $SFL_{l,t}^{k}$ represents the labour slack variables from the LP solution. These will be positive if labour is not fully used or zero if labour is fully used (and if the shadow price is also zero, indicating some alternative production planning solutions might be available). The slacks cannot be negative since the solution would be infeasible and therefore not recorded in the feasible solutions list. The slack variables are useful in the generation of feasible solutions in the earlier part of the heuristic algorithm since they can identify labour classifications where surplus labour availability consistently exists, thus suggesting alternative actions (and the extent of reductions) for the HRM model and also assist in arriving at alternative solutions for the LP model of the production planning problem. However, their value for Heuristic C might lie only in identifying 'tightness' and/or potential for an increase in the overall reduction in labour availability. Note that the mission $Z1_T^k$ and the objective $Z3_t^k$ for HRM are met by all feasible solutions as explained earlier. It is possible that differing $FL_{\iota,t}^k$ values might yield the same solution to the production scheduling problem.

The number of potential 'best practice' solutions generated by the solution heuristic is either K^T or K (if $K < K^T$). Here K^T is the predetermined number of solutions desired for evaluation by Management. In the event that a global optimal solution occurs in the first instance (and no additional solutions required to be generated by Management), K=1. Alternatively, if no solution exists to the LP problem due to an infeasibility *not* associated with labour, then K=0 (as is the case also when there exists no feasible solution to the HRM problem with only natural attrition being accounted for (Step1)). Hence $0 \leq K \leq K^T$.

The purpose of this heuristic is to facilitate Management's determination of what constitutes best practice. This best practice is either a selection from the available list of feasible solutions generated using the first part of the heuristic solution algorithm, or possibly a Management decision that none of the solutions is acceptable and that the objectives *per se* within the HRM mission statement need adjustment. In essence, the heuristic is subjective but has a number of procedures within it to assist the decision making.

In this heuristic a distinction is made between objectives and associated information. For example, the value of $Z2_t^k$ and the associated action $a_{i,\iota,t}^k$, are important in different ways. The $Z2_t^k$ can be readily assessed (objectively), i.e., the bigger the better. The $a_{i,\iota,t}^k$ can also be assessed in terms of whether the strategies adopted here are more or less acceptable (subjective). Thus while one solution has a slightly larger $Z2_t^k$ the actions of the lesser objective function solution are more 'politically' acceptable (for example) for a manager. Thus, for this heuristic, the following pieces from the solution record are 'linked':

For HRM	$Z2_t^k$, $a_{i,\iota,t}^k$	
For Production planning	ZP_T^k, $SFL_{\iota,t}^k$	(22)

The actual allocation of labour within classifications across the planning period ($FL_{l,t}^k$) for the HRM model and the production quantities of final goods across the planning period for the production planning model ($x^*{}_{j,t}^k$), are not all that important in the decision making process. The group that is loosely defined as Management consists of a total of P managers. The Management group would include, CEO, production, HRM, marketing and finance managers at the very least.

The heuristic undertakes the following procedures in an attempt to facilitate Management's decision making with respect to best practice:

(i) each participant is asked to assign a score out of 100 to each of the groupings of important attributes for the models (i.e., for two groups as outlined in (22) above a weight $w_{g,p}$ is assigned where g is the group number (of which there are a total of G) and p is the participant number (of which there are a total of P)).

(ii) a total weight is then obtained:

$$W_g = \sum_{p=1}^{P} w_{g,p} \qquad (g=1,..,G) \qquad (23)$$

(iii) the maximum weighted grouping (g^*) is found thus:

$$W^*_{g^*} = \underset{g}{\text{Max}}\, W_g \qquad (g=1,..,G) \qquad (24)$$

i.e., the g associated with the maximum weighting W^*_g.

(iv) the indexes (g) of the groupings (as in (22)) are then ranked in descending order with the *first* index of the ranked groupings index, g^+ being g^*, i.e., ($g^+ = g^*, ..$).

(v) for the first grouping in g^+, each participant (p) is then asked to assign a score ($S_{g^+,k,p}$) to each of the K solutions in turn (k = 1, . . , K) such that the scores total 100 for all the K solutions for each participant. This is then repeated for remaining groupings in the order indicated by g^+. The most popular solution (k^*) for each grouping in the order indicated in g^+ across all the participants is arrived at viz:

$$TS_{g^+,k} = \sum_{p=1}^{P} S_{g^+,k,p} \qquad \text{for each element of } g^+ \quad (25)$$
$$(k=1,..,K)$$

$$TS^*_{g^+,k^*} = \underset{k}{\text{Max}}\ TS_{g^+,k} \qquad (26)$$

for each element of g^+

i.e., the k^* is the k associated with the maximum weighting ($TS^*_{g^+,k^*}$) in (26).

(vi) A table is then constructed with the 'winning' solution for each g^+ shown, and the final acceptance or request for an alteration of the HRM missions statement made by Management. This latter request would require the entire procedure to be repeated.

An Example of the Determination of Best Practice

Assume that the procedures outlined above in the heuristic solution algorithm have been followed, and that for a simple problem involving two periods, two classifications of labour and two final products the full list of solutions (a total of three) are as summarised in Table 1, using the two groups of solution attributes already discussed with three managers participating.

From Table 1 below it can be seen that the first ranked and the second ranked solution attributes both saw solution 1 chosen as the best practice solution. This would suggest a degree of robustness associated with the solution, in part due to the consistency associated with the reduction of labour over the planning period. The group 2 solution attributes are the ones be used in this case, since they received the highest weightings by Management, with solution 1 in group 2 chosen.

In reality it may well be that the decision making consistency of Management in the Heuristic C above, would be increased by their exposure to 'dummy runs' using hypothetical data in conjunction with the application of Social Judgement Theory as outlined in [18] and [19].

The Heuristic C above, for the behavioural reasons outlined, is considered simple and effective, however, there are others that might well be used. This paper has selected the simplest in order to illustrate the process and the principles involved.

Table 1
List of Solutions by Ranked Groups of Attributes

Solution Group[(a)] (g^+) in ranked order	Solutions [(b)] (k) for each group (g^+)	Management's [(c)] Solution Weighting ($TS_{g+,k}$)
$g^+ = 2$ (k^*, $ZP_T^{\ 1}$ $SFL_{l,t}^{\ 1}$)	1, \$6,500, (12,8,8,7)	180
$g^+ = 2$ (k, $ZP_T^{\ 2}$, $SFL_{l,t}^{\ 2}$)	2, \$6,500, (10,11.5,0,13.5)	30
$g^+ = 2$ (k, $ZP_T^{\ 3}$, $SFL_{l,t}^{\ 3}$)	3, \$6,000, (20,3,4,8)	90
$g^+ = 1$ (k^*, $a_{i,l,t}^{\ 1}$, $Z2_t^{\ 1}$)	1, (0.1,0.2,0.1,0), 1.5, 1.6	150
$g^+ = 1$ (k, $a_{i,l,t}^{\ 2}$, $Z2_t^{\ 2}$)	2, (0.4,0,0,0.1), 1.4, 1.35	90
$g^+ = 1$ (k, $a_{i,l,t}^{\ 3}$, $Z2_t^{\ 3}$) ,	3, (0,0.3,0,0), 1.56, 1.6	60

Notes:

(a) The results of the weighting process across the 3 Management participants was that group 2 attributes ($ZP_T^{\ k}$, $SFL_{l,t}^{\ k}$) were ranked first and group 1 attributes ($a_{i,l,t}^{\ k}$, $Z2_t^{\ k}$) ranked second. (i.e., g = (1, 2), while g^+ = (2, 1) and W_g = (120, 180) for g = 1 and 2 respectively. This indicates that the profits and unused labour were of more interest in determining best practice (on average) than the labour productivity and reduction scheme chosen. Note that the $Z2_t^{\ k}$ values are the sum over the two labour categories, for each time period.

(b) The solutions for group 2 attributes include the solution number, the profit in total in dollars for the two periods, and the unused labour (labour constraint slack variables) for labour category 1 and 2 (period 1) and labour category 1 and 2 (period 2). Note that the solutions are ranked in their order of occurrence and that $K = K^T = 3$.

(c) Using the weighting system described in (25) and (26).

CONCLUDING REMARKS

In this paper a representation of a soft area of a business, namely the human resources management function has been developed. This HRM soft model is linked with a hard production planning model and with the assistance of a heuristic solution algorithm (which is also developed) with direct interaction from Management, best practice is determined. It is hoped that this development will open up a greater awareness of the need for soft modelling and highlight the alternative to the pursuit of optimal solutions, namely, the determination of best practice.

The development of the HRM model together with the heuristic solution algorithm has relied on a significant input from organisation behaviour and management theory to see the modelling develop appropriately and especially the development of Heuristic C, the key to the arrival of best practice. The approach developed in the paper is a good example of mixed-mode modelling, and it is hoped that it will assist management in general in the real world to manage a business more effectively, even if it only highlights the interconnectedness between HRM, for example, and production planning at the highest strategic management levels. It is also stressed that the two business functions selected for this paper were illustrative only, and that in practice, many other functions would need to be introduced as well. This observation also highlights the need for the solution approach developed in this paper.

Another attribute of the modelling approach developed in this paper is the fact that the HRM mission statement can be altered at any time during the planning horizon by environmental factors, such as for example a loss of a large amount of labour from certain categories due to industrial action. The solution process discussed in this paper will allow Management to reassess the situation by running the solution algorithm again with the updated mission statement and determine new best practice that will meet the new circumstances. This *modus operandi* will ensure that 'knee-jerk' reactions need not occur and that reasoned decision making can be undertaken simply, quickly and result in best practice.

REFERENCES

[1] Goldratt, E. M. *What is this thing called the Theory of Constraints?* North River press, Croton-on-Hudson, New York, 1990.

[2] Lehaney, B. Mixed-mode modelling. In *Operations Research Keynote Papers*, Eds., Johnson, D and O'Brien, F, pp 150 - 157, 1996.

[3] Lehaney, B. and Clarke, S. Soft Systems Methodology (and Simulation) for Mixed-mode modelling? In *Operations Research Keynote Papers*, Eds., O'Brien, F and Orman, A., pp 16 - 33, 1997.

[4] Mingers, J. and Brocklesby, J. Multimethodology: Towards a Framework for Mixing Methodologies, *Systemist*, 18, pp 101 –p 131, 1996.

[5] Enright, M and Nicholls, M. G. The Use of Mixed-mode modelling in Production Scheduling to Incorporate the Marketing Function and Human Resources Considerations. *Proceedings of the OR40 Annual Conference*, University of Lancaster, United Kingdom, 8th - 10th September, pp 125, 1998.

[6] Nicholls, M. G., Enright, M., Cargill, B. and Dhir, K. S. The Application of Mixed-mode modelling to the Holistic Solution of Business Planning Problems. *Proceedings of the 29th Annual Meeting of the Decision Sciences Institute*, Eds., Bartkus, K., Parent, M., and Jenson, R., Las Vegas, USA, 21st - 24th November, pp 344, 1998.

[7] Nicholls, M. G and Cargill, B. J. The Development of a Soft Human Resources Management Model and its Interfacing with a Holistic Production Planning Model. *Proceedings of the 30th Annual Meeting of the Decision Sciences Institute*, Eds, Chaney, B. E., Jones, T. W. S and Douglas, D. E., New Orleans, USA, 20th – 23rd November, pp 903 – 906, 1999.

[8] Nicholls, M. G and Cargill, B. J. The Development of a Solution Heuristic for a Mixed Mode Model Incorporating Human Resources Management and Production Planning with a View to Yielding Best Practice. *Proceedings of the 30th Annual Meeting of the Western Decision Sciences Institute*, Eds, xx, April 3rd – 7th, Vancouver, Canada, 2001.

[9] Nicholls, M. G. An Integer Programming Approach to Short-term Production Scheduling in a Tobacco Plant, *Journal of the Operational Research Society*, Vol. 49, No. 11, pp 1117 - 1129, 1998.

[10] Gardener, J. C., Huefner, R. J and Lofti. H. A Multiperiod Audit Staff Planning Model using Multiple Objectives: Development and Evaluation, *Decision Sciences*, 21, No. 1 pp 154 – 170, 1990.

[11] Liang, T and Thompson, T. J. A Large-scale Personnel Assignment Model for the Navy, *Decision Sciences*, 18, No. 2, pp 234 – 249, 1987.

[12] Bergmann, T. J and Martin, G. E. Optimal Large-scale Manpower Recruitment Policies. *Human Resource Planning*, 10, pp 93 – 101, 1987.

[13] Gatewood, R. D and Rockmore, B. W. Combining Organizational Manpower and Career Development Needs: An Operational Human Resource Planning Model, *Human Resource Planning*, 9, pp 81 – 96, 1986.

[14] Burns, R. N and Carter, M. W. Work Force Size and Single Shift Schedules with Variable Demands, *Management Science*, 31, No. 5, pp 599 – 607, 1985.

[15] Tyson, S. *Human Resource Strategy - Towards a General Theory of Human Resource Management*, Pitman, London, 1995.

[16] Schuler, R. S., Dowling, P.J., Smart, J. P. and Huber, V. L *Human Resource Management in Australia* (Second Edition), Harper Educational/West Publishing, Sydney, 1992.

[17] Patrickson, M., Bamber, V. and Bamber, G. (Eds), *Organisational Change Strategies - Case Studies of Human Resource and Industrial Relations Issues*, Longman, Melbourne, 1995.

[18] Dhir, K.S. Formulating policies for faculty promotion and tenure, *Academic Chairpersons: In search of Academic Quality*. Kansas State University: Centre for Faculty Evaluation and Development, 1988.

[19] Dhir, K.S. Analysis of human judgement in the valuation of resources. In *Handbook of Behavioural Economics, Behavioural Decision Making*. Eds., Frantz, R., Singh, H and Gerber, J. Volume 2B, JAI Press Inc., Greenwich, Connecticut, 1991.

10

A SKILL ASSESSMENT PROCESS FOR INFORMATION SYSTEMS PROFESSIONALS

M. Gordon Hunter
Management Information Systems
The University of Lethbridge, Canada

ABSTRACT

There exists a general complacency among employers of information systems personnel. Due to the growth of the industry and a lack of supply there is a shortage of entry-level workers. Because of rapid changes in technology the skills of those currently working in the profession can quickly become obsolete. A lack of training initiative contributes to both unproductive personnel and inappropriate information systems. What is necessary is a consistently reliable human resource practice, which takes into consideration the unique requirements of the information systems profession. Thus, based upon research conducted regarding identifying the qualities of 'excellent' systems analysts, a method is outlined, which may assist in the resolution of the above situation. This chapter describes how the research method may be applied to implement the concepts underlying the Software Engineering Institute's (SEI) People – Capability Maturity Model (P-CMM). The SEI sponsored P-CMM is a personnel management framework for the information systems industry, the purpose of which is to enhance the capability of organizations to manage information systems personnel in order to improve their software development capability. The P-CMM framework provides a description of a continuous improvement process for organizations to adopt in the management of their information systems personnel. P-CMM represents an effective assessment framework, but does not offer implementation guidance. Employing the RepGrid, as proposed

M.G. Nicholls et al. (eds.),
Mixed-Mode Modelling: Mixing Methodologies for Organisational Intervention, 293–317.

in this chapter, will ground the application of the P-CMM framework within the organization and provide an implementation method. This approach represents an innovative mixture of methodologies, both the P-CMM framework for assessment and the RepGrid technique for implementation, for conducting applied research and organizational intervention. The method described here represents an effective way to identify and develop the necessary capability within organizations to address skill shortage and obsolescence.

Keywords: information systems personnel, skills obsolescence, RepGrid, P-CMM.

INTRODUCTION

A study conducted for Employment and Immigration Canada [1] in 1992 suggested a 20% annual growth rate of personnel in the Canadian software industry. Current projections suggest this previously projected growth rate was conservative. Indeed, recent dialogue in the popular press has suggested a figure of 30% would be more appropriate.

While demand for software personnel is high, the concomitant supply of appropriate human resources has not been able to keep pace. Post-secondary institutions represent the traditional source of entry-level software personnel. Unfortunately, just as demand has increased significantly, fewer students are graduating, mainly as a result of under-funding. Further, those who are graduating do not necessarily possess the skills required to perform in the current software industry. For instance, there are many courses where a student can learn COBOL, but very few courses for JAVA.

Another situation, which further exacerbates the above problem, relates to the skill obsolescence of those individuals who are currently working in the software industry. These individuals are plateauing in mid-career, just when they should be their most productive. However, rapid changes in technology and a lack of training initiative leads to unproductive personnel developing inefficient or inappropriate information systems. Rapid changes in technology necessitate a continual effort to maintain up to date knowledge. While the majority of this effort is conducted informally through work assignments, formal training sessions offer an opportunity to obtain knowledge of and experience with current technology.

Further, there is a lack of definition of the IS profession and what skills are necessary to perform the myriad of tasks. There is an absence of consistently reliable human resource practices among employers of software workers. Human resource departments do not seem to be prepared to take into consideration either the unique requirements of the profession or the skills, which must be possessed by IS professionals to perform their assigned duties well. There seems to be a general complacency among IS personnel employers even as they themselves point to personnel shortages and skills obsolescence.

This chapter presents a method for implementing an IS personnel skill assessment process, which will address the uniqueness of the profession and the requirements of a specific organization. The process is based upon the framework of the P-CMM, which is discussed in more detail in the following section. The combination of the P-CMM assessment framework and the proposed implementation method represent an innovative mixing of applied methodologies for organizational intervention.

While the P-CMM framework presents 'what' should be done regarding IS personnel management, it does not specifically outline 'how' to implement the process. The method presented here not only describes 'how' to implement P-CMM, but it also ensures the implemented process is grounded within the specific organization. Overall, a skill assessment process will be developed, which will support the identification of the appropriate types of IS personnel for specific organizations. In turn, the personnel shortages and skill obsolescence situation, described above, will be addressed. That is, the organization, through the assessment process will be able to identify those entry-level personnel who will be most appropriate for the current requirements of the organization. Further, the organization will be able to more appropriately manage the process of assessing the performance of IS personnel. They will have the ability to identify where current skills do not match requirements resulting in the development of necessary skills training programs.

This chapter is organized in the following manner. First, the framework is presented in the form of a description of P-CMM. This discussion outlines the 'what' of the IS personnel skill assessment process. Second, a qualitative in-depth interview technique is presented, which serves to describe 'how' the process may be implemented. Finally, the chapter concludes with a discussion of how the proposed process may be employed, in a mixed-mode modelling context, to address the IS software industry problems presented at the beginning of the chapter.

The P-CMM Framework

The Software Engineering Institute (SEI) is associated with Carnegie-Mellon University and a large number of software development organizations. The overall objective of SEI is to establish and foster an environment within organizations, which supports the development of appropriate information systems, which are both efficient and effective. Originally, to support this objective SEI developed a Capability Maturity Model (CMM) for the assessment of software development organizations. The purpose of CMM is to ensure organizations are capable of conducting well-managed and repeatable information systems development processes.

The People – Capability Maturity Model (P-CMM) represents the next major initiative of SEI. Where CMM has been used to assess organizations in general, P-CMM focuses on a process for the assessment of individuals. The main goal of P-CMM is to enhance the ability of software organizations to manage system development personnel in order to improve the capability to develop and maintain software. P-CMM represents a framework for continuous improvement in the area of management of software personnel. The framework is depicted in five consecutive levels. The components of each level must be implemented before the organization can progress to the next higher level. The implementation of each level will result in an improved approach to the management of software personnel. Progression through the levels will result in fundamental changes to both the culture of the organization and how software personnel are managed.

The five levels may be described as follows:

Level 1 – The Initial Level

At this level there is no consistent approach to the management of software personnel. Management has not been trained to perform personnel management tasks and consequently approach any human resource duties inconsistently.

Level 2 – The Repeatable Level

Policies, procedures, and practices have been implemented within the organization. All associated tasks are performed consistently. Through appropriate training all tasks may be repeated for different individuals, projects and work units.

Level 3 – The Defined Level

Not only is the approach to software personnel management repeatable, it is tailored to the nature of the specific organization. Best practices are identified both from within the organization and as seen in other organizations. The best practices are adapted to suit the current organizational situation.

Level 4 – The Measured Level

The organization implements objective measures for the effectiveness of personnel management and to identify growth in the skills of individuals. Corporate-wide skills can be identified, measured, and improved.

Level 5 – The Optimizing Level

Continuous improvement in the management of software personnel has been implemented. Opportunities to improve effectiveness are pro-actively identified and adapted for the specific organizational context. Innovative approaches are identified and employed corporate-wide, where appropriate.

Each of the above levels consists of five common areas of concentration, known as Key Process Areas, which may be described as follows:

1. **Work Environment**
   This relates to the establishment and maintenance of good quality work environment.
2. **Staffing**
   This relates to the recruitment, selection, and assignment of software personnel.
3. **Performance Management**
   This relates to the establishment of objective evaluation criteria for both individuals and work units. The criteria may be used for both feedback and improvement.
4. **Training**
   This relates to ensuring all software personnel have the opportunity to acquire the necessary skills to perform assigned tasks.
5. **Compensation**
   This relates to ensuring software personnel are compensated equitably and relative to their value to the organization.

The Implementation Process

The dilemma in evaluating professionals, in this case software personnel, is to determine a consensus regarding what is good performance. Even before performance can be evaluated it is necessary to attempt to define just what constitutes the duties of an individual involved in software development. This second point relating to job descriptions will be left to the specific organization. There have been some investigations regarding what may be regarded as good performance, in general, for software personnel. The following paragraphs describe some of these investigations.

Maxwell [2] investigated the characteristics of successful information systems personnel. He employed the critical incident technique to gather data from 197 respondents. Table 1 presents the results of Maxwell's research in the form of a ranked list of characteristics based on frequency of occurrence.

TABLE 1
RANKING ANALYSIS OF SELECTED PERSONAL CHARACTERISTICS FOR ALL RESPONSES

Characteristics	Number of Responses	Percent of Responses	Ranking
Works well with others	70	17.5	1
Compromises	49	12.5	2.5
Communicates well with others	49	12.2	2.5
Thinks, reasons and creates order	46	11.5	4
Functions with objectivity	36	9.0	5
Considered technically competent	28	7.0	6
Possesses high, personal, ethical standards	27	6.7	7
Views a situation as a system	26	6.5	8
Motivates and develops others	22	5.5	9
Manifests patience	21	5.2	10
Manifests a positive nature and personality	12	3.0	11

TABLE 1 cont.
RANKING ANALYSIS OF SELECTED PERSONAL CHARACTERISTICS FOR ALL RESPONSES

A self-starter, motivated	6	1.5	12
Prefers Less-structured environments	3	0.7	13
Pursues organized plan for personal and professional continuing education	2	0.5	14.5
Manifests sensitivity and loyalty to employing organization	2	0.5	14.5
Functions with tact and consideration	1	0.2	16.5
Possesses a career instead of just an information systems orientation	1	0.2	16.5
Total Responses	**401**	**100.0**	

McCubbrey and Scudder [3] asked 10 MIS practitioners to comment on the importance of a supplied list of skills regarding software personnel. The list was the result of previous work by Nunamaker *et al* [4]. The results of the McCubbrey and Scudder [3] research, shown in Table 2, show the identified skills rated based upon participant responses according to a standard Likert scale (Less important 1 2 3 4 5 more important). The results suggest that communication and organizational skills are important for software personnel.

TABLE 2
SURVEY RESULTS

SKILL	AVERAGE
1. People Skills:	
Hear and listen	4.3
Describe behavior by economics/psychology	3.6
Describe/predict task/time behavior	3.2

TABLE 2 cont.
SURVEY RESULTS

2. Model Skills	
Formulate and solve simple models	3.3
Recognize appropriate models	3.6
View situation as system	2.9
Apply system to organisation	2.7
Perform economic analysis	3.8
Present written summary of project	4.0
Present written detailed description of subparts	3.1
3. Computer Skills	
Knowledge of hardware/software	3.1
Program in a higher language	3.6
Program a defined problem	3.0
Develop multiple logical structures	3.0
Develop multiple implementations	3.3
Develop specifications	2.6
Knowledge of sources	3.4
Develop major alternatives for system components	3.5
Develop economic analysis for alternatives	3.6
Create 'rough-cut' feasibility evaluations	3.8
Develop task management and database components	2.6
4. Organisational Skills	
Knowledge of purposeful organisation structure	3.9
Knowledge of functional areas	4.5
Identify functional area key issues and problems	4.3
Knowledge of typical functional roles and behavior	4.0
Identify short-term/long-term effects	3.9
Identify appropriate information needs	3.9
Knowledge of IS needs at organisational levels	4.1
Knowledge of information gathering techniques	4.1
Gathering information systematically	3.9
Specify alternative information transfers	3.5
Make 'rough-cut' analysis of alternatives	3.7
Develop positive and negative impacts	3.9
Develop specifications for needs	2.6

5. Societal Skills

Articulate position on issues	3.5
Perceive and describe impacts on society	3.6
Perform 'rough-cut' specifications of impacts	3.5

Further, Guinan [5] determined that the individuals involved in information system development could improve the quality of their interactions with more knowledge about effective communication.

Cheney *et al* [6] asked 79 senior information managers to comment on skill requirements of software personnel. They concluded that, "The trend for systems analysts/designers is toward increased knowledge of people and problem-solving skills, and away from developing application software." Cheney *et al* [6] (p335).

The above research projects have all identified some skill or set of skills as being important to software development personnel. While these projects have provided valuable input regarding the generic description of skills for software personnel, they have not been able to show how to relate the importance of specific skills to the current situation for one particular organization. In light of this, the following paragraphs describe a technique, which grounds the investigation in the current organization and provides a method for the implementation of the P-CMM framework. The technique is referred to as the RepGrid Technique and is based upon George Kelly's Theory of Personal Constructs [7, 8].

Kelly regarded individuals as 'scientists'. He believed that in order for individuals to respond to their environment they required a way to interpret their past experiences. Thus, based upon their past experiences individuals would, Kelly contended, develop a system of personal constructs which would aid them in dealing with current or anticipated situations in their environment. The RepGrid technique was devised by Kelly to document an individual's personal construct system relative to a specific area of investigation. Kelly employed the technique to document and counsel clients regarding interpersonal relationships. The RepGrid technique has also been used to investigate problem construction [9, 10, 11]; for market research [12]; and expert system knowledge acquisition [13, 14].

The following description of the investigation method is based upon a series of research projects. The results of these projects have been reported in Hunter [15, 16, 17, 18, 19]. Subsequent replications have been conducted and reported by Hunter and Beck [20], Hunter and Beck [21, 22], Hunter and Palvia [23] and Palvia and Hunter [24].

Hunter and his colleagues defined the domain of discourse to be the identification of skills associated with the research participant's interpretation of what constitutes an 'excellent' systems analyst. The investigators did not define the term 'excellent'. In deed, they anticipated the definition would be found in the narrative description provided by the research participants. Other terms, such as 'good' or 'well' could also suffice.

Further, the term 'systems analyst' did not necessarily reflect a specific job description. It was generally interpreted as the individual who, representing the Information Systems Department, interacted with the Business Professional throughout the majority of the systems development life cycle.

Thus, both terms were grounded within the specific organization where the investigations were conducted. This grounding of the data is further supported by the interview technique, which is described in detail later in this section.

Before commencing the interview process, it is important to identify which groups of individuals will be asked to provide their perspectives. The research conducted by Hunter and his colleagues identified five audiences. Figure 1 shows and describes these audiences. Two of the audiences (Systems Analysts and Business Systems Managers) have subsequently been referred to as representing Information Systems Professionals, while the other three audiences (Users, Sponsors, and Clients) have been considered as representative of Business Professionals. Other audiences may also be considered as potentially providing interpretations regarding good performance. These audiences may include such technical specialists as Database administrators, communications experts, or programmers. Other audiences could be senior management, or even customers. The important aspect for audience determination is whether the individuals are considered to have something significant to contribute to the determination of how a subject is interpreted within the local or corporate context.

Interview: Introduction

At the start of the interview a verbal commitment was made regarding the confidentiality of the discussion. This commitment could be made in a more formal manner by introducing a document to be signed by both parties. The important consideration is that the research participant feels comfortable in voicing their interpretation of the subject. Next the research participant was asked to reflect upon their experience with the subject area. Hunter and his

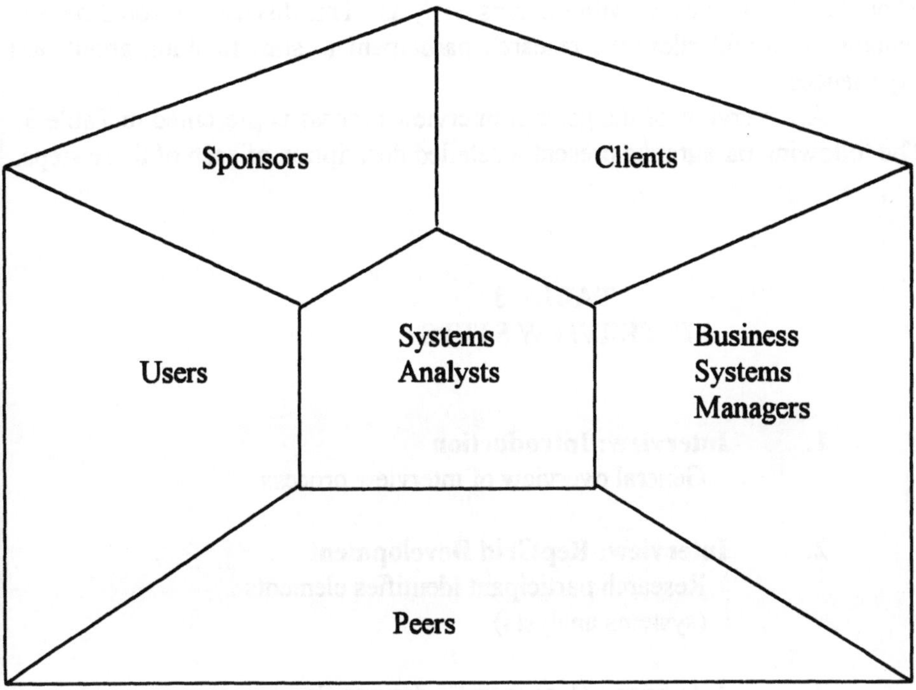

Figure 1. Audiences

Peers: Those individuals who perform the same or similar function as 'Systems Analysts' within the organization.
Business Systems Managers: Those individuals responsible for the administration of the corporate unit to which the functions of 'Systems Analysts' is assigned.
Users: Those individuals who interact directly with the information system as developed or maintained by 'Systems Analysts'.
Sponsors: Those individuals whose corporate budget includes the development or maintenance cost of the information system, or who are responsible administratively for the Users, but do not interact directly with the information system.
Clients: Those individuals who interact directly with the information system, and whose corporate budget includes the development and maintenance cost of the information system, but who are not responsible administratively for Users.

colleagues, at this stage, would ask the research participant to talk about how and when they had interacted with systems analysts. This discussion would be very general. It would allow the research participant to start thinking about past experiences.

An overview of the general interview process is presented in Table 3. The following paragraphs present a detailed description of each of these steps.

TABLE 3
INTERVIEW STEPS

1. **Interview: Introduction**
   General overview of interview process

2. **Interview: RepGrid Development**
   Research participant identifies elements (systems analysts)

3. **Interview: Research Participant's Comments**
   Comments are recorded
   Ratings are documented
   Initial feedback is obtained via "visual focusing"

4. **Interview: Conclusion**
   Exchange of final comments

Then the detailed interview technique was introduced. An overview was presented and the research participant was shown how the technique would be related to the subject of the interview. While the details of how a RepGrid is completed are presented in the next interview step, an example is presented here in Table 4.

TABLE 4
REPGRID

AUDIENCE: Systems Analysts PARTICIPANT: Name

	ELEMENTS							
CONSTRUCTS	1	2	3	4	5	6	7	8
1. Delegator - Does Work Himself	7	2	5	4	2	6	1	9
2. Informs Everyone - Keeps to Himself	8	2	3	3	8	6	1	9
3. Good User Rapport - No User Rapport	5	2	4	2	4	2	1	9
4. Regular Feedback - Inappropriate Feedback	6	1	5	3	5	3	1	9
5. Knows Detail - Confused	2	1	4	3	5	1	1	9
6. Estimates Based on Staff Estimates based on Himself	8	3	4	6	4	6	1	9
7. User Involvement - Lack of User Involvement	6	2	5	5	3	3	1	9

Interview: RepGrid Development

The research participant was then asked to think of the names of up to six individuals (referred to as elements in Kelly's theory) who perform the tasks under investigation and have interacted with the research participant. The interaction should be sufficient to allow the research participant to form an opinion about all of the individuals' performance. While six is a rather arbitrary number, it does allow for sufficient variability in the subsequent elicitation process. The interview can be completed, however, with fewer individuals.

The research participant was also asked to add to the list the concepts of 'ideal' and 'incompetent'. The meanings of these concepts are obvious. They are not meant to depict specific individuals but rather to represent a fictitious person who is currently working in the field. Later in the interview these concepts will serve as 'anchors' for the research participant when discussing aspects of specific individuals. Stewart and Stewart [25] have suggested that in order to determine how a research participant interprets the performance of individuals both effective and less effective ones should be included in the discussion. Therefore, these 'anchors' provide this type of differentiation. The research participant then writes all the names and concepts, on an index card, with one element per card. This facilitates the subsequent elicitation process.

Interview: Research Participant's Comments

Theory refers to this step as the triadic elicitation of constructs. The process is triadic in that three of the eight cards are randomly presented to the research participant. Upon presentation of the three cards, the research participant is asked to describe, in their own words, how two of the cards are the same, yet different from the third. These words, chosen by the research participant, represent a construct, which is the operationalization of Kelly's theory regarding personal construct systems. The research participant was encouraged to separate the two similar cards from the other different card, and to discuss the aspects supporting the decision. These comments were noted and further explored once the construct was documented. In order to understand what a research participant means by a construct, it is necessary to have a label or description for both the similarity and the contrast.

To further understand and document the research participant's interpretation of a particular construct, the process of 'laddering' [25] was pursued. Laddering represents a series of 'how' questions which prompt the research participant to elaborate upon their initial comments about the elicited construct. Responses to this line of questioning are documented in detailed interview notes. Laddering of one specific construct is continued until the research participant can offer no further elaboration. Table 5 shows the results of laddering one construct.

TABLE 5
INTERVIEW NOTES

AUDIENCE: Systems Analysts PARTICIPANT: Name

GOOD USER RAPPORT
- good relationship on all subjects
    - work, interests, family
- user feels more comfortable
- how is this done?
    - good listener
    - finds out user's interests
        - doesn't forget
    - takes time to answer user's questions
        - speaks in terms users can understand
        - provides and answer that users are happy with
        - or learns why and understands

NO USER RAPPORT
- not a good listener
- no concern for user
- aggressive
    - user is intimidated
    - uses big words
- implies that the system is his
    - 'I develop - you use'

After a thorough discussion and explanation of the construct, the research participant was asked to rate each element with respect to the construct. To facilitate this process a continuum was defined using the positive and negative side of the elicited construct. The research participant was asked to place all eight cards along the continuum relative to their interpretation of how the individual performed the activity associated with the construct. Then, the research participant was asked to assign a number to each card along the continuum. A 9-point rating scale was used, where 1 represented the positive end of the construct and 9 represented the negative end. The 9-point scale was used because if provided a mid-point and it allowed for more variability than the number of elements (eight, in this case). Refer back to Table 4 to see the results of the elicitation and rating process. All of this process was repeated until the research participant felt that no further new comments could be made on the subject.

Near the end of the interview a preliminary confirmation of the discussion was obtained through a technique called 'visual focusing' [25]. Thus, the lower the numbers assigned by the research participant for a specific individual, the closer is the research participant's interpretation that the individual is to the concept of 'ideal'. Conversely, the higher the numbers the closer the individual is to the research participant's concept of 'incompetent'. This comparison represents a general confirmation of what the research participant has said and what has been documented in the RepGrid.

Interview: Conclusion

At the end of the interview the research participant was asked for any further comments about the discussion or the interview process. These comments were also documented. Further, there was a re-statement of confidentiality of interview. Finally, an offer was made to provide feedback to the specific research participant after all the interviews were conducted.

DISCUSSION

As described above, RepGrids may be employed as a qualitative research technique, which brings structure to an interview while, at the same time, allowing flexibility and reducing researcher bias. The technique is structured in that it helps the research participant focus on the subject of the investigation through the identification of element values that are familiar to the research participant. There is, however, flexibility and reduced researcher bias because it is the research participant who decides what to say and how to further explain their interpretations.

With regards to the identification of software personnel skills and the implementation of the P-CMM framework the RepGrid technique is appropriate. According to Stewart and Stewart [25] the RepGrid technique supports the gathering of qualitative interview data in some detail with significantly reduced interviewer bias. These authors have suggested that using the RepGrid technique allows the investigator to, "... interview someone in detail, extracting a good deal of information ... and to do this in such a way that the input from the observer is reduced to zero." Stewart and Stewart [25] (p5).

For the research described in this chapter the RepGrid technique was used to generate in-depth, narrative data. The research participant in each interview determined both the element list and the resulting elicited constructs. This approach is referred to as the use of unique grids. The process of laddering facilitated the generation of a research participant's further elaboration of an elicited construct. Subsequent analysis of the elaborations resulted in the identification of themes relating to the domain of discourse.

It is possible to use the RepGrid technique in different ways. The use of common grids requires that either elements or constructs, or both must be the same for the administration of the grid to several research participants. This commonality allows for subsequent statistical analysis of the data within the grid. Principle Component Analysis, for instance, may be used to determine relative similarity and difference between the common elements or constructs.

The use of the RepGrid by Hunter and his colleagues generated extensive interview notes, which were subsequently organized with the assistance of software known as COPE [26]. The following Figure 2 shows how the interview data (See Table 3) from one construct may be organized with COPE.

The maps were constructed from the general to the specific. The top item of the map is the elicited construct. Via the technique of laddering more detailed interpretations of the construct are provided by the research participant. The comments have been built into the COPE map for each elicited construct. The COPE maps were further analyzed using content analysis to identify a theme, which represented each path within the map.

AUDIENCE: Systems Analysts PARTICIPANT: Name

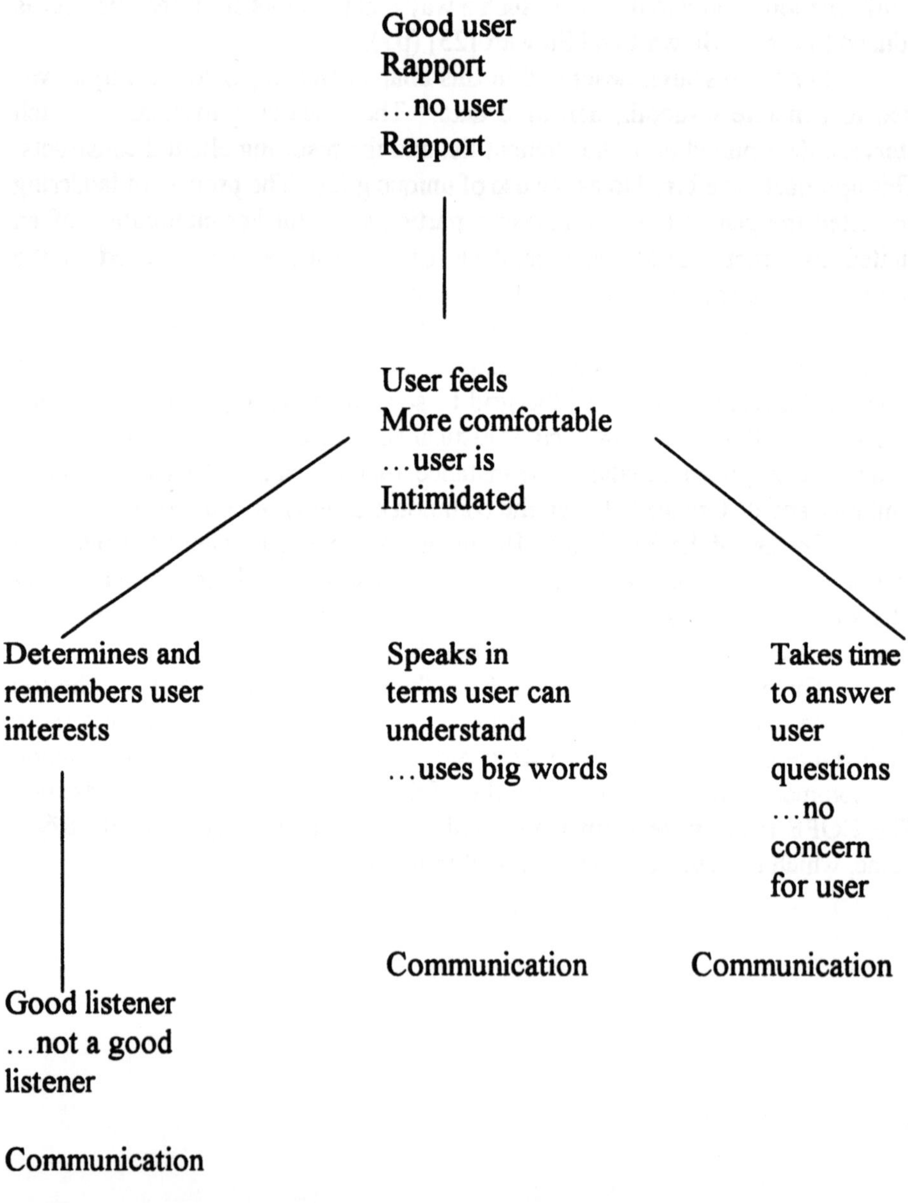

Figure 2. Cope map with paths.

Theme	Users	Sponsors	Clients	System Analysts	Business System Managers	Total
1. Communication	32	18	19	16	26	111
2. Attitude	6	14	1	6	6	33
3. Investigation	8	8	3	7	3	29
4. Thorough	12	0	4	6	4	26
5. Knowledge	11	1	7	2	1	22
6. Involve User	10	2	0	3	5	20
7. Flexible	10	1	0	2	6	19
8. Experience	7	0	3	4	4	18
9. Plan	2	5	2	0	9	18
10. Delegation	0	1	4	7	5	16
11. Design	0	2	3	2	0	7
12. Team Member	0	1	4	0	1	6
Total	98	52	50	55	70	325
Participants	8	5	4	5	5	27

Figure 3. Location C-1 Occurrence of themes by group

Figure 3 represents the themes, which were 'identified' via the above process at one location [16]. This data suggests there are 'universal' themes, which are common for all individuals and groups regarding interpretations of what constitutes an 'excellent' systems analyst. Further, there are 'local' interpretations of the relative importance of these themes. For a further elaboration of the universal and local themes with regards to 'excellent' systems analysts, see [16].

Table 6 presents definitions of the themes based upon data obtained in the interviews. Once consensus is obtained regarding these definitions it is possible to return to an organisation, where the data was gathered, and implement a process, which supports the P-CMM framework.

TABLE 6
DEFINITION OF THEMES

Theme		Definition
Attitude		personal belief about how to approach work, users and staff
	Examples:	"analyst realizes it's his duty to check into reported errors"
		"will work overtime"
		"keen about analysing what user wants"
Knowledge		understanding of a particular subject
	Examples:	"knows how system will interface with other systems"
		"knows which parts of system are correct"
		"knows existing application packages"
Communicate		exchange (send or receive) of messages with others
	Examples:	"can express self well"
		"gives programmers feedback at the end of each project stage"
		"will explain things to team members"

TABLE 6
DEFINITION OF THEMES cont.

Plan	anticipation of activities and organization of tasks
Examples:	"prepares a schedule of who and by when"
	"allows time for each activity"
	"can fit in with other projects"
Investigate	gathering of facts about a particular aspect
Examples:	"determines how request will affect current situation"
	"tries to understand what user wants"
	"finds out from users how they handle the situation now"
Flexible	readiness to change based upon external clues
Examples:	"doesn't have a solution in mind"
	"willing to try different things that are untried"
	"open to suggestions from project team"
Thorough	consideration of aspects at a detailed level
Examples:	"analyst checks out entire system"
	"goes into depth in new system"
	"analyst looks at solution from all sides"
Design	incorporation of necessary functions in a system for current and future use
Examples:	"system provides what user wants"
	"system is easy to use"
	"ensures present system can be changed to meet future needs"
Experience	length of time spent working in an area or on a system
Examples:	"has worked on system for a long time"
	"has worked in this area"
	"doesn't need guidance about how to solve problems"
Involve User	include functional user in tasks

TABLE 6
DEFINITION OF THEMES cont.

Examples:	"will work with user deciding how to make a change" "will offer user other alternatives" "forces user to think more about the request"
Delegate	assignment of duties to staff and monitoring progress
Examples:	"leaves members free to use their own style" "works well with subordinates" "distributes he work load"
Creative	internal generation of new ideas
Examples:	"tries to think in ways not thought before" "generates lots of ideas"

Armed with the knowledge of interpretations of what constitutes good performance within an organization it is possible to implement P-CMM. For instance, one of the Key Process Areas for each level of P-CMM is Staffing, which relates to recruitment, selection, and assignment. The RepGrid technique, suggested in this chapter, will identify what skills and qualities are considered important, and should be obtained through the staffing process. Another KPA relates to Performance Measurement, which suggests the establishment of objective evaluation criteria. It is possible to develop a decision support system for this purpose using the RepGrid data. The 'universal' themes may be employed as decision criteria and the 'local' values for those themes may be used to represent the weights of the criteria. It is then possible to develop an evaluation of a specific individual by determining a rating for that individual relative to each theme (decision criteria). Further, this process may also be used to provide input to two other KPAs, namely, Training, and Compensation. From the above decision support system description it will be possible to determine relative weaknesses, which may require some form of training, and relative strengths, which perhaps could serve to determine compensation rewards.

CONCLUSION

The proposed method gathers data relevant to an individual corporation. Thus, data are grounded in the experience of those individuals within the corporation, and reflect the current organization's environment. The following excerpt from the P-CMM Draft Version 3.0 supports this approach:

> 'Goodness' attributes can only be interpreted in the context of the business environment and specific circumstances of the unit and the organization. Such 'goodness' judgements can be made only by the organization as part of its continuous people management cycle. Perfection is never achieved, and continuous improvement never ends." P-CMM [27] (pp35 - 36).

This chapter has presented a discussion of a research technique, RepGrid, which may be employed to implement P-CMM within a specific company. P-CMM provides a framework, while the RepGrid technique represents a method for grounding the implementation of P-CMM within a specific organization. As outlined at the beginning, there is a shortage of personnel with the required skills.

The approach proposed in this chapter represents an innovative mixture of methodologies, both the P-CMM framework for assessment and the RepGrid technique for implementation, for conducting applied research and organizational intervention. The method described here represents an effective way to identify and develop the necessary capability within organizations to address skill shortage and obsolescence.

REFERENCES

[1] Employment and Immigration Canada. *Software and National Competitiveness – Human Resource Issues and Opportunities*, Ottawa, Canada, March 1992.

[2] Maxwell, Paul David. *"A critical Analysis of the Personal Characteristics of Successful Information Systems Analysts"*. Doctoral dissertation, Boston University, 1986.

[3] McCubbrey, Donald J. and Richard. A. Scudder. "The Systems Analysts of the 1990's". Management of Information Systems Personnel, *Proceedings of the 1988 ACM SIGCPR Conference*, New York, ACM, pp. 8-16, 1988.

[4] Nunamaker, Jay F., Jr., J. Daniel Couger, and Gordon B. Davis. "Information Systems Curriculum Recommendations for the 80's: Undergraduate and Graduate Programs". *Communications of the ACM*, Vol. 25, No. 11, November, pp. 148-149. 1982.

[5] Guinan, Patricia J. *Patterns of Excellence for IS Professionals - An Analysis of Communication Behavior*. Washington, ICIT Press, 1988.

[6] Cheney, Paul H., David P. Hale, and George M. Kasper. "Information Systems Professionals: Skills for the 1990's". *Proceedings of the 22nd Annual Hawaii International Conference of Systems Sciences*, IEEE Computer Society Press, pp. 331-336, 1989

[7] Kelly, G. A. *The Psychology of Personal Constructs*. Norton, New York, 1955.

[8] Kelly, G. A. *A Theory of Personality*. Norton, New York, 1963.

[9] Eden, Colin and Wheaton, G. *"In Favour of Structure"*. Centre for the study of Organisational Change and Development, University of Bath. Working Paper, 80/06, 1980.

[10] Shaw, M. *On Becoming a Personal Scientist – Interactive Computer Elicitation of Personal Models of the World*. London, Academic Press, Inc., 1980.

[11] Eden, Colin and Jones, S. "Using Repertory Grids for Problem Construction". *Journal of Operations Research*, vol. 35, No. 9, pp.779-798, 1984.

[12] Corsini, Raymond and Marsella, Anthony J. *Personality Theories, Research and Assessment*. Itasca, Illinois, Peacock Publishers, Inc., 1983.

[13] Latta, Gail, F. and Swigger, Keith. "Validation of the Repertory Grid for Use in Modelling Knowledge". *Journal of the American Society for Information Science*, Vol. 42, No. 2, March, pp. 115-129. 1992.

[14] Phythian, Gary John and King, Malcolm "Developing an Expert System for Tender Enquiry Evaluation: A Case Study". *European Journal of Operations Research*, Vol. 56, No. 1, January 10, pp. 15-29, 1992.

[15] Hunter, M. Gordon. *"Managing Information Systems Professionals: Implementing a Skill Assessment Process"*. Special Interest Group on Computer Personnel Research, March 26-28, Boston, Massachusetts, pp. 19-27, 1998.

[16] Hunter, M. Gordon. *"People-Capability Maturity Model: A Proposed Implementation Method"*. 8th International Conference of the Information Resources Management Association, May 18-21, Vancouver, Canada, 1997.

[17] Hunter, M. Gordon. "Managing Systems Analysts: A Proposed Decision Making Process". *International Conference on Global Business in Transition, Prospects for the Twenty First Century*, December 14-16, Hong Kong, pp. 527-534, 1995.

[18] Hunter, M. Gordon. ""Excellent" Systems Analysts: Key Audience Perceptions". *Computer Personnel*, April, pp. 15-31, 1994.

19] Hunter, M. Gordon. "A Strategy for Identifying "Excellent" Systems Analysts". *The Journal of Strategic Information Systems*, Vol. 2, No. 1, March, pp. 15-26, 1993.

[20] Hunter, M. Gordon and Beck, John. "Using Repertory Grids to Conduct Cross-Cultural Information Systems Research". *Information Systems Research*, Vol. 11, No. 1, pp. 93-101, 2000.

[21] Hunter, M. Gordon and Beck, John. "A Cross-Cultural Comparison of "Excellent" Systems Analysts". *Information Systems Journal*, Vol. 6, No. 4, pp. 261-281, 1996a.

[22] Hunter, M. Gordon and Beck, John. ""Excellent" Systems Analysts: The Singapore Context". *Asia-Pacific Journal of Management*, Vol. 13, No. 2, October, pp. 25-46, 1996b.

[23] Hunter, M. Gordon and Palvia, Shailendra. "Ideal, Advertised, and Actual Systems Analyst Skills: The Singapore Context". *Information, Technology & People*, Vol. 9, No. 1, pp. 63-77, 1996.

[24] Palvia, Shailendra and Hunter, M. Gordon. "Information Systems Development: A Conceptual Model and a Comparison of Methods Used in Singapore, USA, and Europe". *Journal of Global Information Management*, Vol. 4, No. 3, summer, pp. 5-16, 1996.

[25] Stewart, Valerie and Stewart, A. *Business Applications of Repertory Grid*. London, McGraw-Hill Ltd., 1981.

[26] Eden, C and Ackermann, F. Strategic Option Development and Analysis - using a computer to help with the management of strategic vision. In *Knowledge-based Management Support Systems*. Doukidis, G I, Land, F. and Miller, G. (Eds). Ellis Horwood, Chichester, pp.208-224, 1989.

[27] *People - Capability Maturity Model* (P-CMM), Draft Version 3.0. The software Engineering Institute, Pittsburgh, 1995.

Applied Optimization

1. D.-Z. Du and D.F. Hsu (eds.): *Combinatorial Network Theory.* 1996 ISBN 0-7923-3777-8
2. M.J. Panik: *Linear Programming: Mathematics, Theory and Algorithms.* 1996 ISBN 0-7923-3782-4
3. R.B. Kearfott and V. Kreinovich (eds.): *Applications of Interval Computations.* 1996 ISBN 0-7923-3847-2
4. N. Hritonenko and Y. Yatsenko: *Modeling and Optimimization of the Lifetime of Technology.* 1996 ISBN 0-7923-4014-0
5. T. Terlaky (ed.): *Interior Point Methods of Mathematical Programming.* 1996 ISBN 0-7923-4201-1
6. B. Jansen: *Interior Point Techniques in Optimization.* Complementarity, Sensitivity and Algorithms. 1997 ISBN 0-7923-4430-8
7. A. Migdalas, P.M. Pardalos and S. Storøy (eds.): *Parallel Computing in Optimization.* 1997 ISBN 0-7923-4583-5
8. F.A. Lootsma: *Fuzzy Logic for Planning and Decision Making.* 1997 ISBN 0-7923-4681-5
9. J.A. dos Santos Gromicho: *Quasiconvex Optimization and Location Theory.* 1998 ISBN 0-7923-4694-7
10. V. Kreinovich, A. Lakeyev, J. Rohn and P. Kahl: *Computational Complexity and Feasibility of Data Processing and Interval Computations.* 1998 ISBN 0-7923-4865-6
11. J. Gil-Aluja: *The Interactive Management of Human Resources in Uncertainty.* 1998 ISBN 0-7923-4886-9
12. C. Zopounidis and A.I. Dimitras: *Multicriteria Decision Aid Methods for the Prediction of Business Failure.* 1998 ISBN 0-7923-4900-8
13. F. Giannessi, S. Komlósi and T. Rapcsák (eds.): *New Trends in Mathematical Programming.* Homage to Steven Vajda. 1998 ISBN 0-7923-5036-7
14. Ya-xiang Yuan (ed.): *Advances in Nonlinear Programming.* Proceedings of the '96 International Conference on Nonlinear Programming. 1998 ISBN 0-7923-5053-7
15. W.W. Hager and P.M. Pardalos: *Optimal Control.* Theory, Algorithms, and Applications. 1998 ISBN 0-7923-5067-7
16. Gang Yu (ed.): *Industrial Applications of Combinatorial Optimization.* 1998 ISBN 0-7923-5073-1
17. D. Braha and O. Maimon (eds.): *A Mathematical Theory of Design: Foundations, Algorithms and Applications.* 1998 ISBN 0-7923-5079-0

Applied Optimization

18. O. Maimon, E. Khmelnitsky and K. Kogan: *Optimal Flow Control in Manufacturin* Production Planning and Scheduling. 1998 ISBN 0-7923-5106-
19. C. Zopounidis and P.M. Pardalos (eds.): *Managing in Uncertainty: Theory and Pra tice*. 1998 ISBN 0-7923-5110-
20. A.S. Belenky: *Operations Research in Transportation Systems:* Ideas and Scheme of Optimization Methods for Strategic Planning and Operations Management. 199 ISBN 0-7923-5157-
21. J. Gil-Aluja: *Investment in Uncertainty*. 1999 ISBN 0-7923-5296-
22. M. Fukushima and L. Qi (eds.): *Reformulation: Nonsmooth, Piecewise Smoot Semismooth and Smooting Methods*. 1999 ISBN 0-7923-5320-
23. M. Patriksson: *Nonlinear Programming and Variational Inequality Problems*. A Un fied Approach. 1999 ISBN 0-7923-5455-
24. R. De Leone, A. Murli, P.M. Pardalos and G. Toraldo (eds.): *High Performanc Algorithms and Software in Nonlinear Optimization*. 1999 ISBN 0-7923-5483-
25. A. Schöbel: *Locating Lines and Hyperplanes*. Theory and Algorithms. 1999 ISBN 0-7923-5559-
26. R.B. Statnikov: *Multicriteria Design*. Optimization and Identification. 1999 ISBN 0-7923-5560-
27. V. Tsurkov and A. Mironov: *Minimax under Transportation Constrains*. 1999 ISBN 0-7923-5609-
28. V.I. Ivanov: *Model Development and Optimization*. 1999 ISBN 0-7923-5610-
29. F.A. Lootsma: *Multi-Criteria Decision Analysis via Ratio and Difference Judgemen* 1999 ISBN 0-7923-5669-
30. A. Eberhard, R. Hill, D. Ralph and B.M. Glover (eds.): *Progress in Optimizatio* Contributions from Australasia. 1999 ISBN 0-7923-5733-
31. T. Hürlimann: *Mathematical Modeling and Optimization*. An Essay for the Desig of Computer-Based Modeling Tools. 1999 ISBN 0-7923-5927-
32. J. Gil-Aluja: *Elements for a Theory of Decision in Uncertainty*. 1999 ISBN 0-7923-5987-
33. H. Frenk, K. Roos, T. Terlaky and S. Zhang (eds.): *High Performance Optimizatio* 1999 ISBN 0-7923-6013-
34. N. Hritonenko and Y. Yatsenko: *Mathematical Modeling in Economics, Ecology an the Environment*. 1999 ISBN 0-7923-6015-
35. J. Virant: *Design Considerations of Time in Fuzzy Systems*. 2000 ISBN 0-7923-6100-

Applied Optimization

36. G. Di Pillo and F. Giannessi (eds.): *Nonlinear Optimization and Related Topics*. 2000
ISBN 0-7923-6109-1
37. V. Tsurkov: *Hierarchical Optimization and Mathematical Physics*. 2000
ISBN 0-7923-6175-X
38. C. Zopounidis and M. Doumpos: *Intelligent Decision Aiding Systems Based on Multiple Criteria for Financial Engineering*. 2000 ISBN 0-7923-6273-X
39. X. Yang, A.I. Mees, M. Fisher and L.Jennings (eds.): *Progress in Optimization*. Contributions from Australasia. 2000 ISBN 0-7923-6286-1
40. D. Butnariu and A.N. Iusem: *Totally Convex Functions for Fixed Points Computation and Infinite Dimensional Optimization*. 2000 ISBN 0-7923-6287-X
41. J. Mockus: *A Set of Examples of Global and Discrete Optimization*. Applications of Bayesian Heuristic Approach. 2000 ISBN 0-7923-6359-0
42. H. Neunzert and A.H. Siddiqi: *Topics in Industrial Mathematics*. Case Studies and Related Mathematical Methods. 2000 ISBN 0-7923-6417-1
43. K. Kogan and E. Khmelnitsky: *Scheduling: Control-Based Theory and Polynomial-Time Algorithms*. 2000 ISBN 0-7923-6486-4
44. E. Triantaphyllou: *Multi-Criteria Decision Making Methods*. A Comparative Study. 2000 ISBN 0-7923-6607-7
45. S.H. Zanakis, G. Doukidis and C. Zopounidis (eds.): *Decision Making: Recent Developments and Worldwide Applications*. 2000 ISBN 0-7923-6621-2
46. G.E. Stavroulakis: *Inverse and Crack Identification Problems in Engineering Mechanics*. 2000 ISBN 0-7923-6690-5
47. A. Rubinov and B. Glover (eds.): *Optimization and Related Topics*. 2001
ISBN 0-7923-6732-4
48. M. Pursula and J. Niittymäki (eds.): *Mathematical Methods on Optimization in Transportation Systems*. 2000 ISBN 0-7923-6774-X
49. E. Cascetta: *Transportation Systems Engineering: Theory and Methods*. 2001
ISBN 0-7923-6792-8
50. M.C. Ferris, O.L. Mangasarian and J.-S. Pang (eds.): *Complementarity: Applications, Algorithms and Extensions*. 2001 ISBN 0-7923-6816-9
51. V. Tsurkov: *Large-scale Optimization – Problems and Methods*. 2001
ISBN 0-7923-6817-7
52. X. Yang, K.L. Teo and L. Caccetta (eds.): *Optimization Methods and Applications*. 2001 ISBN 0-7923-6866-5
53. S.M. Stefanov: *Separable Programming Theory and Methods*. 2001
ISBN 0-7923-6882-7

Applied Optimization

54. S.P. Uryasev and P.M. Pardalos (eds.): *Stochastic Optimization: Algorithms and Applications*. 2001 ISBN 0-7923-6951-3
55. J. Gil-Aluja (ed.): *Handbook of Management under Uncertainty*. 2001 ISBN 0-7923-7025-2
56. B.-N. Vo, A. Cantoni and K.L. Teo: *Filter Design with Time Domain Mask Constraints: Theory and Applications*. 2001 ISBN 0-7923-7138-0
57. S. Zlobec: *Stable Parametric Programming*. 2001 ISBN 0-7923-7139-9
58. M.G. Nicholls, S. Clarke and B. Lehaney (eds.): *Mixed-Mode Modelling: Mixing Methodologies for Organisational Intervention*. 2001 ISBN 0-7923-7151-8

KLUWER ACADEMIC PUBLISHERS – DORDRECHT / BOSTON / LONDON

MIX
Papier aus verantwortungsvollen Quellen
Paper from responsible sources
FSC® C105338

If you have any concerns about our products,
you can contact us on
ProductSafety@springernature.com

In case Publisher is established outside the EU,
the EU authorized representative is:
Springer Nature Customer Service Center GmbH
Europaplatz 3, 69115 Heidelberg, Germany

Printed by Libri Plureos GmbH
in Hamburg, Germany